Praise for *Tarot Every*

"A captivating exploration of tarot, presented in a style that is both charming and accessible. This book stands out in its unique approach, blending traditional tarot wisdom with an eclectic mix of magical practices. Dorsey skillfully intertwines the mystical with the practical.... The book is enriched with Dorsey's creative flair, transforming it into a delightful journey through the magickal world of tarot."

—MAT AURYN, bestselling author of *Psychic Witch* and *Mastering Magick*

"Dorsey takes readers on a profound journey into the depths of tarot, illuminating its potential as a sacred tool for magical practice and personal growth.... What sets *Tarot Every Witch Way* apart is its unwavering commitment to diversity and inclusivity... From magical workings, recipes, and purposeful tarot spreads to transformative spells that align with each chapter, this book is a treasure trove of inspiration and practicality."

—JULIET DIAZ, author of *The Altar Within* and *Witchery*

"A multifaceted handbook that will advance your spiritual growth through the cards and leave you with a power-packed, delicious repertoire of recipes. Dorsey is a dynamite storyteller. Her voice, her wisdom, her depths of knowledge and experience shine on every page."

—BENEBELL WEN, author of *Holistic Tarot* and *The Tao of Craft*

"A delightful and engaging read. Alongside helpful descriptions of each card, readers will find a collection of delicious recipes, useful spells, and transformational guided meditations. No matter what type of Witch you may be, you won't want to miss out on this phenomenal book!"

—KELDEN, author of *The Crooked Path* and *The Witches' Sabbath*

"If you're a Witch looking to deepen your understanding of tarot and incorporate it into your magical practice, then you will definitely want to add *Tarot Every Witch Way* to your magical bookshelf.... Moving beyond traditional interpretations, Dorsey explores the rich symbolism of every card, providing a unique set of spells, rituals, recipes, and magical work specific to each. … This book is an indispensable tool on your tarot journey."

—**MICHAEL HERKES**, author of *The GLAM Witch* and *Glamcraft*

"A unique and vital addition to the genuine craft of tarot. Utilizing her remarkable academic and esoteric expertise, the author crafts nothing short of a modern-day grimoire. In it, the tarot cards are associated with herbs, minerals, plants, and spells, offering not just everyday advice and support but also, by deliberately engaging all the senses, potentially unlocking pathways to a more immediate and magical experience of life itself."

—**DAVID BETH**, Haitian Vodou priest and founder of Theion Publishing

"This is the definitive tarot lifestyle book. Lilith starts by defining the cards for divination and then invites you to bring the power of tarot into every sense; making tarot a living, breathing magic. One time through the book is not enough; this is a gem for your magical toolbox to reference repeatedly on your journey."

—**JACKI SMITH**, author of *The Big Book of Candle Magic* and founder of Coventry Creations

"If you are new to the tarot, *Tarot Every Witch Way* will be an essential guide. If you are already familiar with the system, Dorsey's broad and inclusive approach, including discussion of a wide variety of decks to fit an even wider variety of witchy practices, will help you find new insights and revelations among the symbols and spreads."

—**PHILIP H. FARBER**, author of *Brain Magick*

Tarot
Every WITCH Way

© Frances F. Denny

About the Author

Lilith Dorsey, MA, has focused their study and practice on Celtic, Afro-Caribbean, and Indigenous American spirituality. They are the filmmaker of the experimental documentary *Bodies of Water: Voodoo Identity and Tranceformation*, and choreographer/performer for jazz legend Dr. John's *"Night Tripper" Voodoo Show*. They have long been committed to providing accurate and respectful information about magic and are proud to be a published Black author of such titles as *Voodoo and African Traditional Religion* (Warlock Press, 2021), *Love Magic* (Weiser, 2016), the best-selling *Orishas, Goddesses, and Voodoo Queens* (Weiser, 2020), and the award-winning *Water Magic* (Llewellyn, 2020).

Tarot
Every WITCH Way

Unlock the Power of the Cards
for Spellcraft & Magic

Lilith Dorsey

Llewellyn Publications | Woodbury, Minnesota

FIRST EDITION
First Printing, 2024

Book design by R. Brasington
Cover art by Craig Maher
Cover design by Kevin R. Brown

Mermaid Tarot © 2019 Leeza Robertson and Julie Dillon, used with permission
The Orisha Tarot © 2018 Andrew McGregor Oba tilemi, used with permission
Millennium Thoth Tarot © 2019 Lo Scarabeo, used with permission of Lo Scarabeo
Santa Muerte Tarot © 2017 Fabio Listrani, Lo Scarabeo, used with permission of Lo Scarabeo
Tarot of the Vampires © 2023 Charles Harrington and Craig Maher, used with permission
Gustave Doré Tarot © 2022 Lo Scarabeo, used with permission of Lo Scarabeo
Tarot Original 1909 Deck © 2021 with art created by Pamela Colman Smith and Arthur Edward
    Waite. Used with permission of Lo Scarabeo.

Llewellyn Publications is a registered trademark of Llewellyn Worldwide Ltd.

Library of Congress Cataloging-in-Publication Data (Pending)
ISBN: 978-0-7387-7632-3

Llewellyn Worldwide Ltd. does not participate in, endorse, or have any authority or responsibility concerning private business transactions between our authors and the public.

    All mail addressed to the author is forwarded but the publisher cannot, unless specifically instructed by the author, give out an address or phone number.

    Any internet references contained in this work are current at publication time, but the publisher cannot guarantee that a specific location will continue to be maintained. Please refer to the publisher's website for links to authors' websites and other sources.

Llewellyn Publications
A Division of Llewellyn Worldwide Ltd.
2143 Wooddale Drive
Woodbury, MN 55125-2989
www.llewellyn.com

Printed in the United States of America

Other Books by Lilith Dorsey

Voodoo and Afro-Caribbean Paganism (Citadel, 2005)

Love Magic (Weiser, 2016)

Water Magic (Llewellyn, 2020)

Orishas, Goddesses, and Voodoo Queens (Weiser, 2020)

Voodoo and African Traditional Religion (Warlock Press, 2021)

Acknowledgments

A million thanks and much love to Priestess Miriam Chamani, Gros Mambo Bonnie Devlin, Ochun Olukari Al'aye, Awo Robert Ogbe Di, Nia Dorsey, Aria Dorsey, Grace Buterbaugh, Alice Licato, Prudy Dorsey, Edith Licato, Alfred Licato, Suss, Christian, Siona, Vincent, Tish, Bast, Shannon, Eric, Queenie, Yogi, Harriet Barnes-Duke, Elie Barnes, Sadie Gordon, Sam Visnic, Ezra Visnic, Liam Nadeau, Phoenyx Precil, Bellavia, Cayne Miceli, Jorge Lopez, Risa Sharpe, Louis Martinié, Mishlen Linden, Jason Winslade, Margot Adler, Tansy Undercrypt, Angie Buchanan, Courtney Alexander, Rachel True, Mat Auryn, Dorothy Morrison, Bernadette Montana, Taylor Ellwood, Andrieh Vitimus, Deborah Lipp, Heather Greene, Spencer Adams, Shelby Quave, Laura Westbrook, Tammany Baumgarten, Sunpie Barnes, Rosie Rosato, Witchdoctor Utu and the Dragon Ritual Drummers, Dr. John (a.k.a. Mac Rebennack), and all my honored ancestors. I value your words, your guidance, your grace, and your support each and every day.

Contents

Spells and Recipes—xiii

Card Spreads—xvii

Foreword by Silver RavenWolf—xix

Introduction—1

Chapter One: Into, Around, and Deep Down into Tarot—9

Chapter Two: The Fool—19

Chapter Three: The Magician—27

Chapter Four: The High Priestess—35

Chapter Five: The Empress—43

Chapter Six: The Emperor—51

Chapter Seven: The Hierophant—57

Chapter Eight: The Lovers—65

Chapter Nine: The Chariot—73

Chapter Ten: Strength—81

Chapter Eleven: The Hermit—89

Chapter Twelve: Wheel of Fortune—97

Chapter Thirteen: Justice—105

Chapter Fourteen: The Hanged Man—113

Chapter Fifteen: Death—121

Chapter Sixteen: Temperance—127

Chapter Seventeen: The Devil—133

Chapter Eighteen: The Tower—141

Chapter Nineteen: The Star—149

Chapter Twenty: The Moon—157

Chapter Twenty-One: The Sun—165

Chapter Twenty-Two: Judgement—171

Chapter Twenty-Three: The World—177

Chapter Twenty-Four: Wands—183

Chapter Twenty-Five: Cups—189

Chapter Twenty-Six: Swords—195

Chapter Twenty-Seven: Coins—201

Chapter Twenty-Eight: Choosing a Deck—207

Chapter Twenty-Nine: Your Cards and You—215

Chapter Thirty: Tarot Altars and Shrines—225

Chapter Thirty-One: Crystals, Herbs, and Gardens—239

Chapter Thirty-Two: Tarot Questions and Spreads—253

Conclusion: The End and the Beginning—267

Recommended Reading—269

Bibliography—271

Contributor Biographies—273

Spells and Recipes

Magical: Fool's Gold Oil—22

Culinary: Fool's Deviled Egg—22

Culinary: Very Berry Fool—23

A Fool and a Foot Spell—25

Culinary: The Magician's Coffee Cup—30

Culinary: Minted Carrots—31

Salted Protection Spell for Home Blessing—33

Magical: High Priestess Oil—38

Culinary: High Priestess Pomegranate Salad—39

Culinary: Pistachio Stuffed Dates—39

Culinary: Lemongrass Iced Tea—40

High Priestess Tarot Blessing Spell—42

Magical: Empress Oil—45

Culinary: Foxy Pumpkin—46

Culinary: Empress Olive Salad—47

Empress Gris-Gris Bag Spell—49

Magical: Power Pack Oil—53

Culinary: Maple Bacon Delight—54

Culinary: Hot Nuts—54

Emperor Power Powder Spell—56

Magical: Sacred Wisdom Oil—60

Culinary: Sacred Sangria—60

Culinary: Lemon Pound Cake—61

Hierophant Helping Hand Floor-Wash Spell—63

Magical: Lovers Oil—68

Culinary: Lovers Carrot Apple Salad—69

Culinary: Fig Jam—69

Lovers Dream Pillow Spell—71

Magical: Sturdy Chariot Oil—76

Culinary: Protection Pot Roast—76

Culinary: Spice Cookies—77

Chariot Gris-Gris Bag Spell—79

Magical: Strong Medicine Oil—83

Culinary: Fortitude Fried Chicken—84

Culinary: Orange Marmalade—85

Strength Spray Spell—87

Magical: One Love Oil—92

Culinary: Healthy Hermit Bars—92

Culinary: Sage Stuffing—93

Meditation Bath Spell—95

Magical: Lucky Gold and Silver Oil—100

Culinary: Nutty Mushroom Bites—100

Success Sprinkling Spell—103

Magical: Court Case Oil—107

Culinary: Garlic Chicken—108

Culinary: Herbal Delight Pea Soup—108

Justice Jar Spell—110

Magical: Rebalancing Oil—116

Culinary: Traditional Pesto—116

Culinary: Roasted Red Grapes—117

Hanging Balance Bath Spell—119

Magical: Ashes and Earth Oil—123

Culinary: Vanilla Poppy Seed Cake—124

Death Becomes Us Water Spell—126

Magical: Fire and Ice Oil—129

Culinary: Ginger Pecan Spread—130

Temperance Gris-Gris Bag Spell—132

Magical: Down and Dirty Devil Oil—136

Culinary: Black Cherry Jello Shot—137

Culinary: Lil Devil Cupcake—137

Devil Walks Spell—139

Magical: Taking Down the Tower Oil—143

Culinary: Licorice Brownies—144

Tower Truth Candle Spell—146

Magical: Star-Crossed Oil—152

Culinary: Apple Cranberry Chutney—152

Star Uncrossed Candle Spell—154

Magical: Full Moon Magic Oil—160

Culinary: Mango Muffins—161

Moon Card Spell—163

Magical: Sun and Success Oil—167

Culinary: Sunshine Salsa—168

Sunshine Day Bath Spell—170

Magical: Maman Brigitte Oil—173

Culinary: Divinity—174

Judgement Clarity Candle Spell—176

Magical: Wider World Oil—179

Culinary: Magic Herb Bread—179

Spell for the World—182

Wands Incense—187

Cups Incense—192

Swords Incense—198

Coins Incense—204

Candle Blessing Spell—210

First Food Blessing Spell—211

Tarot Blessing Jar Spell—212

Tarot Bag Working—213

Card Spreads

Yes/No Spread—256

Open/Close Spread—257

Past/Present/Future Spread—257

Celtic Cross Spread—258

Wheel of the Year Spread—259

Ancestral Message Spread—260

Daily Tarot Spread—261

Rainbow Spread—261

What Is Happening Spread—263

Spiritual Path Spread—263

Ring around the Faeries Spread—264

High Priestess Spread—265

Foreword
by Silver RavenWolf

The night fills with so many sensory experiences that my mind reels with delight. The thick humidity hangs in the air, infused with the sweet, heavy, smoky scent of incense. My eyesight blurs as the spirits, the smells, the sounds, my vision, and my heartbeat become one. The drums sing with enticing joy. I am filled with the power of human ritual that we cannot see. All of my being is encompassed in the moment.

And I am ecstatic.

She moves with purpose, sometimes smiling softly, other times thoughtful and focused. The mother of the ritual, her presence and abilities fill me with peace and connection to divinity as she moves about the courtyard, fulfilling her purpose.

Reverence—I see her embrace the elements and the universal energies of honor.

Joy—I watch her dance, her feet moving in perfect rhythm with the drums creating the pathway that we will all follow.

Compassion—I admire her welcoming spirit of others. No judgment. Only joy. A free spirit that celebrates the happiness of her companions with true openness.

At the conclusion of the ceremony, I watch the participants—laughing, smiling, discussing the wonderful power of their experience. They disperse not alone but carrying with them the glowing remembrance fashioned by Lilith Dorsey, the author of this book.

I met Lilith in New Orleans and have always admired her many talents and her occult knowledge. When she asked me to write the foreword for this book, I was honored. I have been reading the tarot since I was sixteen years old—over fifty-one years—and I am delighted to share with you my endorsement of this amazing body of work. Innovative, dynamic, and ya know what? Interesting! Lilith's interpretation helps us navigate the sometimes jumbled mass of psychic information, shaking off the confusion to find the deeper meaning of the reading or cleanly unveiling the solution we need to a particular problem. From discovering how to use the energy of crystal grids to strengthening your readings and your psychic knowledge through distinctive and enjoyable techniques, this book will help you dig deep into the ways in which you can incorporate tarot into your physical well-being, from gardens to cooking to artistic fulfillment! Lilith provides a plethora of good, solid ideas, correspondences, and associations that you can use right now, today, at this minute. You'll want to place this book on your "go-to" shelf of magickal goodies!

Truly, it is one of those books that you won't want to lend out because you'll be afraid you won't get it back!

Embracing the power of magic and ritual to encourage change has been a part of human existence since the beginning of time. Such acts of ritual, study, and contemplation hold a special place in our lives, helping us mark essential moments and transitions, connect with our spirituality, and find meaning in our daily routines. In this book, you will delve into the sweetly deep world of interpretation and creative rituals of the tarot, exploring an incredible array of unique and interesting information. Guided by thirty-five years of Lilith's experience, you will find the joy of using the tarot as a positive force in your daily life through the author's distinctive and powerful perspective. Whether you want to deepen your spiritual practice, create meaningful ceremonies for yourself or others, or gain a better understanding of the role of the tarot in your life, this book has something for everyone. With personal anecdotes, practical advice, and inspiring examples, it will guide you on a journey of discovery and transformation. This book represents a wonderful path of clarity through a sometimes confusing subject. So come, let us embark on this journey and unlock the power of the tarot in your life through the expertise and definitive knowledge of Lilith Dorsey!

Introduction

Tarot is ancient, mysterious, powerful, and prescient. Honestly, there are probably as many ways to interpret the cards as there are individuals reading them. Cards contain the power to unlock the future, traverse space and time, and even discover important insights about yourself and those around you. Individuals can use them to read for themselves or others, or even expand the scope and do readings about the wider world.

One of the things that I am most excited about in modern society is that it has become a wonderful wide open world of Witches. I actually always hoped it would happen. The ancient ways have come home; well, honestly, for some of us they never left. There are those who identify as Water Witches, Fire Witches, Green Witches, Kitchen Witches, Herbal Witches, House Witches, Hedge Witches, Eclectic Witches, Traditional Witches, Art Witches, Love Witches, Urban Witches, and many, many more kinds. It may not surprise you that almost all of them are interested in tarot. This book is for every single one of them. You may identify as one of these Witches, all of these Witches, or none of these Witches, but nevertheless, and ever the more, you will find something useful in these pages. This book will show you how to utilize your inherent talents and apply them to this ancient tool for both divination and self-discovery.

Me and My Tarot

To tell the truth, I've always wanted to write a tarot book. My persistent dream was for a comprehensive book that covers every which way people use and grow through the cards. After so many years, I'm proud to truly say this is it.

My first book was published in 2005, and over the years, I've written seven more books. A few have won awards, and a few books have gone on to become international bestsellers. I am sincerely grateful and honestly humbled—I'm the High Priestess card in the Tarot of the Boroughs deck and the Hierophant in the Melanade Stand Tarot. So why did I wait so long to write this tarot book? There are a few good reasons, I promise you.

A good place to start is at the very beginning. I started reading tarot over four decades ago now, and for the past thirty-five years, I have been a professional tarot reader. I've done readings for people from all walks of life. I've done tarot readings in dirty dive bars and Grateful Dead show parking lots. I've read for famous artists, musicians, and government officials, and I've also read for homeless people. I would never write a book about anything I didn't have a deep and abiding knowledge of. After all these years, I finally feel like my tarot book is ready to birth itself into the wide world. Are you ready? I hope so.

Academically, I'm trained as an anthropologist and a plant scientist. While magically I'm an initiated priestess of New Orleans Voodoo, I'm also a long-time practitioner of Hoodoo, a practitioner of La Regla Lucumi (Santería), and a Witch. While some of these are initiatory traditions with closed practices, all of the workings in this book are for honoring and designed to be done by anyone who can approach the topic respectfully.

Part of the idea for this book was born out of a workshop I started doing back in 2005. The workshop was in turn based on a major arcana deck I had created at the time called the Tarot of Cruelty. Despite the name, it probably isn't what you think it is. For better or worse, I was in graduate school at New York University at the time. One of the precious few elective classes I was taking dealt with Antonin Artaud and his legendary theater of cruelty. To explain it as simply as I can, this experimental theater style emphasizes both mysticism and the power of the extreme.[1] The theater style includes references for everything from the Marx Brothers to the Tarahumara (Rarámuri) Ritual to

---

1.   Antonin Artaud, *Antonin Artaud: Selected Writings* (Berkeley: University of California Press, 1988), 1–35.

Shakespeare. Using humor, shamanism, and poetry, Artaud shows the reader how to unlock their creative bodies and their minds. For me, his musings begged to be incorporated into the language and imagery for a tarot deck. Artaud was also fascinated with mysticism. His methodology was influenced by the nontraditional and allowed people to understand these concepts on a meta level. I wondered if only this could be incorporated into the discipline of reading tarot cards.

Around this time, I was also doing tarot readings for clients privately and at the numerous witchy workshops and events I participated in. One day, a very concerned mom came to me for a consultation about her relationship with her teenage son. He was severely disabled and had recently become violent in his interactions with her. She was distraught and almost at her wit's end. Through the reading, we determined that she would need to use nontraditional ways to communicate with him to bring peace and understanding to their relationship. His verbal communication was limited, so we brainstormed ways to bring peace to the situation through foods, scents, songs, and other ways. We talked about his favorite meals, his favorite music, and hers too. Each individual card in the reading was associated with something other than mere words. We researched the corresponding herbs, sounds, animals, and the like that represented the cards in her reading. Now she could cook the accompanying foods and play the appropriate music notes that were necessary for his healing. At the end of the process, what we had created was not only glorious but also proved to be highly successful. Her interactions with him became more peaceful and full of understanding on both their parts. I realized this technique might also help others who were getting and giving tarot readings. Books on tarot meaning are extremely plentiful and so are books on divination correspondences; however, a book combining all these methods has yet to be fully explored. The genesis of this book, *Tarot Every Witch Way*, was born. Every day, I thank the Goddess that it was. Everyone has their own personal strengths and weaknesses, and these methods celebrate this in every way.

Exploring Every Witch Way to Use Tarot

There are a lot of benefits to be gained by reading the tarot for yourself and others. I won't go so far as to say all your problems can be solved with tarot, but most certainly most of them can. Even if the solution is only seeing things in a new light and with a better understanding of the situation at hand.

The first chapter of this book is titled "Into, Around, and Deep Down into Tarot." Here the book will examine the history of what some have called a "wicked" deck of cards, the origins of tarot in Italy, and how it evolved into the complex system now known today. In modern times, people have begun to associate tarot with both psychological and mythological processes. This helps users utilize it to explore either internal or external phenomena. Both are possible with tarot cards.

It is certainly possible to be more than one kind of Witch. You can be a Kitchen Witch who thrives in an urban environment and considers themselves an Urban Witch as well. You could be an Elemental Witch who also utilizes sex magic and many other ritual techniques—maybe that also makes you an Eclectic Witch. Fortunately, it is ultimately up to you. You decide your path because you alone are walking it. This first chapter will also explore in more detail what it means to be each of these Witches and how that particular slant may help you better utilize your cards. The process of becoming a Witch also allows you to own your own power and the keys to your success. You can 100 percent use tarot to help you along this journey, and this book will guide you toward ways to do that successfully.

The second chapter is an in-depth investigation of the first card of the major arcana, the Fool. In each of these major arcana chapters, Kitchen Witches will find the food for this card. Actually, each chapter holds recipes and spells to utilize the power of these tarot trumps. Sea Witches will find formulas for ritual baths and floor washes to help them dive deep into these cards. Fire-focused Witches will learn how to dress candles and make fire blessing packets to salute the energy of the cards. Incense blend suggestions are here to please our air-focused Witches, while Green Witches can ground their concept of the tarot through the growth of corresponding herbs and formulas. The Fool is numbered zero, which places it before any of the traditional trump cards. It makes a glorious place to start our study of this system.

Chapter 3 is dedicated to the card called the Magician. Many equate it with masculine power in the traditional sense. The force of the magic wand or staff bursting through into existence is often depicted and always implied in decks.

The High Priestess is numbered two in the tarot deck. She is the focus of chapter 4. She represents feminine power and the strong force of the Goddess in all her crowning glory. This is only the introduction, but I want to start out by saying that even though words like "masculine" and "feminine" are used here, it must be clear that this is not a binary system. Each of these cards inherently implies a fluidity. Tarot, just like gender, is a beautiful spectrum of possibility.

The next three chapters deal with the Empress, the Emperor, and the Hierophant. These represent different kinds of power and dominion than the previous cards. Here is the Emperor as a force of commanding intelligence. Ruling over lands and people, he is a different flavor of traditional masculine power. The same holds true for the Empress, examined in chapter 5. Some equate her with the maternal forces of the universe and humanity. She is a commanding ruler in her own right. As with all the chapters, there are recipes, correspondences, and suggestions for better understanding these cards.

The subsequent three chapters of this book talk about the next three trumps: the Lovers, the Chariot, and Strength. Tarot here begins to move away from individuals and shift toward deeper concepts and things. Union, connection, bonding, and melding all come together in the bodies depicted and evoked in the Lovers card. The Chariot is about movement, the vehicle you choose, and the ride you take to get where you are going. Strength shows us that we can and do have great fortitude to tame the beasts we find in our lives.

Next, the tarot moves on from looking at our individual selves and concepts into the wider universe with the Hermit, Wheel of Fortune, and Justice cards. They show us how our inner journey moves from internal to external and beyond. Chapter 11 focuses on the Hermit and how it illustrates that one can find peace, strength, and wisdom in the silent and solitary moments. The Wheel of Fortune is examined in chapter 12. This card spins us through the vicissitudes of our own personal destiny. Chapter 13 is about Justice. For better or worse, this card is about the structure and rules of the situations humans find themselves involved in. Justice reminds us of the laws of both humans and the universe, pointing out that no one is above these rules. Together, these cards provide necessary lessons and experiences to help guide individuals through life.

The Hanged Man, Death, and Temperance are the focus of chapters 14, 15, and 16, respectively. Outside of the court cards, these are probably the most puzzling ones dealt in a tarot deck. The Hanged Man shows us times of indecision and the cosmic need for balance. Death, often shrouded in darkness and fear, also points to the ultimate transformation and regeneration that awaits us all. The Temperance card, sometimes called Art, illustrates the power that can come through both adversity and creativity.

Chapter 17 examines the Devil card. The locks and chains we have forged for ourselves often show their ass in the Devil card. In other words, they reveal themselves plainly. Some decks even feature partially nude figures for this card in literal chains. We can choose to live with our chains or break free however we can. The Tower card is the subject of chapter 18, and it can be one of the most challenging in the tarot deck. It invariably points to the crumbling of the structures and situations the seeker finds themselves entangled with. Chapter 19 is dedicated to the Star card. In almost every deck I have seen, the Star card is associated with destiny. Each individual's journey toward their destiny will involve challenges, many of which play out in the archetypal situations depicted in the tarot, but if the challenges are navigated effectively, anyone can stay the course toward success.

The following three chapters take us from the single star to the Moon, the Sun, and Judgement cards. The Moon, covered in chapter 20, is our closest heavenly body, responsible for the tides of the planet and the ebb and flow of our emotions. The word "lunacy" springs to mind, which comes from the Latin word *luna*, meaning "moon." While the card doesn't necessarily mean madness, it does encompass the entirety of the meanings and conditions associated with the Moon. Chapter 21 revolves around the meanings for the Sun card. These often turn to great joy and happiness, the feeling you get when you are bathed in sunshine. The Judgement card is the focus of chapter 22. It is often connected to the concept of final judgment from a spiritual or cosmic perspective. When I find this card in a reading, very often the rewards given to the seeker will be in direct connection to the effort and character of the individual.

Chapter 23 is an examination of the final major arcana card, the World. It represents the utmost success and positive outcomes on the way. The lessons learned and the battles won through the journey up until this point are being rewarded in the best possible ways. Some decks refer to this card as the Universe; here the entire solar system is your oyster, your playground, yours to enjoy as you will.

From there, the next focus in *Tarot Every Witch Way* is the minor arcana cards. Chapter 24 deals with wands in all their fiery and energetic glory. The twenty-fifth chapter dives into the suit of cups and its watery depths. The suit of swords is the subject of chapter 26. Cutting to the point with great skill and intellect, the tarot reader sees how this plays out in a natural progression. Chapter 27 deals with the suit of coins or pentacles. From ace to king, all levels of earthly manifestation are made clear.

In the last third of the book, we'll move away from card descriptions and look at putting the cards into action. These sacred tools are meant to be utilized. Chapter 28 talks about your own cards and their unique relationship to you. This chapter will also cover getting to know your cards and getting your cards to know you. I find this to be a vital step for both accuracy and confidence when you are giving readings for yourself or others. Chapter 29 is next, covering reading basics. Mastering the basics is necessary before attempting to further your knowledge of any discipline. Things like reversals, best ways to practice, and advice from famous Witches and tarot authors are also included here.

Chapter 30 highlights tarot altars and shrines. Here you will find instructions on crafting a sacred space for your tarot cards to operate in. This can be as elaborate or as simple as you need to make it. It can be contained in a small candy tin or spread out across an entire room.

The powerful universe of tarot crystals, herbs, and gardens is explored in chapter 31. Here are detailed crystal workings with your cards, as well as plants and gardens you can use to help you supplement the power of tarot. This may be of particular interest to both Crystal Witches and Earth Witches reading this book. It will help you discover how to use the energy of crystal grids to strengthen your readings and your psychic knowledge. Then the book will dig deep into the ways in which individuals can incorporate tarot into their gardens and growing spaces. You may be wondering if this is of any use to you if you have little or no outdoor garden space; not to worry, this chapter will also cover gardening in window boxes, houseplants, and guerrilla gardening efforts in vacant lots and abandoned locales.

There are probably as many tarot spreads as there are tarot readings, so this is why all of chapter 32 deals with this subject. Here you will find traditional spreads like the Celtic cross and past/present/future explained. However, there will also be instructions for more unconventional spreads and unique ways to create your own spreads designed specifically for the question you are seeking solutions for. The all-important questions and how to best formulate them are also covered here.

In the conclusion, we will be able to springboard into integrating practice every "Witch" way. Maybe you have been reading cards for five days, or maybe you have been reading them for five years. In any case, you will be ready to go forward turning a new leaf, or should I say a new card.

Tarot Your Way

Tarot is a lifelong study. Always remember tarot is a valuable asset that will help you improve your other witchy strengths. Author and psychic Mat Auryn explains, "One of the reasons I love working with tarot is that it helps me make sense of psychic information that may not be entirely clear. When I receive psychic information, it often comes through in a jumbled or fragmented way, making it difficult to understand. However, using tarot as a tool, I can create a framework or structure around the information and gain a clearer understanding of it."[2] This book is designed to help you figure out all the different ways you can use tarot working to complement all your other talents.

---

2. Mat Auryn, interview conducted by Lilith Dorsey, April 25, 2023.

Chapter One
Into, Around, and Deep Down into Tarot

Fully understanding the origins of tarot is almost as complicated as understanding the cards themselves. People have infused myths with the magic, and unpacking the truth is no simple task. However, it makes sense to start by trying to discover the origins of the word itself. The word "tarot" as it is known in English has its roots in the Romance languages. *Tarot* is a French word that describes a deck of seventy-eight cards used for both playing games and telling the future.[3] Linguists have traced the word origins to Italian, where the cards were referred to as *tarocco*.

The earliest written references to the cards date to the 1440s, although many believe they were already in use as a popular card game similar to bridge or hearts. These early decks contained suits similar to the decks most readers are familiar with today. These were cups, swords, batons or wands, and coins or disks. They were joined with trumps, beginning with the Fool, assigned the number zero, and twenty-one trump cards. The trumps were originally called *trionfi* in Italian, which translates to the word "triumphs."[4] These cards were allowed to *triumph* over the other suits during the course of gameplay.

---

3. Cynthia Giles, *The Tarot: History, Mystery and Lore* (New York: Fireside, 1994), 3.

4. *Encyclopaedia Britannica Online*, s.v. "tarot," by David Parlett, accessed August 26, 2022, https://www.britannica.com/topic/tarot.

In these very early decks, there were neither names nor numbers. Players were required to memorize their order and ranking. While they may not have come with a name, they always seemed to represent a message or a concept. The images found on the trumps have been described as being allegorical or archetypal in design. They are chameleons transforming themselves into whatever the need is at hand and also phoenixes allowing the reader to fly forth through the flames of whatever situation he is enslaved inside.

The trump cards are also referred to as the "major arcana." They can be seen as archetypes, angels, spirits, or guiding internal or external forces. "Arcana" is derived from the Latin word *arcanus*, which translates to "secret." It is this limitless possibility that allows for its true brilliance as a system of discovery. Psychic and tarot expert Mat Auryn explained, "I must express my deep appreciation for the rich occult history of tarot. Its origins can be traced back to medieval Europe, where it was initially used as a game and later evolved into a tool for divination. The tarot's symbolism draws from a wide range of esoteric and mystical traditions, including astrology, numerology, Kabbalah, and alchemy. The depth and complexity of the tarot provides endless opportunities for exploration and discovery."[5]

Unfortunately, much of the early origins of tarot still remains clouded by history. Tarot scholars, however, do agree that one of the earliest surviving decks is the Visconti-Sforza Tarot. There are over fifteen different decks created between 1420 and 1450 still in existence.[6] Today there are thousands of decks on the market, and each appeals to a particular type of Witch or psychic reader.

In this book, I will expand these early ideas even further and give you recipes, scents, plants, musical notes, crystals, art, and much more for each card, so you can truly explore all these realms for yourself.

Which Witch Is Which?

So many Witches, so many glorious manifestations of magic. It doesn't take too much to be a Witch—just a belief in yourself and the forces around you. Each witchy specialty will allow us to truly maximize our talents as practitioners while crafting our way through this world. Some of these classifications

---

5.   Mat Auryn, interview conducted by Lilith Dorsey, April 25, 2023.

6.   Giles, *The Tarot*, 12.

are traditional, while others are newly crafted. In preparation for this work, I spent weeks seeing the different ways Witches identify themselves both online and at events in person. There's a wide variety here, showing that some define themselves by the type of Witchcraft and others by how one actually practices. Feel free to align with whatever you choose.

You can be all of these Witches or none of them. You can be half of one and 100 percent another, or it can change daily or with the seasons and situations you find yourself in. Ultimately, the point is to make magic. Magic that makes things better. Here are a few of the types of Witches you can choose to identify with. Discover what you need and leave the rest.

Art Witches

An Art Witch is just what it sounds like: a Witch who uses art or focuses on art in their practice. Within this category, there are also subclassifications, such as Stitch Witch and Crafty Witch, which explain the ways in which they choose to express themselves. A Stitch Witch prefers sewing and fabric as their primary medium. They might choose to make tarot patches, tarot altar cloths, or other tarot-inspired items of clothing or art. A Crafty Witch will use all different types of media to express and craft their magic. People identifying as an Art Witch are in luck when it comes to tarot because, first and foremost, tarot is an artistic medium. There are many different tarot decks in existence, and each one beautifully illustrates a particular form of artistic expression. They come from authors, artists, and readers from every walk of life. Artists can use these images as tools for both inspiration and self-exploration. One of the best pieces of advice I have is if this is your chosen witchy specialty, don't limit yourself. If you work with fabric by making clothes, try a different expression of art, like a tarot quilt or embroidering tarot symbols and vice versa. This will help you unlock both your creative potential and your magical potential by forcing you to take a different perspective.

Beginner Witches

I was not sure if I should include Beginner Witches on this list. That's because it is a stage rather than a type of Witch. "Beginner Witch," sometimes called "Baby Witch," is just a common way of referring to a Witch new to the practice. We all have to start somewhere, don't we? Everyone was a Baby Witch once, no matter how old they are chronologically. Even if someone came into this lifetime as an old soul, there is always something new to learn. Fortunately, with time, experience, and some luck, no one will stay a Beginner Witch forever. Our knowledge and experience will eventually help us blossom into our full expression of power. I've also heard newcomer Witches referred to as Witchlets and Newbie Witches. Embrace what you already know, even if it is just accepting that you are a Witch and taking it from there. In regard to tarot, it will help to start with the basics, choosing a simple deck as a starting point, learning it inside and out, and then expanding from there.

Chaos Witches or Magicians

One of the most misunderstood types of practice is that of Chaos Witches or magicians. The word *chaos* implies disorder to some extent, but this type of Witchcraft is more focused on fluidity and embracing the unexpected. Andrieh Vitimus, author of *Hands-On Chaos Magic: Reality Manipulation through the Ovayki Current*, describes the practice as "an attitude, a philosophy that promotes experimentation, play, and creativity while discarding dogmatic rules."[7] Very often these Witches combine tactics and techniques to bring about their desired results. When applying chaos magic to tarot, remember nothing is accidental; pay special attention to synchronicities and references to tarot however they appear.

Cosmic Witches

This type of Witch relies heavily on astrology and planetary influences. They make the most of the powers of the planets, stars, moons, and galaxies. Within this classification, we could also include Astrological Witches, Sun Witches, Moon or Lunar Witches, and Stellar Witches. Each one will have their own unique take on using this system in combination with astrology. The answers may be within, but it helps when we look to the stars. This book will help this type of Witch explore the ways their unique practice resonates with the astrological correspondences of the tarot cards.

---

7. Andrieh Vitimus, "Chaos Magic: The Misunderstood Path," *Llewellyn Journal* (blog), last modified January 12, 2009, https://www.llewellyn.com/journal/article/1799.

Cottage Witches

This type of Witch and their magic are focused on the home, which is similar to a Hearth Witch. The residence of a Cottage Witch is truly magical, frequently containing plants, animals, altars, and shrines to help assist them with their magic. They embrace nature in a multitude of ways. It will help to learn about the accompanying plants, animals, and other elements associated with tarot. For these Witches, their home or "cottage" is the space where they feel the most power, and they can use tarot to help amplify that in every way. It may mean adding tarot art to your home, choosing plants that represent your favorite or most challenging tarot cards, or even setting up tarot shrines in your temple space. The representations are completely up to you.

Coven-Focused Witches

Coven Witches prefer the connection and power that can be gained through the strength of a coven, which is the opposite of a Solitary Witch. A coven is a group of Witches, traditionally numbering between three and thirteen, who meet on a regular basis to practice magic. They also celebrate holidays together, such as sabbats and full moons. These can be traditional or eclectic and fluid. Customarily, they are led by a high priestess and a high priest, and recently the public has seen these positions being filled by individuals regardless of gender identification, thank Goddess. Coven-focused Witches will be guided by the dictates of their particular coven, but there are plenty of suggestions in this book to help them expand their practice in new and exciting ways. They may benefit themselves and their coven as a whole by bringing their tarot knowledge and practices to rituals and events.

Crystal Witches

Crystal Witches turn first to crystals and stones when they need to do their magic. Since crystals come from the earth, there is probably some overlap here with Earth Witches. Crystal Witches may delight in carrying crystals, creating crystal grids, and more. As far as tarot is concerned, they may feel better placing crystals in their tarot bag or creating elaborate crystal grids when they prepare to do a reading. Instructions for doing all those things in detail are presented in these pages. Crystal Witches may gain a greater understanding of the meaning of specific tarot cards by exploring their crystal correspondences and associations and approaching the matter that way.

Elemental Witches

There are four types of Elemental Witches corresponding to each of the elements: earth, air, fire, and water. These can also be broken down astrologically according to one's specific natal chart. Most people are familiar with their sun sign, but it is also helpful to look to the placement of the moon, rising sign, and other dominant influences in your chart to help you figure out where your witchy strengths lie.

Earth Witches

Earth Witches, similar to Green Witches, will find strength in nature and plants. They may enjoy growing things in their garden, or even surrounding themselves with houseplants in their home. When using the tarot, Earth Witches will gain strength by paying attention to botanical correspondences and how these may relate to the energy of the tarot cards. In these pages you will find a variety of herbal suggestions for including in your magic. Earth Witches may feel particularly fond of cards like the Empress, which features a verdant garden, or the suit of pentacles, which is said to represent the element of earth as a whole.

Air Witches

Air Witches are said to thrive on intellect and knowledge. Magically, they are said to resonate with incense and music. Each of the major arcana cards comes with a corresponding musical note that Air Witches may try to include in their tarot meditations or other practices. They may feel a connection to the suit of swords in the minor arcana, which is known to represent air.

Fire Witches

Fire Witches burn with passion and energy. The tools they are drawn to are most likely candles and other items where fire is directly present. There are many ways these can be used to increase the energy of the tarot. These Witches may feel a particular spark from the cards that are associated with the sun or fire in general, like the suit of wands.

Water Witches

Water Witches utilize and honor the magical energy of water in the form of seawater, ocean water, pond water, spring water, and more. Some practitioners choose to specify within this element and identify as Sea Witches, River Witches, and so on. Each one will have their own special practices, but they may feel particularly drawn to cards like the Moon or the suit of cups that are associated with water. Whichever element you identify with, it is an easy thing to integrate with your tarot readings and practice.

Eclectic Witches

Just as the name implies, Eclectic Witches make up their practice from a wide range of sources. They may include crystals, elemental workings, or any of the other techniques mentioned here as part of their Witchcraft, creating a beautiful bricolage of magic. They may also wish to pick and choose from the many different ways to explore tarot cards in this book. The Eclectic Witch may want to play to their strengths and explore the sections of the book that are similar to their own established practices or branch out and reach toward something new.

Faery Witches

Also called Fae Witches, these practitioners center their practice on the fae folk. They frequently have a special reverence for nature, animals, and sacred spaces directly in nature. My only warning is that folklore has shown us that faeries can be tricky, and if this is your path, please remember that things are not always as they seem. Certain herbs, crystals, or techniques detailed in this book may help you honor the Fae while also learning more about the use of tarot. There are traditional schools of Witchcraft focusing on this type of magic, but one could choose to be solitary and take their cues directly from the faeries themselves.

Green Witches

I certainly identify at heart as a Green Witch. I've always had a deep and abiding love of plants that has carried throughout my life. Here in New Orleans I have my own community garden, and I even had to take a break from the writing of this to be an official judge for the New Orleans Spring Garden Show. Green Witches can be Witches who have a general love of gardening or who have a special niche that they are drawn to, such as Goth plants, medicinal herbs, native plants, and so on. Having a better understanding of how different botanicals relate to the tarot will help with improving your magic in both areas. Remember you don't have to have a giant garden to be a Green Witch—even apartment dwellers can have houseplants and a grow light if necessary to bring their practice home. Many Green Witches have also taken a liking to guerrilla gardening and have begun to seed bomb empty lots and untended public spaces.

Healing Witches

As the name clearly states, Healing Witches focus their magic on healing. When I first started formally studying the craft, one of my teachers pointed out that in reality all magic can be considered healing magic. Obviously, the first thing that comes to mind is the healing of illness, but these Witches can also focus on healing someone's financial or romantic situation or even healing the planet. Some of these Witches utilize reiki or therapeutic touch with their healing work. Tarot and other divination methods can often be utilized to find out where and how healing efforts should be focused. Healing Witches should also take special care to utilize the cleansing and protective techniques used in this book. Being a Healing Witch comes with its own baggage, and you must remember to shield yourself from the unhealthy energy you are frequently coming in contact with.

Hedge Witches

The Hedge Witch is associated with the hedge or special plants that create the boundaries for property. It has been this way for centuries. Hedge Witches are seen as belonging to this liminal or special in-between area, a space where magic happens and anything is possible. Their craft often focuses on plants, herbs, animal guides, intuition, and time-honored formulas. They also frequently live a solitary lifestyle on the edge of both society and town. In many ways this is similar to a Folk Witch, whose beliefs are also centered on herbs, animals, and family or folk-honored traditions. Every one of these can be supplemented with individual cards or readings about your practices. Each Hedge Witch may have methods that differ from others; that is perfectly fine. Remember that nothing is set in stone.

Hereditary Witches

A Hereditary Witch is one whose focus is on inherited magic from their ancestral line. For these Witches, family traditions, including recipes, spells, workings, rituals, customs, and the like, are all incorporated into their belief systems and ways of doing things. If you ask my opinion, I think all Witches have some sort of hereditary power, even if they don't know it, and those ancestral Witches' names have been lost to time. Many of these Witches may have been taught the use of tarot cards and other divination methods from their elders. They may use the techniques in this book to expand upon the ancestral knowledge they have been given. Some of it may even seem familiar to what they have been taught their whole lives.

Kitchen Witches

Just as the name implies, Kitchen Witches find their strength in the power of food and cooking. They view every recipe, every bite even, as an opportunity to make magic happen. Throughout this book, they will find so many different foods and recipes corresponding to the tarot cards. It is my sincere hope that some of these will find their way onto these Witches' magical tables. We all have to eat. Why not make it magical? Eating the related foods will allow you to internalize and understand the cards in a whole different way.

Solitary Witches

To be a Solitary Witch means that you prefer to practice magic on your own, without the aid of a coven or larger group. I've met a lot of these Witches over the years, in part, I believe, because people's connection with nature and also deity can be very personal. Many of you may have grown up in an environment where it wasn't safe or cool to be a Witch and practices were kept secret. This was a necessity for a very long time. Even Coven Witches and Traditional Witches still do magic for themselves when they are not at a ritual or event, so at some time or another everyone is a Solitary Witch. There is a power that comes with solitude, and mastering that is a wonderful skill to possess. We see this particularly highlighted in the Hermit card in the major arcana.

Traditional Witches

Back when I first started studying magic and the occult in New York City in the 1970s, Traditional Witchcraft was about all there was available. Individuals following this type of system traced their lineage back to some of the earliest practitioners of these old ways. Sadly, many of these icons, such as Margot Adler and Herman Slater, are no longer with us. Luckily, many have picked up the mantle and continued to make sure these time-honored traditions are still practiced today. This type of Witch may feel more comfortable with traditional decks like Rider-Waite-Smith or Thoth tarot and using traditional spreads like the Celtic cross.

This list is by no means complete. There are House Witches, Tech Witches, Sex Witches, Ceremonial Witches, and lots more. As I said earlier, there are probably as many types of Witches as there are people practicing Witchcraft. The previous list is included here as a good starting point so readers can attempt to identify their strengths and maximize these in every way possible. Nothing is permanently set in stone, and nothing needs to be decided before you start to use this book. Ultimately, more will be revealed as you take your own magical journey through these pages. Maybe you will discover a scent that speaks to you or a recipe you find particularly tasty. These will help you find ways to improve your Witchcraft and your sacred relationship with the tarot cards.

Chapter Two
The Fool

The Fool card is the start of the tarot deck. It is the beginning of the hero's journey into life—wild, weird, and wonderful. We see our archetypal hero, or just maybe we see ourselves. The Fool starts us on our way.

Numbered zero in the tarot deck, the Fool card comes before or after everything else. It is outside and in-between just like fools themselves. This is a liminal space. In many decks, the Fool doesn't even have both feet on the ground. The Fool card, in a way, is absolutely everything in the tarot and absolutely nothing. It evokes the deep darkness that comes before the illumination of light and vice versa. It is the alpha and omega, and here completely anything is possible. The joy of the Fool is in the beginning. The fact it is assigned the number zero is quite fitting. Like the Ouroboros, the mythological serpent eating its tail, it represents both beginnings and endings. The Fool represents endless cycles that are always turning.

The earliest Fool card still in existence is from the Visconti-Sforza tarot and is part of the Morgan Library collection housed in New York City. This specific image dates from the late 1400s. The image of the Fool is scantily clad in only a coat and loincloth, wears feathers in his hair, and carries a large club. Not present are the dog, the sun, or the ominous cliff often represented in later decks.

Sometimes the Fool is depicted with a stone; some believe this is in reference to the "stones of folly," which were said to be embedded in the heads of the insane and a cause of madness.

The oldest decks seem to paint this figure as a beggar with disheveled clothing and wild, unkempt hair. In some decks, the Fool carries a sack. This raises the question from many tarot readers "What is in the sack?" Could it be riches, money, knowledge, or potential, or is it empty? The world may never know. It is important to note that this is the start of a journey. The Fool has little other than himself, and a trusty dog to get through the trip. But maybe that is all they need.

Certain decks, like the New Orleans Voodoo Tarot by Louis Martinié and Sallie Ann Glassman, feature an egg as one of the primary symbols for this card. I love this because it invites thoughts of beginnings and birth, creation as the ultimate first journey everyone takes. It also raises the question of which came first, the chicken or the egg? Or in this case, the snake or the egg? If this is your first time looking at this card, think about why you are taking this journey with these mysterious cards and where you hope it will lead. Think about beginnings and endings and the cycle that connects them on every level.

The Fool card that appears on the left at the start of this chapter is from the Orisha Tarot deck by Andrew McGregor Oba tilemi. It shows the Orisha Elegguá or Esú, who is seen as the wise trickster who must be consulted before anything is to be done. He is the energy of the crossroads, of choices and possibility. His lessons are always powerful for those who are smart and cunning enough to understand them. Very often he is pictured as a child, which also highlights the fact that the fool is always at the beginning of his journey.

Meanings and Correspondences

Popular meanings for the Fool card include new beginnings, transformation, innocence, change, spontaneity, inspiration, fearlessness, possibility, liberation, development, and growth. Here are other correspondences and magical associations for this card.

Crystal Correspondences

Amazonite—This stone is said to focus the mind on what is important. Amazonite allows you to see all sides to a situation, which makes it very helpful when doing divination with cards in which multiple perspectives can be represented.

Aventurine—Aventurine is a crystal of awareness and infinite possibility. It helps with growth and the transformations that need to take place in order for this progress to happen.

Clear Quartz—Clear quartz is an all-purpose stone that can be used in almost every aspect of magic, including divination. It will amplify and complement any other crystal it is used with.

Herbal Correspondences

Ginseng (*Panax ginseng*)

Frankincense (*Boswellia sacra*)

Peppermint (*Mentha ×piperita*)

German Chamomile (*Matricaria chamomilla*)

Cypress (*Cupressus sempervirens*)

Rose (*Rosa* spp.) (Note: in many decks, the flower that the Fool holds is actually a rose.)

Other Correspondences

Animal—Dog

Astrological—Mercury, Uranus

Musical Note—E

Magical and Culinary Recipes

Here are a few recipes that are associated with the Fool card or work with its energy.

Magical: Fool's Gold Oil

This is a recipe designed for new beginnings. It is made to bring joy, happiness, and protection.

Ingredients

Small glass bottle

½ ounce sweet almond oil

9 drops frankincense oil

9 drops cypress oil

9 drops rose oil

Gold glitter

Directions

Get all the ingredients together and place them on your tarot altar or shrine. If you don't have one of these, please find a clean and quiet space to work in where you will not be disturbed. First, add the sweet almond oil to the bottle. Then add the frankincense, cypress, and rose oils. Add the gold glitter. Cap the bottle. Rub the bottle quickly between your two palms. Throw it gently in the air and catch it. These practices allow the mixture to be blessed and charged with your energy and the energy of the Divine. Now it is ready for use.

Culinary: Fool's Deviled Egg

One of the foods associated with this card is deviled eggs. It is one of my favorites. The egg is a symbol of new beginnings, and yet because so many of us grew up with deviled eggs at holiday time, it evokes the past as well. This recipe contains old standby ingredients like dill and onion, plus a few spicy new additions like chipotle mayonnaise and smoked paprika. I hope you enjoy it while you contemplate the past, celebrate the future, and meditate on everything in between.

Ingredients

8 hard-boiled eggs	1 tsp garlic powder
⅛ cup chipotle mayonnaise	1 tsp onion powder
⅛ cup plain mayonnaise	1 tsp minced chives
3 tbsp sweet relish	2 tsp smoked paprika
2 tsp dried dill	Salt and pepper to taste

Directions

Peel the eggs and slice them in half. Scoop out the yolks into a large bowl. Mash with a fork. Add the remaining ingredients, minus salt and pepper. Mix well, then add salt and pepper to taste. Spoon the filling back into the cooked egg whites. Keep refrigerated until serving. Makes 16 halves.

Culinary: Very Berry Fool

While the Fool is a tarot card, it is also a dessert and a valued part of English cuisine for hundreds of years. It is sublime in its simplicity, and many believe that's how it got its name. Traditionally, the dish is prepared with gooseberries, but those particular berries can be difficult to find, so the following recipe substitutes blueberries and strawberries. You may, however, use whichever fruit you wish in this dish. The original recipes also involved custard, though modern cooks use whipped cream instead. While this recipe might be simple, it's also delicious and the perfect thing to help you ponder your new beginnings ahead heralded by the Fool card.

Ingredients

2 cups whipping cream	1 tsp white sugar
1 pint blueberries, washed	1 tbsp rose water
1 pint strawberries, washed and sliced	

Directions

Beat the whipping cream until stiff; divide into 2 bowls. Heat the berries over low heat in a nonreactive saucepan along with the sugar and rose water. After

5 minutes, remove from heat and let cool until room temperature. Take half the cream and fold it into the berry mixture. In a large glass bowl or trifle dish, spread a layer of whipped cream, followed with a layer of the berry mixture, and continue layering until you run out of cream and berries. Chill in the refrigerator and serve cold. Makes 8–10 servings.

Journeying with the Fool

Part of my wish for this book is that it helps to guide everyone on their own unique journey with the cards. There are thousands of books that will provide generic meanings and stock answers, but ultimately, it is your own personal connection to the cards and their sacred journey that will unlock the keys it holds for you. This meditation journey will help you unlock the major arcana meanings for yourself, no matter which Witch you are. It may help to record the following journey working and play it back as you listen to it in a comfortable space, where you will be undisturbed by the outside world as you travel through this sacred space. Alternatively, if you are new to this type of working, it may help to have a friend or partner read the following to you, helping you along the way. Whichever tactic you use, do your best to clear your mind, sit down, close your eyes, and immerse yourself in the full flavor of the experience.

The Fool is where each and every one of us starts our journey. Imagine yourself at the top of a staircase. The steps are numbered in descending order. You are at the top step, number ten. See your feet on the step. Look at the number written there. Slowly step down to step number nine. See the number written there. Do you see letters or numbers? Really look at what is in front of you. When you see it clearly, step down to number eight. Continue stepping down through the numbers seven, six, and five. See the numbers and your feet going down to number four, number three, then number two, and finally down to number one. When you get to the bottom of the stairs, you see a large golden door. Open the door and step through.

Walk into the world on the other side. Look around you. The space in the card is a cliff on a mountain. You are on this cliff. Look around; there are mountains in the distance. Is there snow on the mountaintops? Are they mostly green? Do your best to remember what you see here. It will help your memory to answer these questions out loud even if you are alone. Plant your feet firmly on the ground and look down. What do you see? Are there grasses? Are there plants? Do you see flowers?

You hear a puppy in the distance. It is running and playing. It comes toward you. You hold out your hand for it to smell. How does the puppy react? You see a figure up ahead. They are carrying a sack. Greet them. Ask them if they have anything to tell you. What do they say? If you like, you can ask them more questions about their journey or yours. What else do you see here? When you have taken it all in as best as you can, turn and walk back toward the door where you came into this place.

When you come to the door, open it slowly and cross the threshold. In front of you are the exact same numbered steps you came down earlier. This time you are going to walk up these stairs. See your feet climbing up the first step to the second. Then on to the third step, fourth, going higher and higher up. Up the fifth, the sixth, the seventh. Continue on up to the eighth, the ninth, the tenth. Now you are back at the top. Open your eyes.

It may help to write down all the things you discovered during this working in a tarot journal or notebook. You can refer to this whenever the Fool card comes up in your reading, playing an important yet puzzling part.

A Fool and a Foot Spell

In many traditions, feet and shoes are blessed as part of a ritual to make sure the individual is walking in the right direction. This simple spell does the same. All you need are your shoes and some simple things to get started.

Ingredients

1 tbsp dried peppermint   Small bowl

1 tbsp dried rose petals   Your favorite pair of shoes

3 drops cypress oil

Directions

Gather all ingredients (except the shoes) together on your working altar or tarot shrine. Place the peppermint and the rose petals in the bowl, adding the cypress oil on top. Mix well. Leave the mixture outside for 24 hours to bless it with the rays of the sun and the moon. After the time is up, it is ready to use. Place a small pinch in each of your shoes whenever you feel you need help with guidance and direction. Repeat as often as necessary.

Chapter Three
The Magician

I - THE MAGUS

An entire world of possibility is presented in the tarot card numbered one and dedicated to the Magician or Magus. The image on the right is from Millennium Thoth tarot and includes both traditional imagery and radiant brilliance.

The Magician card evokes manifestation, power, and commanding forces. Here is the archetypal hero taking the first purposeful steps in this journey called life. In many decks, we see the Magician figure raising one hand high up toward the sky and the other down toward the earth. This implies dominion in both realms, illustrating the principle "as above, so below." There is a sacred balance highlighted here, one that the tarot reader is to be mindful of on every level. The Magician card is the fulcrum on which this delicate balance hinges.

The figure represented here is a skillful magician able to manifest his deepest desires at will. He grabs the world with both hands, and power flows energetically from his fingertips. The ability to transmogrify, or magically transform, has been attributed to some iconic religious figures over time, most notably Jesus Christ and the Buddhas. However, the process can also be found in nature, such as the process of a caterpillar metamorphosing into a butterfly. The Magician owns this power.

In certain decks, the Magician is called the Magus or the Juggler. This second description is a clue to the tricky nature of this card. Several balls or issues are up in the air. The power is in figuring out which to catch ahold of next. As if to complicate the matter further, the trickster featured here often speaks in complicated riddles. It is as if the truth and commanding skill he holds have to be decoded by the willing and the worthy. The same holds true for the tarot cards themselves, and we should never forget it.

Very often the imagery of this card features the tools of the minor arcana suits, namely a coin, a cup, a wand, and a sword. All of this is present in the Millennium Tarot Magus pictured on the previous page. This again reinforces the Magician's mastery over not only magic but also the elements, which are represented by these suits. The popular Rider-Waite-Smith deck places red roses and white lilies in a garden at the feet of the Magician. This symbolism has also been echoed in many of the tarot decks created in the following years. The red rose is traditionally a signifier of love and passion, while white lilies are frequently associated with purity and the Virgin Mary. Also ever-present in the Magician card is the infinity symbol above the figure's head. This can be seen to represent the eternity or limitlessness of the magic represented here.

This is a card of crafting, and through this skillful crafting comes manifestation. It should not be lost on the reader that the word "craft" means many different things. As children, we create with simple tools: blunt scissors, popsicle sticks, foam, indestructible beads, tasty globs of paste, and more compose our beginning forays into art and magic. We create representations of what we see and also what and who we want to be. Crafting in our adult bodies very often refers to magic—and maybe the occasional Pinterest board. Hopefully, we still use what we see to create what and where we want to be. The Magician card reminds us that we have skills and tools to help us achieve all our goals right at our fingertips.

The majority of decks depict the Magician as a single figure. This is their choice. Yet in many ways, they are not alone: they are imbued with the sacred knowledge and the versatile tools they need to be successful. The importance of this cannot be ignored. On a deep level, this is a card of abundance, not necessarily in a traditional way. It is an abundance that is like a spark of energy leaping from one's magical fingertips to bring about much-needed change.

Meanings and Correspondences

Popular meanings for the Magician card include communication, consciousness, confidence, power, discernment, knowledge, energy, perception, potential, magic, manifestation, transformation, imagination, and resourcefulness.

Crystal Correspondences

Agate—This is a power stone of rebalancing. Agate will help unify and harmonize your mind, body, and spirit. During a tarot reading, it can assist with concentration and perception.

Citrine—This light yellow stone is a form of quartz. It is useful when doing readings for love or healing. Citrine brings clarity, psychic awareness, and growth.

Fire Opal—This stone is known to help align you with the higher realms and psychic perception. It is known to have held special significance for ancient Maya and Aztec cultures and was said to grant both joy and luck.

Herbal Correspondences

Cedar (*Cedrus* spp.)

Marigold (*Calendula officinalis*)

Myrrh (*Commiphora myrrha*)

Rosemary (*Salvia rosmarinus*)

Red Rose (*Rosa* spp.)

White Lily (*Lilium candidum*)

Yarrow (*Achillea millefolium*)

Other Correspondences

Animal—Raven, fox, snake, unicorn

Astrological—Mercury, Jupiter

Musical Note—E

Magical and Culinary Recipes

The foods associated with this card are mint, fennel, dill, rosemary, and coffee. The following recipes incorporate some of these and are a great way of symbolically taking this card's meaning and drinking it in.

Culinary: The Magician's Coffee Cup

A traditional Irish coffee is made with only four ingredients: coffee, sugar, cream, and whiskey. This recipe takes that classic a step further but can also be made without alcohol for those in recovery or those who choose not to imbibe. I chose this recipe because it is designed to do two things. The first is to wake you up and keep you alert and awake for this journey you are about to undergo. For the tarot is most definitely a journey, and at the beginning is the Magician. The second reason is to serve as an offering for our ancestors, as liquor is something that many of us use for this purpose. Many drank in life and continue to require alcohol now that they have crossed over to the other side. Therefore, even if you choose not to drink this yourself, you might wish to consider leaving this as an offering for your ancestors.

Ingredients

1 cup hot chicory coffee

1 tbsp cream

1 tbsp Irish whiskey

1 tsp sugar

Dash of cinnamon

Dash of nutmeg

Directions

Combine the chicory coffee, cream, Irish whiskey, and sugar in a tall coffee mug. Stir well. Sprinkle with cinnamon and nutmeg. Enjoy. Makes 1 cup.

Culinary: Minted Carrots

Carrots are full of vitamin A, which helps strengthen the eyes. There's a reason your elders told you to eat you carrots. It just so happens that they have the ability to strengthen your psychic sight as well. This recipe is one I have enjoyed for years, and it is both simple and delicious.

Ingredients

2 tbsp butter

1 tbsp chopped fresh basil

3 tbsp chopped fresh mint

2 cups sliced carrots

½ cup water

Directions

Place the butter, basil, and mint in a saucepan and cook over low heat until the butter is melted. Add the carrots and water. Stir frequently. Continue to simmer until the carrots are slightly tender and most of the water has been absorbed. Remove from heat and serve warm. Makes 3–4 servings.

Journeying with the Magician

The following journey working is designed to help you uncover the Magician inside yourself. It is an exploration into your own personal power and strength. While this exercise involves exploring the unconscious, it will also help you make a clear connection with your conscious self. Workings like this may be difficult for some; feel free to move at your own safe pace, and remember you are ultimately in control of your own destiny. I've encountered a lot of people who think about journey work as a path to their shadow self; while it can be, it is also a path to your shinier self. This is the road everyone travels on here. You may wish to record this meditation and play it for yourself if you are alone; alternatively, you can have a friend read it for you. For this meditation, you may use the traditional imagery detailed in the following journey, or choose a Magician card from your favorite deck and use that as your focus. If you choose your own specific deck, you will need to alter the following instructions to correspond directly with the imagery presented in that card.

Close your eyes. Imagine yourself at the top of a staircase. The steps are numbered in descending order. You are at the top step, number ten. See your feet on the step. Look at the number written there. Slowly step down to step number nine. See the number written there. Do you see letters or numbers? Really look at what is in front of you. When you see it clearly, step down to number eight. Continue stepping down through the numbers seven, six, and five. See the numbers and your feet going down to number four, number three, then number two, and finally down to number one. When you get to the bottom of the stairs, you see a large golden door. Turn the handle and step into the world of the Magician.

In the distance you see a table. Walk toward it. Upon it, you see the traditional tools, but they are not generic in any way. These are your tools, the ones specifically given to you to achieve your purpose. There is a wand; reach out and pick it up. Examine it. What is it made of? It will help your memory to answer these questions out loud even if you are alone. Is it wood? If so, what kind? Is it ash, alder, oak, maple, or something else you see? Perhaps it's made of metal. Is it copper, a shining silver, or a glistening gold? How does it feel in your hand? Heavy or light?

When you are done inspecting, put it back down on the table and look for your chalice. This chalice is more than just a simple cup: it is the sacred grail filled with the elixir of life. Take a long, hard look at it. Again, notice and really accept what it is made of and what this might mean for you. Is it crystal, catching all the glimmers of light that fall upon it? Maybe it is made of wood or even metal. Pick it up and discover what the liquid inside looks like. Remember this is your own personal vessel of power. Smell it. Drink it if you like. How do you feel afterward? Really feel that feeling and remember it on a cellular level.

What else do you see on the Magician's table? The suit of pentacles is often represented as a coin or coins. Do you see a coin in front of you? If so, pick it up. What is it made of? Are there words or symbols on it? Is it old or new? Maybe you don't see a traditional coin. What round metallic item is there? Feel the weight of it in your hand.

Turn it over. Is something different on the flip side? Does it look familiar? Does it look foreign? If you can, do your best to memorize and mentally record what you see in your hands.

Place the coin back on the table if you wish, and turn your attention to your last magical item, the sword. Is it a sword, or is it maybe an athame or other sacred blade? Is it straight or curved? What is the handle made of? Could it be bone, leather, or wood, or is it something else? This is your power tool to cut out whatever isn't working in your life. You can use it to protect and to help you persevere. What color is it? Mentally record as many details as you can and then place it back on the table. Now it is time to return to the doorway.

Walk back toward where you entered this place. When you come to the door, open it and walk through to the other side. In front of you are the same numbered steps you came down. This time you are going to walk back up. See your feet climbing up the first step to the second. Then on to the third, fourth, going higher up. Up the fifth, the sixth, the seventh. Continue on up to the eighth, the ninth, the tenth. Now you are back at the top. Open your eyes.

It may help to write down the things you discovered during this working in a tarot journal or notebook. You can refer to this whenever the Magician card comes up in your reading.

Salted Protection Spell for Home Blessing

Magic begins at home. It's a place for living, sleeping, and manifesting our dreams. Making sure your home is spiritually blessed and protected is one of the most important first steps you can take toward success. This spell incorporates all the tools of the Magician tarot card to help you build a strong foundation at home. It may speak to Elemental Witches of all types, or those focused on the home. Even if you don't identify as one of these, it may be helpful to make sure your home is protected for whatever the future has in store. Also remember you can do this as often as needed, such as whenever there is tension or disruption in the home or when things just don't feel right.

Ingredients

½ cup sea salt	1 cup tap water
1 tsp dried basil	Glass bowl
1 tsp iron filings	3 drops myrrh oil
Glass jar	1 small white candle
1 cup spring water	

Directions

Begin by gathering all ingredients on your working altar or tarot shrine. If you don't have one, please check out the instructions in chapter 30. Place the sea salt, basil, and iron filings in the jar. Cover the jar and shake well. Next, put the spring water and tap water in the glass bowl. Add the myrrh oil. Put the candle in the center of the bowl and light it. As it burns, visualize its energy radiating out and covering your home in a protective light. See the light radiating out to all corners of the space. When it has burned down (never leave a burning candle unattended), take the remaining wax floating in the water and put it in the trash.

Take the salt mix in the jar and sprinkle some on your doorstep. Traveling counterclockwise, go throughout your home sprinkling a pinch of the mix on the windowsills, under the sinks, and under your bed. Dispose of whatever remains after you have done this in the garbage. Next, take the remaining water in the bowl and sprinkle it around your home. Start at the front door and sprinkle it on the threshold. Traveling clockwise, sprinkle a small amount on the windowsills, doorways, and under the beds. Pour the remaining mixture down your drain. The spiritual working is now complete. You may repeat this as often as you like.

Chapter Four
The High Priestess

THE HIGH PRIESTESS

Masterful and mysterious, serene and commanding, the High Priestess holds dominion over all in her sacred gaze. The featured image on the left is from Santa Muerte Tarot. It shows the power she wields even in other realms. Her throne is adorned with crystals, allowing her to hone and channel her gifts.

The High Priestess card in the tarot can be seen as the ultimate representation of the divine Goddess in all her glory. For many, myself included, this is one of the best cards in the deck to receive in a reading. It evokes feminine power at a meta level. Some visualize this as a specific goddess, and this card has been attributed to Isis, Astarte, Artemis, Lilith, Mary Magdalene, Pope Joan, Santa Muerte, Sophia, Kali, Persephone, Maya, Miriam, Voodoo Queen Marie Laveau, and many others. Everyone has access to the sacred feminine regardless of gender, and this card salutes that in every possible way.

When we examine the imagery here, it is ripe with meaning. Many traditional decks feature two pillars inscribed with the letters B and J. It has been theorized that this has biblical significance and refers to the columns outside the Temple of Solomon that bore the words or names "Jachin" and "Boaz." This also holds significance for Freemasons. Like the biblical King Solomon, this priestess is known to possess great wisdom and insight. Other common symbolism on the card includes a crescent moon and an equal-armed cross. A crescent moon is said to be symbolic of the Egyptian goddess Hathor. Hathor was known to be a goddess of love, beauty, and pleasure as well as a strong protector of women. Because of this inclusion of the crescent moon, many believe this card to be influenced by the moon. The three phases of the moon are said to be represented in the headdress worn in the classic Rider-Waite-Smith tarot deck.

There is a stillness in the High Priestess card. She sits as the ultimate spiritual power taking it all in and waiting poised for the time to act. She is guided by her intuition and knowledge from the otherworlds. The Rider-Waite-Smith deck features a curtain of pomegranates behind her, which evoke the story of Persephone and the Underworld. In all realms, in all ways, this knowledge is there for you to explore.

When I first began reading cards, this particular one spoke to me of the Triple Goddess, specifically the Goddess in both her Maiden and Crone aspects. The High Priestess embodies all the excitement and exuberance individuals have in their youthful maiden aspect, while also possessing the great wisdom and experience that can only be held by someone in their crone time. When she graces your reading, explore that balance in the situation, the dance of young and old in perfect equilibrium.

Meanings and Correspondences

Popular meanings for the High Priestess card include intuition, feminine power, subconscious, occult wisdom, prophetic dreams, truth, honesty, awareness, faith, balance, and supernatural happenings. Here are a few more associations for this card.

Crystal Correspondences

Moonstone—This milky white stone can help with all levels of psychic ability and accessing the unknown. It is a stone of truth and honesty. Just like the moon itself, it is also used to remind us that everything is caught in a larger cycle of change and transformation.

Garnet—Garnet will help with energy and courage. It can be used in combination with your tarot cards, as it helps with clarity and insight into yourself and the people you are reading for.

Pearl—Pearls can be formed in the ocean or in fresh water by oysters and mussels, respectively. They can also be man-made. Since the beginnings of civilization, they have been associated with sacred femininity and the Goddess. They are especially helpful with full moon readings and workings. Water Witches may find pearls helpful because they are literally born of water.

Lapis Lazuli—Lapis is said to work directly to improve psychic energy and connections. It is a stone that assists with revealing and also releasing that which is unnecessary. A true stone of the Priestess, this can help you actively listen during a tarot reading.

Jet—Magically, this powerful stone enables you to accurately express and manifest your psychic abilities. It gives strength and deflects negativity for all who wear or carry it. Jet has been used since ancient times for protective amulets and talismans.

Herbal Correspondences

Clary Sage (*Salvia sclarea*)

Iris (*Iris* spp.)

Lemon (*Citrus ×limon*)

Ylang-Ylang (*Cananga odorata*)

Date Palm (*Phoenix dactylifera*)

Dahlia (*Dahlia pinnata*)

Vetiver (*Chrysopogon zizanioides*)

Myrrh (*Commiphora myrrha*)

Jasmine (*Jasminum* spp.)

Other Correspondences

Animal—Cat, owl

Astrological—Moon, Mercury

Musical Note—G#

Magical and Culinary Recipes

The following formulas and recipes showcase the bounty and sovereign power that is present in this card. The foods that are used most often for her are pomegranates, dates, and lemongrass, and they feature prominently in these recipes.

Magical: High Priestess Oil

The following recipe is designed to help you connect with the forces of the divine feminine specifically through the energy of the High Priestess card. It is especially helpful to wear it while doing tarot readings.

Ingredients

½ ounce sweet almond oil

1-ounce (or larger) glass bottle

9 drops myrrh oil

9 drops vetiver oil

9 drops amber oil

9 drops jasmine oil

Pinch of orris root

Directions

Gather all your ingredients together on your magical altar or shrine. If you don't have one, please check out the instructions in chapter 30. It is best to begin crafting this formula on the eve of the full moon. Place the sweet almond oil into the bottle. Add the myrrh, vetiver, amber, and jasmine oils. Then add the pinch of orris root. Shake well to combine. Cap it tightly and place it under your pillow or bed overnight to charge it with your energy. The formula is then ready for use.

Culinary: High Priestess Pomegranate Salad

The sacred energy of the High Priestess is complex. She is both Maiden and Crone. She is also both hot and cool. It is for these reasons that I created this refreshing recipe.

Ingredients

2 tbsp extra virgin olive oil

2 tbsp balsamic vinegar

2 tbsp pomegranate juice

Juice from 2 oranges

Salt and pepper to taste

3 cups salad greens (lettuce, arugula, or similar)

2 medium cucumbers, peeled and diced

3 tbsp finely chopped green onions

Seeds from 1 pomegranate

¼ cup black olives

½ cup feta cheese crumbles

Directions

Combine the olive oil, balsamic vinegar, pomegranate juice, and orange juice in a small bowl. Mix well. Then add salt and pepper to taste. In a large bowl, place the salad greens, cucumbers, green onions, pomegranate seeds, and black olives. Sprinkle feta cheese on top. Drizzle the oil mixture over the salad greens. Serve immediately. Makes 3–4 servings.

Culinary: Pistachio Stuffed Dates

Since the date palm tree is featured in many classic tarot decks for the High Priestess, it makes perfect sense to include a date recipe here. This recipe would be appropriate for any ceremonial gathering or feast and would be an extra special addition to a sister or moon circle.

Ingredients

12 Medjool dates

½ cup ricotta cheese

¼ cup shelled pistachios

1 tsp minced lemon zest

Directions

Cut the dates in half lengthwise and remove the pits. Chop the pistachios coarsely. In a medium-size bowl, combine the cheese, pistachios, and lemon zest. Stuff dates with the cheese mixture. Serve immediately. Makes 24 halves.

Culinary: Lemongrass Iced Tea

This tea is said to be healing for both mind and body. As with everything, please consume in moderation.

Ingredients

    1 stalk lemongrass, chopped

    2 cups spring water

    Ice

Directions

Boil water in a nonreactive pan. Add the chopped lemongrass after the water begins to boil. Turn the heat down to low and simmer for 10–12 minutes. Remove from heat and let cool completely. Strain the mixture. Serve over ice.

Journeying with the High Priestess

You may wish to record this meditation and play it for yourself if you are alone. Alternatively, you can have a friend read it for you. For this meditation, you may use the traditional imagery detailed in the following paragraphs, or choose a High Priestess card from your favorite deck and use that as your focus. If you choose your own specific deck, you will need to alter the following instructions for the imagery presented in that card.

Close your eyes. Imagine yourself at the top of a staircase. The steps are numbered in descending order. You are at the top step, number ten. See both of your feet on the step. Look at the number written there. Slowly step down to step number nine. See the number written there. Do you see letters or numbers? Really look at what is in front of you. When you see it clearly, step down to number eight. Continue stepping down through the numbers seven, six, and five. See the numbers and your feet going down to number four, number three, then number two, and finally down to number one. When you get to the bottom of the stairs, you see a large silver door. Turn the knob and step through.

On the other side of the door is a curtain. It is gold and silver, embroidered with deep burgundy pomegranates. Push it to the side, really feeling the weight of it. This is like nowhere you have been before. The fabric fruits give way to real fruits, vines, and trees. In the distance, you see a throne. Walk toward it. On either side of the throne are pillars. One pillar is black. Carved deep into the stone is the letter B. Feel it with your fingers. Is it rough? Smooth? Cool to the touch or warmed by the sun? It will help your memory to answer these questions out loud even if you are alone. You feel drawn to explore all aspects of this place. Soon your attention is drawn to the other pillar. On it is carved the letter J. It is white. Before you is a study in opposites, in balance, in duality in its highest forms. Feel the differences. Explore the similarities. Between these pillars is a throne. Is it made of wood? Stone? Or is it some other material? Is it carved? Run your hands across it. What does it feel like on your fingertips? Do you want to sit on the throne? If so, take a seat. Get comfortable. Beside you is a scroll. Open it. Read it. Remember what it says here. When you are done experiencing this place to the fullest, turn and walk back toward the way you entered this sacred space.

When you come to the door, open it slowly and cross the threshold. In front of you are the exact same numbered steps you came down earlier. This time you are going to walk back up these stairs. See your feet climbing up the first step to the second. Then on to the third, fourth, going higher and higher up. Up the fifth, the sixth, the seventh. Continue on up to the eighth step, then the ninth, the tenth. Now you are back at the top. Open your eyes.

It may help to write down the things you discovered during this working in a tarot journal or notebook. You can refer to this whenever the High Priestess card comes up in your reading in an important or even a confusing way.

High Priestess Tarot Blessing Spell

This working is engineered to bring the maximum amount of spiritual energy and blessings from the High Priestess to your deck. You can perform it when you get a new deck or whenever you think your old deck needs a bit of a boost. This working is best performed on the eve of the full moon, but you can perform it anytime if you need to.

Ingredients

Blue cloth

Your tarot cards

1 small piece moonstone

Pinch of myrrh

Pinch of sandalwood

Small white tea light

Candleholder

1 drop lemon oil

Directions

Spread out the blue cloth on your altar or shrine. Remove the High Priestess card from your deck. Shuffle and cut the deck however you choose. Then place the High Priestess card back on the top of the deck.

Place the deck in the center of the cloth. Put the moonstone on top of the deck, followed by the myrrh and sandalwood. Place the tea light in the candleholder. Put the drop of lemon oil on the candle and light it. Place the candle on the cloth between you and the cards. Envision the light from the candle moving back and forth between you and the tarot deck. It may help to play your favorite witchy music at this time. Look at your cards, seeing the energy shining off them.

When you feel the raising of energy is complete, put the candle out and dispose of it in the trash. Put the moonstone in your tarot bag or on your altar. Shake the myrrh and sandalwood onto the cloth and fold it up. Place your cards in your tarot bag or on your altar. Shake the folded cloth outside on the earth to distribute the sandalwood and myrrh. They are biodegradable and will break down over time. Now the working is complete and your cards are ready to use.

Chapter Five
The Empress

III · The Empress

The next card in the deck is the kind and nurturing Empress. If we view the cards as a spiritual journey, here are our earliest teachers and caregivers, those charged with responsibly protecting us and guiding us through this ride called life. Each one provides its own specific guidance and advice. The more

I work with tarot, the more I see its ability to not only help us decode the future but also make sense of the past and how it influences us today.

The maternal aspect of the divine feminine is present in this card. Soft and nurturing, this card represents care and concern on every level. Her number is three, evoking the family and also the Holy Trinity in all its forms. It is rampant and abundant growth and fertility in all realms. Mother Nature and Mother Earth reside in this card, as do Venus, Cybele, Demeter, Ishtar, Hera, Aphrodite, Eve, and many more primal mothers birthing the seeds of humanity. The Empress chooses you before you are even born. Her magic and mastery are as ancient as the hills. Now is the time to be enraptured by her loving kindness and support.

This card is that of the accomplished woman. She has learned much, and she has much to share with those she loves. She has also seen much, but getting her to share those tales is a bit more complicated.

A large majority of tarot decks portray this card as a woman surrounded by the bounty of nature. It is here that she feels most at home, surrounded by her beloved birds and beasts. Her heart and her garden are in full bloom. Some readers see this card as a natural extension of the Queen of Pentacles: here is another woman grounded and stable in her power. An Empress commanding and ruling with a loving and gentle hand. There is both physical and emotional security that she freely possesses and gives. Her energy is that of the best hug that you didn't even know you needed.

Meanings and Correspondences

Popular meanings for the Empress include beauty, initiation, success, motherhood, and expression. Here are other associations and correspondences for your reference and use.

Crystal Correspondences

Rose Quartz—This variety of quartz is said to help with love in all its forms. It was used in ancient Persia, in ancient Egypt, and in historic Asian beauty spells, and you can certainly utilize its great benefits today. Rose quartz can be used as an offering for Freya, Yemaya, Venus,

Isis, and Hathor. This ancient crystal is prized by many goddesses and is ultimately used to contact the divine feminine.

Peridot—This is a stone used to bring great joy. It also helps with physical and spiritual growth in all ways. Traditionally, peridot was worn to help combat negativity and psychic attack. It can help with your tarot readings by giving confidence and clarity.

Turquoise—This stunning blue-green stone grants protection, success, and luck. It was particularly prized by a number of Indigenous North American peoples.

Emerald—This popular gemstone is said to help with memory and intelligence. It is said that even the legendary Cleopatra wore one as a display of her power.

Herbal Correspondences

Hyacinth (*Hyacinthus orientalis*)

Water Lily (*Nymphaeacae*)

Motherwort (*Leonurus cardiaca*)

Rose (*Rosa* spp.)

Ylang-Ylang (*Cananga odorata*)

Other Correspondences

Animal—Dolphin, deer

Astrological—Venus, Saturn

Musical Note—F#

Magical and Culinary Recipes

Enhancing your readings by making magical concoctions and feasts allows for a greater understanding of what the cards are trying to tell you. These recipes can be used to help connect you with the divine feminine in all her aspects.

Magical: Empress Oil

The oil contains sweet florals that are often associated with this card.

Ingredients

½ ounce sweet almond oil	6 drops orange blossom oil
6 drops ylang-ylang oil	6 drops amber oil
6 drops hyacinth oil	Small glass bottle

Directions

Gather the ingredients together on your working altar or shrine. If you don't have one, please check out the instructions in chapter 30. Combine all ingredients in the small glass bottle. Shake well to combine. Hold the bottle between your palms and rub it back and forth quickly to charge it with your energy. It is then ready to use. Use generously.

Culinary: Foxy Pumpkin

This culinary recipe contains olives, wheat, and pumpkin, which are often associated with this card.

My spiritual family and I have enjoyed this recipe for years. Because of its use of pumpkin, it can be eaten to celebrate the bounty of nature and the fertility of the divine feminine in all its forms.

Ingredients

½ cup diced red onion	¾ cup mashed pumpkin
2 tbsp minced garlic	¾ cup seasoned breadcrumbs
3 tbsp chopped fresh sage	1 egg, beaten
3 tbsp olive oil	Dash of salt and pepper
3 tbsp chopped fresh parsley	

Directions

Fry the onions, garlic, and sage in olive oil until browned, remove from heat. In a separate bowl, combine the parsley, pumpkin, breadcrumbs, and egg. Mix well, then add the onion mixture. Stir well to combine. Form the mix into balls approximately 1 inch in diameter. Place them on a lightly greased baking sheet and cook at 375 degrees Fahrenheit for 20–25 minutes.

Culinary: Empress Olive Salad

I wanted to include as many recipes as possible that are vegetarian and healthy in every way. This recipe is both. Make this salad to help nurture your soul and fuel your body.

Ingredients

1 cup large green olives, pitted

1 cup large black olives, pitted

3 tbsp chopped red onion

¼ cup chopped celery

¼ cup chopped carrots

1 tsp minced garlic

3 tbsp extra virgin olive oil

2 tbsp balsamic vinegar

1 tbsp minced fresh basil

2 tsp minced oregano

2 tsp minced parsley

¼ tsp black pepper

Pinch of salt

Directions

Combine the olives, onion, celery, carrots, and garlic in the bowl. Mix well. Pour the oil and vinegar on top. Then sprinkle the rest of the ingredients over the top. Combine well. Cover and refrigerate for at least 3 hours, and then it will be ready to serve. Makes 5–6 healthy servings. This will keep 3–4 days in the fridge, so you can make it ahead if necessary.

Journeying with the Empress

You may wish to record this meditation and play it for yourself if you are alone. Alternatively, you can have a friend read it for you. For this meditation, you may use the traditional imagery detailed in the following paragraphs, or choose an Empress card from your favorite deck and use that as your focus. If you choose your own specific deck, you will need to alter the following instructions for the imagery presented in that particular card.

Sit down and get comfortable. Close your eyes. Imagine yourself at the top of a staircase. The steps are numbered in descending order. You are at the top step, number ten. See your feet on the step. See the number written there. When you are ready, slowly step down to step number nine. Look closely at the number written there. Do you see letters written out or actual numbers? Really look at what is in front of you. When you see it clearly, step down to number eight. Continue stepping down through the numbers seven, six, and five. See the numbers and your feet going down to number four, number three, then number two, and finally down to number one. When you get to the bottom of the stairs, you see a large golden door. Turn the handle and step into the world of the Empress.

On this side of the door, you see a lush garden, a forest, a jungle, a universe of verdant green. What plants do you see? What flowers? What does it smell like here? Take it all in. It will help your memory to answer these questions out loud even if you are alone. In the distance, there is a throne. Walk toward it at your own pace. Notice what the earth feels like beneath your feet. Pay attention to the trees, flowers, and other plants you find there. When you get to the throne, take a long look at it. What is it made of? Is it adorned with crystals or intricate carvings? Are they familiar to you? Do your best to remember all you see and feel here. You may sit in the throne if you like. How does that feel? Look around the area. Do you see a scepter or other tool? Look further into the distance. Do you see a river, mountains? What is out there? Feel the sun shining down on your skin. Feel its warmth. Explore as much or as little as you like. When you feel ready to return, begin walking back toward the door to the steps.

When you come back to the golden door, open it and walk through. In front of you are the same numbered steps you came down earlier. This time you are going to walk up these stairs. See your feet climbing up the first step to the second. Then on to the third step, the fourth, going higher and higher up. Up to the fifth, the sixth, the seventh. Continue on up to the eighth, the ninth, the tenth. Now you are back at the top. Open your eyes.

It may help to write down the things you discovered during this working in a tarot journal or notebook. You can refer to this whenever the Empress card comes up in your reading, especially if she appears in a prominent or even a confusing position in your tarot spread.

Empress Gris-Gris Bag Spell

A gris-gris (pronounced *gree gree*) bag is a little bundle of magic. It is traditionally made from natural fabric filled with herbs, oils, crystals, and charms to
help you achieve your goals. This bag is in honor of the Empress tarot card. It
will help provide joy and nurturing when you most need it. Earth Witches may
find it especially helpful, as it contains both herbs and crystals from the earth.

Ingredients

4-inch square natural fabric in
    your favorite color or design

1 small piece rose quartz

1 tsp dried rose petals

1 tsp gardenia petals

3 drops ylang-ylang oil

6-inch piece leather or jute cord

Directions

Gather all the ingredients together on your working altar or shrine. If you
don't have one, please check out the instructions in chapter 30. Place the fabric
square in the middle of the space. Next, put the rose quartz in the center of the
fabric. Place the rose and gardenia petals and on top of that. Finally, sprinkle
the ylang-ylang oil over the herbs. Gather the corners of the fabric together
and tie it with the cord. Throw the bag gently into the air and catch it. This will
allow it to travel into the world of the invisibles to get a blessing. Now the bag
is ready to use. Carry it in your pocket or place it under your pillow whenever
you need a little extra comfort and nurturing.

Chapter Six
The Emperor

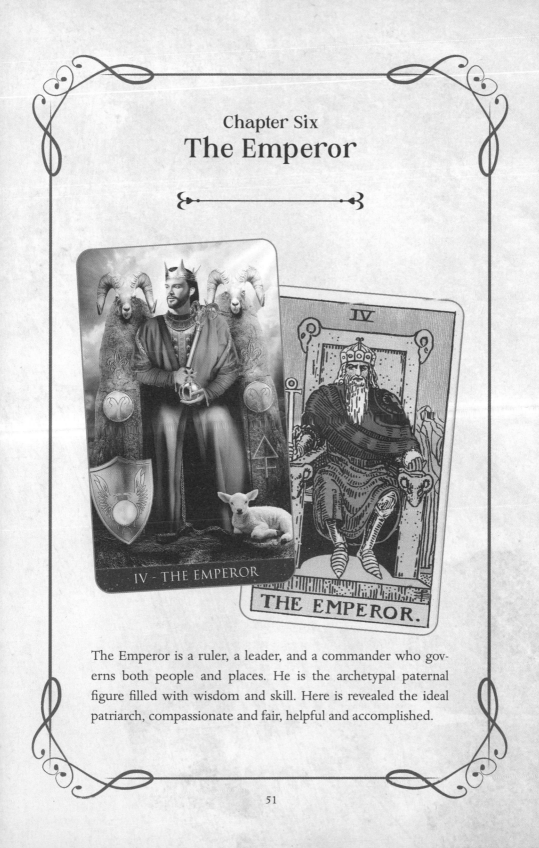

IV - THE EMPEROR

THE EMPEROR.

The Emperor is a ruler, a leader, and a commander who governs both people and places. He is the archetypal paternal figure filled with wisdom and skill. Here is revealed the ideal patriarch, compassionate and fair, helpful and accomplished.

The Emperor card shows us how to manage and organize chaos so it becomes order. Many liken this card to some of the more phallic gods, such as Jupiter, Apollo, Osiris, Poseidon, and Legba. In many ways, this is the counterpart of the Empress card. The Emperor sits upon a throne, a visual symbol of authority. Some decks also feature a ram's head, a symbol for the zodiac sign of Aries, implying dominion and authority. The left image featured on the previous page is from the Millennium Thoth deck and shows several different rams: two on the throne, one on the scepter, and even a baby at the Emperor's feet. This is clearly an accomplished ruler. Time and again, he has done the impossible, and it has made him mighty.

This card is numbered four, which represents stability and foundations. In a reading, this card can mean a paternal figure in your life providing important lessons and expert guidance. He gives wise counsel, which everyone would do well to listen to. Alternatively, this could also be representative of yourself and the ways in which you mentor and guide others seeking your help. The Emperor is honest and truthful, yet also serious and kind.

Meanings and Correspondences

Popular meanings for the Emperor include power, protection, dominion, authority, achievement, ambition, and skill. Here are more correspondences relating to this card for your use.

Crystal Correspondences

Red Jasper—This fiery-colored jasper uncovers hidden problems concerning the situations that arise in the tarot reading. It also helps with remembering your dreams and could be useful when using tarot in concert with dreamwork.

Ruby—Ruby is an energetic stone that can both motivate and protect. When used in conjunction with your tarot readings, it can help you get a clear picture of the issues at hand. It is known to grant a heightened awareness of things and assist with concentration.

Fire Agate—This protective stone surrounds you with a shield of spiritual fire. It grants both courage and psychic fortitude.

Herbal Correspondences

Hemlock (*Conium maculatum*) (poisonous)

Pine (*Pinus* spp.)

Oak (*Quercus* spp.)

Geranium (*Pelargonium* spp.)

Ginger (*Zingiber officinale*)

Calamus Root (*Acorus calamus*)

Other Correspondences

Animal—Ram, goat

Astrological—Mars, Jupiter, Aries

Musical Note—C

Magical and Culinary Recipes

Enhancing your readings by making magical concoctions and feasts allows for a greater understanding of what the cards are trying to tell you. The oil honors the supreme power of the Emperor card and can be used when you need confidence and the ability to succeed. The most common foods for the Emperor card are ginger, bay leaf, and nuts. All three of these feature in the creations that follow.

Magical: Power Pack Oil

At the end of making this recipe, you will have a tiny bottle of oil packed with power.

Ingredients

3 drops pine oil

3 drops ginger oil

3 drops geranium oil

3 drops sandalwood oil

1 bay leaf, crushed

½ ounce sweet almond oil

Small glass bottle

Directions

Gather all the magical ingredients together on your altar or shrine. If you don't have one, please check out the instructions in chapter 30. Combine the oils and bay leaf in the small glass bottle. Throw the bottle gently up in the air to bless it with the energy of the Divine. Don't forget to catch it on the way down. Then it is ready to use.

Culinary: Maple Bacon Delight

This is one of those simple recipes that you can't stop eating. It is great to have as part of a holiday brunch or feast. I use it for the Emperor card because it makes you feel powerful just eating it.

Ingredients

1 lb bacon, cooked

¼ cup maple syrup

¼ cup brown sugar

¼ cup walnuts, chopped

1 package crescent rolls

Directions

Form the crescent rolls into a large rectangle on a baking sheet. Drizzle with the maple syrup. Next, crumble the bacon into pieces and sprinkle it over the top. Do the same with the brown sugar and walnuts. Bake in a 350 degree Fahrenheit oven for 15–20 minutes until it begins to brown. Serves 4–6. Enjoy.

Culinary: Hot Nuts

This hot and spicy nut recipe can be made for a special occasion, but it is so delightful you may find yourself making it every few weeks just to have on hand as a healthy snack for you and your loved ones. All nuts are said to be connected to the Emperor card.

Ingredients

1 tbsp melted butter

1 tbsp extra virgin olive oil

1 tsp garlic powder

2 tsp chili powder

¼ tsp ground cayenne pepper

1 tsp onion powder

½ tsp black pepper

¼ tsp salt

| 1 cup peanuts | 1 cup walnuts |
| 1 cup almonds | 1 cup cashews |

Directions

Preheat the oven to 350 degrees Fahrenheit. Mix the butter and oil together in a measuring cup. Add the garlic, chili, cayenne, onion, black pepper, and salt. Stir well until it is thoroughly mixed. Add the nuts to a large bowl. Pour the oil and spice mixture over the nuts, stirring well to make sure they are well coated. Line a cookie sheet with parchment paper. Spread the nuts out over the parchment. Bake for 10 minutes. Remove from the oven and stir. Return to the oven and cook 10 minutes more. Remove from oven and cool. Makes 4 cups.

Journeying with the Emperor

You may wish to record this meditation and play it for yourself if you are alone. Alternatively, you can have a friend read it for you. The Emperor is about getting in touch with power, both inside and out.

Sit down and get comfortable. Close your eyes. Imagine yourself at the top of a small staircase. The steps are numbered in descending order. You are standing at the top step, number ten. See both of your feet on the step. See the number written there. When you feel ready, move on to step nine. See the number written there. Do you see letters or numbers? Really look at what is in front of you. When you see it clearly, step down to step eight. Continue stepping down through the numbers seven, six, and five. See the numbers and your feet going down to number four, number three, then number two, and finally down to number one. When you get to the bottom of the stairs, you see a large red door. Turn the doorknob and step into the world of the Emperor.

On the other side of the door you see a throne. It is highly decorated. The arms of the chair are carved. Examine the detail. Do you see horns, skulls, or something else? It will help your memory to answer these questions out loud even if you are alone. There is a scepter near the chair. It has an ankh at the top. Look at it. What is it made of? Is it metal, stone, or something else? What else do you see while you are here? Is there someone here? What do they have to say? Ask them what you need to know about this place, if you feel comfortable. Explore as much or as little as you like. Remember as much as you can about the experience. When you feel that you are ready to return, begin walking back toward the door to the steps.

When you come to the door, open it and walk through. In front of you are the same numbered steps you came down earlier. This time you are going to walk up these stairs. See your feet climbing up the first step to the second. Then on to the third, fourth, going higher and higher up. Up the fifth, the sixth, the seventh. Continue on up to the eighth, the ninth, the tenth. Now you are back at the top step. You can now open your eyes.

It may help to write down the things you discovered during this working in a tarot journal or notebook. You can repeat this whenever the Emperor card comes up in a prominent place in your reading or when you are having trouble understanding how his power manifests.

Emperor Power Powder Spell

This spell working is designed to help you gather your own power and authority in a situation. It can be used in work or school situations where you can sprinkle it around the corners of the place and also put some in your pocket or desk.

Ingredients

1 tbsp chopped dried calamus root	3 drops bergamot oil
1 tsp powdered ginger root	Glass bowl
3 drops vetiver oil	Wooden spoon

Directions

Combine the roots and oils in the glass bowl. Stir the ingredients three times counterclockwise and then three times clockwise to charge the mix with your energy. Then it is ready to use.

Chapter Seven
The Hierophant

V · The Hierophant

Tradition and spiritual knowledge are the watchwords of the Hierophant. Surrounded by ancient wisdom, the Hierophant urges us to follow the advice of those who have come before. They are first and foremost a sacred teacher, one who imparts wisdom firmly grounded in faith, tradition, and ethical belief.

Many envision this, most likely stemming from their upbringing, as a rabbi, priest, or guru. The card can be this, but it can also represent less orthodox leaders as well. Spiritual teachers in less mainstream religions can be found here, yet still adhering to convention. While intuition can always be useful, it is also important to consider those who have walked these paths before and how Witches from all walks of life can benefit from their successes and also their failures.

The word "hierophant," meaning "sacred reveal," originates from ancient Greece: clad in purple robes, celibate men in Eleusinian cults renounced their former names and became known simply as *hierophantēs*.[8] These figures were responsible for chants and other holy duties during the religious rites.

Many of the depictions of the Hierophant portray them carrying a large book. This is thought to be a holy book containing sacred knowledge and rites. The knowledge contained herein is important enough to be both seriously studied and carefully guarded.

I mentioned earlier that I have been photographed for two different tarot decks. In the Melanade Stand Tarot, I was chosen to portray the Hierophant card. It was a real honor, something quite fitting as I began to think about it. I've written several books, and tradition has always been a big part of my practice. I see the deep value in learning from and also honoring my elders. In Witchcraft, there are some guidelines, and without them, your results may not come out the best. Don't we all want to be our best? This is one of the core virtues the Hierophant represents—the care and protection that can come from having a trained spiritual teacher. When supplemented with one's own intuitive magic, this can make one highly successful hopefully in every area.

One of the most common images featured in this card is a large and imposing throne. This is more than just a chair for sitting, it is a high seat of sacred power. The throne comes with the job, as do a whole host of responsibilities and wisdom. If you take the throne, you must also take the responsibilities that accompany it. The image shown on the right on page 57 is from the Mermaid Tarot by Leeza Robertson and Julie Dillon. It shows the Hierophant in a library consulting sacred texts. Books are common features in this card, symbolic of

---

8. *Encyclopaedia Britannica Online*, s.v. "hierophant," last modified January 15, 2015, https://www.britannica.com/topic/hierophant.

the wisdom contained within. Another frequently used symbol in this tarot card is keys. The keys show that the Hierophant is the one who grants access to what it is we need to see and do. These keys are both literal and metaphorical. They open countless doors in the real and invisible worlds. In some tarot decks these keys are replaced by a large ankh, symbolizing access to both the masculine and feminine mysteries.

Two pillars are actually featured in this card, just like the High Priestess. Some people refer to this as the High Priest card. There are many sacred similarities you can uncover here. Ideally, individuals can internalize all this holy information and use it to progress. This isn't a card of ego, instead utilizing one's spiritual talents and knowledge to help craft a better tomorrow for us all.

Meanings and Correspondences

Popular meanings for the Hierophant include consulting, connecting, authority, established truths, rituals, conventions, teachings, and divine guidance. Here are more correspondences and other associations for this card for use in your workings.

Crystal Correspondences

Smoky Topaz—This type of topaz helps with truth telling and spiritual development. It can also assist with your confidence and problem-solving. Utilized correctly, it can help to boost all your magical efforts.

Hematite—Use this stone for both divination and journey work. It will help unify all aspects of your mind, body, and spirit. Hematite can also be used to help with concentration and focusing on the tasks at hand.

Citrine—A pale yellow stone that is actually a form of quartz, citrine can be useful when doing tarot readings for love or healing. Citrine can grant great clarity, psychic awareness, and spiritual growth.

Sapphire—Another name for sapphire is wisdom stone. It is useful with intuition and psychic power. Sapphire can help to curb wishful thinking in a reading and get to the real truth of the matter.

Herbal Correspondences

Gardenia (*Gardenia jasminoides*)

Lavender (*Lavandula angustifolia*)

Other Correspondences

Animal—Bull

Astrological—Taurus, Earth

Musical note—C#

Magical and Culinary Recipes

Enhancing your readings by making magical concoctions and feasts allows for a greater understanding of what the cards are trying to tell you. The food most commonly associated with this card is lemon, which you can find in the culinary recipes here.

Magical: Sacred Wisdom Oil

This oil blend is great for accessing higher realms and spiritual knowledge. It is also helpful when looking for a spiritual teacher.

Ingredients

½ ounce sweet almond oil

6 drops lavender oil

6 drops gardenia oil

6 drops frankincense oil

3 drops lime oil

Small glass bottle

Directions

Gather all ingredients together on your altar or shrine. If you don't have one, please check out the instructions in chapter 30. Add the sweet almond oil, lavender oil, gardenia oil, frankincense oil, and lime oil to the bottle. Cap the bottle and shake well to cover. Leave it overnight on your tarot altar or shrine to charge, and then it is ready to use.

Culinary: Sacred Sangria

I chose to include a sangria recipe for this card because even the name implies blood and sacredness, as it comes from the Latin *sangre*, which means "blood."

It features lemon slices, peaches, apples, and strawberries. This is a fantastic recipe to prepare and share for a feast day or other sacred celebration.

Ingredients

750 mL bottle or 3 cups red wine, preferably Primitivo or Zinfandel

½ cup brandy

1 lemon, sliced and seeds removed

1 peach, sliced

1 red apple, sliced

6 strawberries, sliced

¼ tsp cinnamon

Directions

Take a large clean carafe. Add wine, brandy, cinnamon, and fruits. Stir well with a wooden spoon. Place in the refrigerator to chill. Serve cold and drink up! Makes 3–4 servings.

Culinary: Lemon Pound Cake

Just like the Hierophant, this recipe is a classic. There are a few modern day changes, however, and the traditional creaming method is sped up with the use of a blender or food processor.

Ingredients

1½ cups cake flour, plus more for coating pan

1 tsp baking powder

½ tsp salt

2 sticks (16 tbsp) unsalted butter

1¼ cup white sugar

2 tbsp lemon zest

Juice from 2 lemons

4 extra large eggs

2 tsp vanilla extract

Directions

Preheat the oven to 350 degrees Fahrenheit. Grease a 9-by-5-inch loaf pan and dust with flour. In a large bowl, whisk together the flour, baking powder, and salt. Melt the butter in a medium saucepan over low heat, being cautious not to let it brown, then let it come to room temperature. In your blender or food processor, mix the sugar and zest until combined. With the blender or processor going, add butter in a steady stream through the tube or top opening in the blender. Mix for approximately 20–30 seconds. Transfer this mix to a large bowl. Mix the eggs, juice, and vanilla. Using a sifter, add the flour mix gradually over the egg mixture, stirring after each addition to combine. Pour the batter into the pan and bake for 15 minutes. Reduce the oven heat to 325 degrees and cook for an additional 30 minutes or until a toothpick inserted into the center comes out clean. Cool to room temperature. Serves 8–10 people.

Journeying with the Hierophant

For this meditation, you may use the traditional imagery detailed below, or choose a Hierophant card from your favorite deck and use that as your focus. If you choose your own specific deck, you will need to alter the following instructions for the imagery presented in that unique card. You may wish to record the following and play it back while you complete the journey work. The Hierophant card speaks deeply of sacred knowledge. This meditation will help you find and utilize this knowledge.

Sit down and make yourself comfortable. Take a deep breath. Close your eyes. Go slowly and take your time. Imagine yourself at the top of an old stone staircase. The steps are numbered in descending order. You are at the top step, number ten. See your feet on the step. See the number that is written there. When you are ready, slowly step down to step number nine. Hold on to the railing if necessary. See the numbers written on the steps. Look carefully at what is in front of you. When you see it clearly, step down to the number eight step. Continue stepping down through the numbers. Down to seven, six, five. See the numbers and your feet going down to number four, number three, then number two, and finally down to the final step, number one. When you get to the bottom of the stairs, you see a large stone door. Turn the handle and step into the world of the Hierophant.

When you cross the threshold, you find yourself stepping into a sacred building. It is large, yet comforting. You smell sacred incense in the air. Does it smell familiar? Take a deep breath. It will help your memory to answer these questions out loud even if you are alone.

What else do you see here? Are there sacred symbols? Have you seen them before? Do you know what they mean? Do your best to remember all you see and feel here.

Is there a throne? Is someone sitting in it? If so, introduce yourself and ask them whatever questions you seek. If not, maybe you want to sit there. How does it feel? What does the vantage point look like from there? Is it comfortable? Do you feel different? Are there keys there? Maybe there is an ankh. If so, pick them up. How do they feel in your hand? What are they made of? Brass? Silver? Do they look familiar? Maybe you have seen them before. In front of you there is a book. Try to pick it up. Try to open it. What is written there? Can you read it? Do your best to remember what it says. Take your time. Absorb all that you can from the book, the keys, everything in this place.

When you are ready, turn and walk back toward the door where you first entered. Turn the handle. Step across the threshold. In front of you are the same numbered steps you came down earlier. This time you are going to slowly walk up these stairs. See your feet climbing up the first step to the second one. Then on to the third step, the fourth one, each time going higher and higher up. Up to the fifth step, the sixth step, the seventh. Continue on up to the eighth, the ninth, the tenth and final step. Now you are back at the top step. You can now open your eyes.

It may help to write down the things you discovered during this working in a tarot journal or notebook. You can repeat this whenever the Hierophant card comes up in a prominent place in your reading, or just whenever you to access these realms of spiritual knowledge.

Hierophant Helping Hand Floor-Wash Spell

Many people don't use floor washes as part of their magic. Maybe they don't know about floor washes. Maybe they don't wash the floor, maybe they're nasty. I am a great believer in floor washes. They allow you to bless your space fully. This one can be used to help sanctify and protect your space. It would be especially helpful used in your temple room or space. This type of magic may hold a special appeal for both Water Witches and Hearth Witches.

Ingredients

Bucket

1 gallon spring water

1 gallon tap water

¼ cup Florida water

9 drops myrrh oil

9 drops frankincense oil

9 drops lavender oil

Mop or rag

Directions

Begin by making sure the space you are going to wash is already physically clean. Then gather all ingredients together. Take the bucket and add the waters and oils. First, stir counterclockwise three times with the mop or rag. Then stir three times clockwise. Start in the farthest corner of the space and wash the floor with the mixture. Continue washing, going around the space clockwise. When you get back to where you started the process, you are finished.

Chapter Eight
The Lovers

VI · The Lovers

In this card, the two become one. The Lovers manifest in a divine paradise. We are seeing the major arcana shift from showing us single players to multiple ones and then to events and qualities. There is a lot happening in this card.

The Lovers card in the tarot represents the sacred moment of blissful union. This sacred embrace is one filled with love and joy. This doesn't involve erasure of the individuals, but rather a situation where they complement each other perfectly. Minds, bodies, hearts, and everything else come together to make each one better. They strengthen each other, and together they function as a glorious invincible team. In this moment, they are simultaneously one and also none. This card takes love off your mind and straight into your heart.

Very often this card is represented by two figures holding each other tightly. They are truly and completely in love. They fill each other's empty spaces and smooth out their otherwise rough edges. They feel seen, heard, and accepted. I'm very pleased that some of the more recent decks choose to depict couples that are same sex or gender fluid. The image on the previous page from the Mermaid Tarot adds its own unique imagery: a mermaid figure who seems to be peering at themselves in a mirror, except that the reflection seems to show a yearning for a different life, a life on land. If one is to see themselves in the cards, there must be room for accurate representation and inclusivity, which for some may be a love for an idea, rather than a person. This is a card of kindred spirits and genuine acceptance on every level.

Many decks feature a sun or a moon at the top of the card shining down on the two figures clinging together in an embrace. Sometimes there is also an angel present looking down on the pair. This is a union truly blessed from above and also below.

The number six is the number assigned to this card. If one looks to numerology, this is assigned the characteristics of destiny, beauty, and love. Some decks feature Adam and Eve blissfully living in the garden of Eden. Very often this card also features a serpent. The Thoth Tarot deck, created by Lady Frieda Harris and Aleister Crowley, also features bees, a lion, and an eagle. Upon examination, we see that the eagle and lion are skilled predators, and I can't help but think their presence here is not accidental. We need both strength and fortitude to succeed at the game of love. If this appears in a reading, look to the seeker's partners, both new and old, to see how this particular twist of fortune is playing out. I will add that most often this refers to romantic love, even if it hasn't played out in the physical realm ... yet.

Meanings and Correspondences

Popular meanings for the Lovers include love, marriage, union, connection, harmony, togetherness, balance, and inspiration. Here are more correspondences for your use as you get to know this card.

Crystal Correspondences

Rose Quartz—This pink variety of quartz is said to help love in all its forms. A valued stone everywhere, including in ancient Persia, in Egyptian tombs, and in Asian beauty spells, you can certainly utilize its great benefits today. Rose quartz is an acceptable offering for Freya, Venus, Isis, and Hathor. This ancient crystal is prized by many goddesses and is ultimately used to commune with the divine feminine forces.

Unakite—Unakite is a stone that can grant great vision and guidance. It aligns our emotions with the spiritual forces. It can also help to ground and center oneself after a reading or journey work.

Apatite—This crystal comes in many different colors: blue, green, pink, purple, and gold. Metaphysically, apatite will help you communicate with higher realms, enhance your insight and intuition, and boost your confidence.

Desert Rose—This stone is also called sand rose or selenite rose. Magically, the stone will help bring you confidence, protection, harmony, and love.

Chrysocolla—Chrysocolla is a stone of hope and harmony, communication, and connection. To be honest, this is one of my favorite crystals, I am almost intoxicated by its sparkling beauty and sublime power.

Jade—Jade is a stone known to grant wisdom and reveal hidden knowledge. It can be especially helpful when used with dreamwork or journey work.

Herbal Correspondences

Lavender (*Lavandula angustifolia*)

Apple Blossom (*Malus domestica*)

Bergamot (*Citrus bergamia*)

Rose (*Rosa* spp.)

Ylang-Ylang (*Cananga odorata*)

Other Correspondences

Animal—Bee, eagle, lion

Astrological—Gemini, Mercury

Musical Note—D

Magical and Culinary Recipes

Enhancing your readings by making magical concoctions and feasts allows for a greater understanding of what the cards are trying to tell you. Several of the above scents associated with this card are utilized in the magical oil, while the popular foods apples, avocados, and figs are represented in the culinary recipes.

Magical: Lovers Oil

I published the bulk of my love recipes and formulas in my book *Love Magic*, but there were a few that I saved for myself. This is one of them. It will help with both love that is already established and also attracting new love to you in every way.

Ingredients

Small glass bottle

1 drop honey

5 drops amber oil

5 drops carnation oil

5 drops cinnamon oil

5 drops rose oil

5 drops orange blossom oil

½ ounce sweet almond oil

Directions

Gather all the listed ingredients together on your working altar or tarot shrine. Make extra sure that the space is clean and you will not be disturbed during this process. I make special mention of this here because more than any of the other oil formulas in this book, you want to be able to make sure the results of this one are pure and unadulterated by any extra energy around. To the glass bottle, add the drop of honey. Next add the amber, carnation, cinnamon, rose, and orange blossom oils. Then add half of the sweet almond oil. Cap the bottle and shake vigorously. Rub it between your palms quickly to warm it and make sure everything is well blended. Then add the remaining sweet almond oil. Cap and shake well again. Leave the bottle outside during the full moon overnight. In the morning after you have done this, the oil will be ready to use.

Culinary: Lovers Carrot Apple Salad

This is one of the recipes that I like to make to represent the Lovers card because it blends phallic carrots with the apple, evoking memories of temptation and the garden of Eden. The recipe is both healthy and refreshing and makes a delightful dish to share with your lover.

Ingredients

2 tbsp apple cider vinegar

2 tbsp grapeseed oil

Juice of 1 lemon

2 cups shredded carrots

1 red apple, grated

¼ cup parsley, finely chopped

1 clove finely minced garlic

Pinch of salt

Directions

In a small bowl, mix together the vinegar, oil, and lemon juice. In a different large bowl, mix together the carrots, apple, parsley, and garlic. Pour the oil and vinegar mixture over the top. With a large wooden spoon, mix until all ingredients are coated with the oil mixture. Add salt to taste. Chill for 1 hour or longer. Serve chilled. Enjoy! Makes 5–6 servings.

Culinary: Fig Jam

Here in New Orleans lots of us have fig trees, and when the time is right, there are figs everywhere. This simple recipe makes a great treat for your loved ones and yourself.

Ingredients

¾ cup sugar

¾ cup water

2 cups sliced fresh figs

Juice from 1 lemon

Zest from 1 lemon

Directions

In a medium saucepan, cook the sugar and water over low heat, stirring occasionally until the sugar is melted. Add the figs, lemon juice, and lemon zest. Turn up the heat and bring to a boil. Turn the heat down to low and cook partially covered for 50–60 minutes. Stir occasionally, and mash down the figs periodically with a masher. Remove from heat and cool. Mash again. If it is too chunky for your liking, you can blend the jam in your blender or food processor. Store in a jar and refrigerate for up to 2 weeks. Makes approximately 2 cups.

Journeying with the Lovers

For this meditation, you may choose to use the conventional imagery detailed in the following paragraphs or choose a Lovers card from your favorite deck and use that as your primary focus. If you choose your own specific deck, you will need to alter the following instructions for the imagery presented in that unique Lovers card. You may wish to record the following and play it back while you complete the journey work.

Sit down and close your eyes. Get yourself comfortable. Take a long, deep breath. Exhale. Imagine yourself at the very top of a staircase. Take your time. The steps before you are numbered in descending order. You are at the top step, number ten. See your feet on the step. Look at the number that is written there. Slowly step down to step number nine. See the number. Do you see letters or numbers? Really look at what is in front of you. When you see it clearly, step down to number eight. Continue stepping down through the number seven, down to six, then five. See the numbers and your feet going down to number four, number three, then number two, and finally down to number one. When you get to the bottom of the stairs, you see a large red door. Grasp the knob, turn it, and step through into the world of the Lovers.

In front of you is a lush and grassy field. The field is full of beautiful flowers in bloom and teeming with life. Off in the distance are two figures. Walk toward them. Do you recognize them? What do they look like? Are they young or old? What are they wearing? What are they saying? Do they have anything to tell you? What would you like to ask them? They are calm, peaceful, and there to help you with the answers you seek. Behind each of them is a tree. Look closely at the trees. Do they have leaves? Are there flowers or maybe even fruit? Do your best to remember what you have learned here. It will help your memory to answer these questions out loud even if you are alone.

Look up toward the sky. Do you see clouds? Maybe you see a rainbow? Maybe the clouds are forming shapes. What are the shapes? Take in how the grass feels under your feet or what it smells like in this delightful place. This is a space of great love and boundless joy. Do your best to remember these feelings deep inside you. Finally, turn and walk back toward the red door where you entered this place.

Turn the handle on the door. In front of you are exactly the same numbered steps you came down earlier. This time around you are going to slowly walk up these stairs. See both of your feet climbing up the first step to the second one. Then on to the third step, the fourth, going higher and higher up. Up to the fifth step, the sixth one, the seventh. Continue on up to the eighth step, the ninth, the tenth. Now you are back at the top step. You can now open your eyes.

It may help to write down the things you discovered during this working in a tarot journal or notebook. You can repeat this whenever the Lovers card comes up in a prominent place in your reading. You can also take out the Lovers card and do this journey working whenever you are struggling with issues concerning love in your life. Feel free to repeat it whenever you like. You may discover something different each time.

Lovers Dream Pillow Spell

One of the first bits of magic that I crafted was a dream pillow. It makes me laugh now, looking back almost thirty years, because I can't sew worth a damn. However, I managed. Anyone can. But for those of you Stitch Witches out there, this one is especially for you. Feel free to embellish the pillow with beads, ribbons, and anything else you like.

Ingredients

3 tbsp dried red rose petals

3 tbsp dried lavender petals

3 tbsp dried gardenia petals

3 tbsp dried chamomile flowers

1 tbsp minced and dried orange peel

Large bowl

Wooden spoon

Two 6-inch square pieces of fabric (red or pink)

Red or pink thread

Natural cotton filling

Items like beads or buttons for decoration

Directions

Gather all items together on your tarot altar or shrine. If you don't have one, please check out the instructions in chapter 30. Place the rose petals, lavender petals, gardenia petals, chamomile flowers, and orange peel into the bowl. Mix well with a wooden spoon. Next, take the fabric squares and put them on top of each other. If you choose a printed fabric, place the printed sides of the fabric together before sewing. Sew three of the sides together. Sew the last side ¾ of the way, then turn it inside out. Place some of the cotton in the bag. Next, add a few tablespoons of the flower mix and then add more cotton. Repeat this process until the bag is filled all the way up. Sew the rest of the bag shut. If you like, you can decorate it with beads, buttons, ribbons, and anything else. Then it is ready to use. Place it under your pillow to help receive messages and solutions relating to love in your dreams.

Chapter Nine
The Chariot

THE CHARIOT

THE CHARIOT.

Chariots are the stuff of legend. They are vehicles of victory and of triumph. The Chariot is one of those tarot cards that presents with multiple meanings. This is the first card in the deck in which we are focused on an object as opposed to people. A vehicle is depicted here, often pulled by horses, that appears to be either traveling or returning from battle. In some decks the horses are black and white sphinxes, speaking in riddles and urging us "to know, to will, to dare, and to keep silent."[9]

For me this card has always meant the process of doing what needs to be done in order to be successful, no matter how difficult or inconvenient. The left card image on page 73 is from the Santa Muerte Tarot, and it shows a covered wagon reminiscent of the style used by the Roma people. These travelers faced hardships and challenges in the hopes of a better life. The Chariot is an actual vehicle but also a feeling, that of victory.

As I was writing about this card, I received a call from a good friend. He said that a famous tarot deck creator, who is no longer with us, once told him that the problem with writing about tarot is that you must live each of the cards. I already suspected this was true, and I wondered how this card would manifest in my strange universe. I didn't have to wait long because that night I accompanied my best friend to an art opening.

Like most events here in New Orleans, it was filled with colorful art and colorful people. One of the artists in attendance sparked up a conversation with me, and one of the first sentences out of her mouth was "Would you like to see my chariot?"

"Why, yes, I would," I replied.

She then proceeded to show me an elaborate chariot they had created, designed to be pulled by a bicycle and featuring elaborate levels and windows, all intricately decorated. "We use it for sarcastic puppet shows, like Statler and Waldorf."

"Amazing," I replied. I marveled at the way a chariot had found its way into my path and how colorful the people inhabiting it were. Magic happens indeed, and you never know how and where it will manifest. The chariot is ultimately a vehicle: it will get you from here to there. It may be a cart, it may be a bicycle, it may be a limousine—get in, strap up, and feel the wild ride.

---

9.   "Term: Powers of the Sphinx," Llewellyn Worldwide, accessed May 16, 2024, https://www.llewellyn.com/encyclopedia/term_print.php?a_sec=Powers+of+the+Sphinx.

Meanings and Correspondences

Popular meanings for the Chariot include action, conquest, movement, triumph, victory, and willpower.

Crystal Correspondences

Amber—In truth amber, is not a crystal at all; it is a solidified form of tree resin. The sap becomes hard over time and is fossilized. This stone can be of particular interest to both Earth Witches and Green Witches, as it comes directly from plants. Amber is said to grant motivation and intelligence. When used with your tarot reading, it can assist with decisions and special messages from both the ancestors and the higher realms.

Howlite—This popular crystal is said to help unlock spiritual realms. Howlite grants knowledge and insight into problems. It is especially useful for divination and also astral travel.

Fluorite—This is a great stone for help with focus and confidence. When used with your tarot cards, it can help you choose exactly which meaning for the cards applies to the situation at hand.

Chalcedony—This is a telepathic stone that can exist in white, pink, blue, red, or gray color. It is said to create a positive mindset and optimism.

Ruby—Ruby is a highly energetic stone that motivates and protects. Used in conjunction with your tarot readings, it can help you get a clear picture of the situation at hand. It is known to grant a heightened awareness of things and assist with concentration.

Herbal Correspondences

Nasturtium (*Tropaeolum majus*)

Rosemary (*Salvia rosmarinus*)

Cilantro (*Coriandrum sativum*)

Other Correspondences

Animal—Horse, turtle, sphinx, whale

Astrological—Moon

Musical Note—D

Magical and Culinary Recipes

Enhancing your readings by making magical concoctions and feasts allows for a greater understanding of what the cards are trying to get across to you. Carrot and cloves are the foods most often associated with this card, and they are included in the recipes below.

Magical: Sturdy Chariot Oil

This oil will help to take you where you need to go. It is useful when traveling or beginning any new adventure. This could be a new relationship, a new job, a new home, or whatever else involves big changes and includes many moving parts.

Ingredients

½ ounce sweet almond oil

6 drops myrrh oil

6 drops sandalwood oil

6 drops carrot oil

3 drops clove oil

Small glass bottle

Directions

Gather all ingredients together on your tarot altar or shrine. If you don't have one, please check out the instructions in chapter 30. Combine all the oils together in the small glass bottle. Place the cap on the bottle tightly. Rub it between your hands quickly to charge it with your energy, and then it is ready for use.

Culinary: Protection Pot Roast

This classic recipe is one that screams victory to me. It is one for a celebration or a holiday.

Ingredients

3 tbsp all-purpose flour

1 tsp salt

1 tsp black pepper

2 tsp onion powder

3–4-lb boneless rump roast

3 tbsp vegetable oil

3 cups water or vegetable stock

2 cups carrots, sliced into 1- to 2-inch pieces

4 cloves garlic, minced

1 red onion, minced

4 red new potatoes, quartered

1 cup small mushroom caps

1 tbsp dried or 3 tbsp fresh
minced basil

1 tbsp dried or 3 tbsp fresh
minced parsley

1 tbsp dried or 3 tbsp fresh
minced thyme

Directions

Begin by mixing flour, salt, pepper, and onion powder together. Rub this mixture all over your roast. Heat a large frying pan over medium heat and add the oil. After 2 minutes, add the roast and turn to brown it on all sides. Turn off heat. Place roast in a large pot with 3 cups hot water or vegetable stock. You can alternatively make this roast in a slow cooker. Turn heat to low. Add carrots, garlic, and onion. After 1 hour has passed, add the potatoes, mushroom caps, and herbs. Remember to turn the roast every hour, and cook for a total of 2½–3 hours or until the meat easily shreds with a fork. Remove from pot; let rest 15–20 minutes, then slice. Remove larger vegetables from pot with a slotted spoon. Cook the remaining liquid down over medium heat for 30 minutes. Taste and add additional salt and pepper as needed. Use this as your gravy. This roast serves 5–6 people.

Culinary: Spice Cookies

This recipe contains cloves and lots of other magical spices. It is great to make when you might be going on a spiritual trip to meet up with fellow Witches and need to pack a snack.

Ingredients

1 cup softened butter or
shortening

1 cup white sugar

1 cup dark brown sugar

2 eggs, beaten

1½ tsp vanilla extract

2 cups flour

1½ tsp ground cinnamon

¾ tsp ground cloves

½ tsp ground nutmeg

1 tsp baking powder

1 tsp baking soda

½ tsp salt

1 cup walnuts

Directions

Preheat the oven to 375 degrees Fahrenheit. Cream the butter or shortening and add the white sugar and brown sugar. Next, add the beaten eggs and vanilla. Stir well to combine. In a separate bowl, combine flour, spices, baking powder, baking soda, and salt. Whisk together to combine. Add the flour mix to the egg mixture gradually, stirring well after each addition. Last, mix in the walnuts. Drop rounded teaspoonfuls onto a greased cookie sheet. Bake for 12 minutes or until the cookies are browned. Remove from oven and let cool. Makes approximately 3 dozen cookies.

Journeying with the Chariot

For this meditation, you may use the traditional imagery detailed in the following paragraphs, or choose a Chariot card from your favorite deck and use that as your focus. If you choose your own specific deck, you will need to alter the following instructions for the imagery presented in that card. You may wish to record the following and play it back while you complete the journey work.

Get comfortable and find a safe, undisturbed place to sit. Close your eyes. Take a long, deep breath. Exhale. Imagine yourself at the top of a staircase. The steps before you are numbered in descending order. You are at the top step; on it is written the number ten. See your feet on the step. Clearly look at the number written there. When you are ready, slowly step down to step number nine. See the number written there. Look carefully at what is in front of you. When you see it clearly, step down to number eight. Continue stepping down through the numbers seven, six, and five. See the numbers and your feet going down to number four, number three, then number two, and then last down to number one. When you get to the bottom of the stairs, you see a large black and white door. Turn the handle and step into the world of the Chariot.

In front of you there is a road. What is it made of? Dirt? Gravel? Is it paved with asphalt? It will help to answer these questions out loud even if you are alone. See the road in front of you. In the distance coming toward you is a chariot. It is making a victory lap, returning home from a hard-won battle. The cart is pulled by two sphinxes. They move with the majestic footprints of a lion. Hear their purposeful paws as they move toward you. See the majesty before you. Look at the cart. This is a vehicle not only for travel but for triumphant return. It is covered in ribbons and garlands. What colors do you see? Can you see the billowing fabric printed with stars waving in the wind? Is anyone in the cart? How do they look? Are they waving? Are they singing? Do your best to mentally take in all you see here on this road of victory. Look at the sphinxes. Regal and commanding, they look toward you. Ask them if they have anything to share. Do they answer? Take it all in and do your best to remember all you have seen. When you have done your best to experience all you can here, turn and walk back toward the black and white door you came through earlier.

Walk through the door. In front of you are the exact same numbered steps you came down when you started your journey. This time you are going to walk up these stairs. Up back toward the world of the present you left above. See your feet climbing up the first step to the second one. Continue on to the third step, fourth, going higher and higher up. Up to the fifth, the sixth, the seventh one. Climb on up to the eighth one, the ninth, and finally the tenth. Now you are back at the top step. You can now open your eyes.

It may help to write down the things you discovered during this working in a tarot journal or notebook. You can repeat this whenever the Chariot card comes up in an important place in your reading or when you are confused about what message it holds for you at this time. It may also help to do this journey working before any big trips or moves you may have coming up. This can help you gain clarity and insight into what lies ahead.

Chariot Gris-Gris Bag Spell

This little bag of magic is made to protect you while traveling from place to place. You can put it in your car, hang it off your bike, or even pack it into your suitcase.

Ingredients

1 dried comfrey leaf

1 tbsp dried lavender flowers

2 tbsp dried basil

1 tbsp dried rosemary

6-inch square of green or yellow natural fabric

1 piece ribbon

Directions

Gather all ingredients on your tarot altar or shrine. If you don't have one, please check out the instructions in chapter 30. Put the comfrey, lavender, basil, and rosemary into the center of the cloth. Pull the corners of the fabric together and tie it with your ribbon. Leave the packet on your windowsill overnight where the moon's rays will touch it. In the morning, it is ready to use.

Chapter Ten
Strength

The Strength card in the tarot tells us about the inner and outer strength we need to complete our objectives. We are never fully aware of the challenges life has for us, so cultivating this strength is a wise choice. While strength means different things to different people, the tarot card can mean many things too: physical strength, emotional strength, psychic strength, strength against adversity, and more.

The Rider-Waite-Smith and other traditional decks often feature the figure of a woman on the card. She is holding open the jaws of a fierce beast (usually a lion). Lions customarily represent strength and courage. The king of beasts knows no fear. The left image featured on page 81 comes from the Santa Muerte Tarot and features a *luchador*, or wrestler, battling the beasts of the past. This is a modern-day image, but it still shows the struggles that are present in the world. Another popular feature typical of this tarot card is an infinity symbol placed above the head of the woman. This is an echo of the infinity symbol we see in the Magician card. Here too it evokes the concept of eternity, an eternal strength that can be called upon to defeat all obstacles in the visible and invisible world.

One interesting thing about this card is that it is often interchangeable with the Justice card, meaning some decks feature Justice as the eighth card, while others have Strength in this position. This makes one wonder about deeper concepts of strength and justice, and which comes first.

In the Thoth Tarot deck, created by Aleister Crowley and Lady Frieda Harris, this card is not called Strength but instead Lust. Here the meaning leans toward passion, both unbridled and transformative. This is a sacred and all-consuming lust that is responsible for the seeds of creation.

If this card shows up in your reading, it can point to a time when great strength is needed. Hold your head up high and walk boldly into the situation at hand.

Meanings and Correspondence

Popular meanings for Strength include strength, fortitude, perseverance, tenacity, instinct, courage, and freedom. Here are a few others for your magical workings.

Crystal Correspondences

Malachite—This is a classic stone. Malachite is wonderful for removing negativity from past trauma and for strength and healing on every level. When used with your cards, it will help you improve both confidence and accuracy.

Tiger's Eye—Tiger's eye is said to enhance psychic awareness and ability. In conjunction with your tarot readings, it can assist in bringing clarity and differentiating between wishes and reality.

Herbal Correspondences

Basil (*Ocimum basilicum*)

Borage (*Borago officinalis*)

Comfrey (*Symphytum officinale*)

Masterwort (*Astrantia major*)

Moringa (*Moringa oleifera*)

Plantain (*Musa ×paradisiaca*)

Thyme (*Thymus vulgaris*)

Other Correspondences

Animal—Lion, serpent

Astrological—Leo, Sun

Musical Note—E

Magical and Culinary Recipes

Enhancing your readings by making magical concoctions and feasts allows for a greater understanding of what the cards are trying to tell you. The Strength card is frequently associated with the foods plantain, orange, and thyme, some of which are included in the recipes here.

Magical: Strong Medicine Oil

Use this oil to help with healing, joy, and focus. Healing Witches may wish to check this one out.

Ingredients

Small glass bottle

½ ounce sweet almond oil

3 drops frankincense oil

3 drops thyme oil

3 drops bergamot oil

3 drops lavender oil

Directions

Add all the sweet almond oil to the bottle. Then add the frankincense, thyme, bergamot, and lavender oils. Close the bottle, then rub it quickly between your hands to charge it with your energy. Leave it on a sunny windowsill or in a safe place outside for 24 hours to charge with the rays of both the sun and moon. When the time is up, the oil is ready to use.

Culinary: Fortitude Fried Chicken

While thinking of recipes that could embody the soul of this card, I very quickly settled on fried chicken. Here in the US, fried chicken is a food that was traditionally eaten by enslaved Black people, as chickens were one of the few animals they were allowed to keep.[10] To complete this monumental journey, they needed strength, courage, tenacity, and luck. They also needed some hearty protein that could go the distance with them.

Ingredients

1½ lbs chicken pieces (breasts, thighs, or legs)

2 cups buttermilk

¾ cup flour

1 tsp garlic powder

1 tsp onion powder

3 tbsp paprika

½ tsp black pepper

½ tsp ground sage

½ tsp finely chopped thyme

1 tsp finely minced parsley

1 tsp finely minced basil

Pinch of salt

Vegetable oil for frying

Directions

Clean the chicken and pat it dry. Place it in a bowl and cover with buttermilk. Let it sit in the refrigerator overnight. Place the dry ingredients and herbs in a large plastic bag and mix well. Drain the chicken and place it into bag. Shake well to coat. Heat the oil in a large pan or fryer. When the oil is warm enough to brown a cube of bread quickly, add chicken in a single layer and fry 5–10 minutes on each side. Frying time will depend on the size of pieces and tem-

---

10.   Buki Elegbede, "Table For All: The Underground Railroad," PBS, last updated May 11, 2022, https://www.pbs.org/video/explore-the-underground-railroad-in-nj-with-buki-elegbede-ay5sak/.

perature of the oil. Fried chicken is a challenge to cook, and I have seen many a reality show contestant go home trying to make this classic recipe. Make sure the juice of the chicken runs absolutely clear when poked with a fork. Remove the chicken from the pan and drain on brown paper or parchment paper. Eat as soon as possible, or freeze the chicken for those trips down the road.

Culinary: Orange Marmalade

This is one of the few recipes I have left from my grandmother Edith. She was one of the strongest women I have ever met. The recipe is at least a hundred years old, so the directions are slightly less detailed than you may be used to.

Ingredients

4 oranges	Water
2 grapefruit	¼ tsp salt
2 lemons	Sugar

Directions

Peel all the fruit, being sure to remove the pith from the skins. Cut the skins into thin strips. Place the skins in a large pan and add 1 qt water. Bring to a boil. Boil for 10 minutes. Cut up the fruit and make sure the seeds are removed. When the skins are done boiling, pour off the water. Add the cut-up fruit and juice to the skins and measure how much you have. Return the mix to the pan and add twice as much water to the mixture. Boil for 40 minutes, stirring frequently. Remove from heat and cool. Measure the mixture again. To this, add an equal amount of sugar and ¼ tsp of salt. Return to heat and boil for 50–60 minutes until thickened, stirring occasionally. Remove from heat and let cool. Then it is ready to serve. Keep in the refrigerator for up to 2 weeks. Makes approximately 1–2 cups.

Journeying with Strength

This journey is all about strength and where you can find it in your weakest moments. For this meditation, you may use the traditional imagery detailed in the following paragraphs, or choose a Strength card from your favorite deck and use that as your focus. If you choose your own specific deck, you will need to alter the following instructions for the imagery presented in that card. You may wish to record the following and play it back while you complete the journey work.

Sit down and make yourself comfortable. Close your eyes. Take a long, deep breath. Exhale. Imagine yourself at the top of a staircase. The steps before you are numbered in descending order. You are at the top step; on it is written the number ten. See your feet on the step. Clearly look at the number written there. When you are ready, slowly step down to step number nine. See the number written there. Look carefully at what is in front of you. When you see it clearly, step down to number eight. Continue stepping down through the numbers seven, six, and five. See the numbers and your feet going down to number four, number three, then number two, and then finally down to number one. When you get to the bottom of the stairs, you see a large gold door. Turn the handle and step into the world of Strength.

The sun is shining and you have walked into a world of abundant green. The grass beneath your feet is lush and soft. Walk forward. Pay attention to your surroundings. Up ahead you see a cat. It is purring and playful. What kind of cat is it? A house cat? A friendly lion? It will help to answer these questions out loud even if you are alone. Ask the cat if you may approach. Wait for a clear response. If you are allowed to approach, ask it what you need to know to continue you journey in the best possible way. Again wait for a clear response. Thank it and ask if there is anything else it needs to tell you.

After this exchange is done, turn and walk back toward the door where you entered. Turn the handle. In front of you are the same numbered steps you came down earlier. This time you are going to slowly walk up these stairs. See your feet climbing up the first step to the second one. Then on to the third step, the fourth, going higher and higher up. Up to the fifth step, the sixth, the seventh. Continue on up to the eighth, the ninth, the tenth. Now you are back at the top step. You can now open your eyes.

It may help to write down the things you discovered during this working in a tarot journal or notebook. You can repeat this whenever the Strength card comes up in a prominent place in your reading.

Strength Spray Spell

One of my favorite magical things to make is a spray. Essentially, you are making a ritual water that can be used in a bath, as a floor wash, or as a spray. Putting the ingredients into a spray bottle makes for better and easier delivery to wherever you need it to go. This particular one is great for when you need a little bit of extra strength and courage. Be sure to spray the corners of your space thoroughly as you envision yourself being infused with strength and power.

Ingredients

Small spray bottle

¼ cup tap water

¼ cup spring water

3 tbsp Florida water

10 drops lavender oil

6 drops frankincense oil

6 drops sandalwood oil

Directions

Gather all your ingredients together on your tarot altar or shrine. If you don't have one, please check out the instructions in chapter 30. Pull out the Strength card from your deck and put it in front of you. Take the spray bottle and add the waters. Cap and shake well. Add the lavender, frankincense, and sandalwood oils. Cap the bottle. Throw it gently into the air and catch it. This will place it in the hands of the invisibles and allow it to gain a special blessing. Next, put the bottle on top of the card and leave it for 24 hours. After the time is up, your spray is ready to use.

Chapter Eleven
The Hermit

IX - THE HERMIT

THE HERMIT.

The word "hermit" has its origins in Greek, and it originally meant "solitary" or "dwelling in the desert." This solitude is never to be confused with loneliness.

Nine is the number assigned to the Hermit. This is a card of introspection and solitude. If we view the tarot as a sacred journey, as many do, this is the part of the path that requires the seeker to take comfort in solitude. This is a powerful, purposeful time of being alone.

One of the practices highlighted here is meditation. The Hermit urges us to be mindful. It is about stilling our thoughts and earthly cares and submitting to the silence. Here are precious moments saluting both the breath and the body so they may tell us what we need. Instead of looking to external sources of help, we turn our attention inward to find solutions. This is also a card of sincere prayers, asking higher powers, however you reckon them, for assistance and guidance through complicated situations. Many religions observe times of silence and seclusion as part of their necessary spiritual training. The Hermit asks us to think about where we might need to pause and contemplate. An element of this seclusion is also rest. An overly busy mind and body cannot find true calm and clarity. This should not be seen as a detrimental experience but instead a time for self-care and a much-needed recharging of your physical and mental batteries.

There are a few constants that we see across various manifestations of this card. The first is the robed figure. Heavy robes cloak the Hermit, almost as if their clothes are so heavy the individual is forced into inaction. The image featured on the right on page 89 from the Millennium Thoth deck shows this clearly. In this card the figure is also located in a cave and surrounded by rock. Movement here is very slow, if present at all, and extremely purposeful. It reminds me of when people are fasting or in extreme conditions where they must conserve every tiny piece of energy available. Another common element shown in this card is the staff. Strong and supportive, this big wand is there for stability and protection. The seeker can lean on it and ground themselves with it. A large lantern is also frequently pictured in this card. Moving slowly and in darkness, it is almost as if the Hermit holds the literal key to illumination in their hand.

Some readers tend to think of this as a negative card. I think that viewpoint is a bit myopic. What we have here is beneficial solitude, not unhappy loneliness. It is a time of introspection that allows for necessary rest and transformation through self-care.

Meanings and Correspondences

Popular meanings for the Hermit include solitude, seclusion, silence, patience, reflection, and rest. Here are a few other connections for this card.

Crystal Correspondences

Amethyst—This is a stone used to bring clarity, spirituality, joy, and self-awareness. One of the most popular stones, amethyst is known to heal both physical and emotional pain. It is a wonderful stone to use with tarot because it can be very valuable when doing spiritual journey work, help you to connect with higher realms, and give you insight in all situations.

Apatite—This crystal comes in a variety of colors: blue, green, pink, purple, and gold. Metaphysically, apatite will help you access higher realms, while improving your insight and intuition and boosting your confidence.

Calcite—This crystal will strengthen your vision and improve your psychic abilities. It amplifies whatever is happening in your situation. Calcite will also help with memory and recalling information discovered in other realms.

Peridot—Peridot is known to bring great joy. It also helps with physical and spiritual growth in all directions. Peridot was worn to help combat negativity and psychic attack. It can help with your tarot readings by giving confidence and clarity.

Watermelon Tourmaline—Tourmaline in general is said to block and transform negativity, and this variety is no different. It is said to help greatly with understanding and finding joy in difficult situations.

Herbal Correspondences

Sage (*Salvia officinalis*)

German Chamomile (*Matricaria chamomilla*)

Other Correspondences

Animal—Lamb

Astrological—Virgo, Earth

Musical Note—F

Magical and Culinary Recipes

Enhancing your readings by making magical potions and feasts allows for a greater understanding of what the cards are trying to tell you. Molasses is the food associated with this card, and the recipe below highlights this ingredient.

Magical: One Love Oil

It is often said you can't get your life right until you get your heart and mind right. This oil is designed to help you contemplate and unify all aspects of yourself so you can be your best. Wear it whenever you need a little boost back on the path toward self-love and success. The Hermit speaks to self-love on a deep level, as those times of solitude can quickly turn to loneliness if we don't remember out greatness and divine power.

Ingredients

6 drops lotus oil

6 drops myrrh oil

6 drops gardenia oil

6 drops sandalwood oil

6 drops lemon oil

½ ounce sweet almond oil

Glass bottle

Directions

Gather all ingredients together on your tarot altar or shrine. If you don't have one, please check out the instructions in chapter 30. Combine all the oils in the glass bottle. Rub the bottle back and forth between your palms to charge it with your energy. Wear the blend as needed, especially during meditations.

Culinary: Healthy Hermit Bars

Lucky for us, this tarot card even has its own dessert, namely the hermit cookie or bar. No one is exactly sure how these treats got their name—maybe from the fact that they will keep forever, or maybe because they originally looked like they were draped in the robes that we see here in this card.[11] Whatever the case, these long-lasting bars are easy to make and absolutely delicious.

Ingredients

2 cups all-purpose flour

½ tsp salt

2 tsp baking soda

1 tsp ground ginger

1 tsp ground cinnamon

½ tsp ground nutmeg

½ cup butter, softened

1 cup dark brown sugar

¼ cup molasses

1 egg

⅓ cup raisins

⅓ cup dried cranberries

Directions

Sift together the flour, salt, baking soda, ginger, cinnamon, and nutmeg. In a large bowl, cream together the butter and brown sugar with a hand mixer until fluffy. Then add the molasses and egg. Mix until combined. Slowly add in the flour mixture, continuing to beat until combined. Fold in the raisins and cranberries. Place dough in the refrigerator for 1 hour. As the dough is chilling, preheat the oven to 375 degrees. Remove the chilled dough and cut it in half. Shape each half into a rectangle approximately 1 foot long. Place each rectangle on a separate cookie sheet and bake for 15 minutes or until they begin to crisp. Remove from oven. Wait 5–10 minutes, then slice the rectangles into bars. Makes approximately 15–16 bars. They can be stored in an airtight container for up to a week.

Culinary: Sage Stuffing

When I think of comfort food, I almost always turn to stuffing. It is a holiday favorite that often finds its way to the dinner table on other occasions too. Almost every stuffing recipe I have ever seen includes a healthy amount of sage, and this is no different.

---

11. Cynthia R. Greenlee, "Hermit Cookie," Bon Appetit, accessed December 7, 2022, https://www .bonappetit.com/story/hermit-cookie-reclusive-recipe.

Ingredients

4 tbsp butter

½ large red onion, diced

½ cup mushrooms, sliced

2 cloves garlic, minced

1 loaf sandwich bread, cut into
cubes

1 medium celery stalk, diced

1 large egg, beaten

1½ cup low-sodium chicken broth

1 tbsp minced fresh sage

1 tbsp minced fresh parsley

2 tsp onion powder

1 tsp garlic powder

½ tsp salt

¾ tsp black pepper

Directions

Preheat the oven to 350 degrees Fahrenheit. Melt 2 tbsp of butter in a sauce-pan. Add the onion and mushrooms and cook until they begin to brown. Add the garlic and cook for 2 minutes more. Remove from heat. Add the bread, celery, and egg to a large bowl. Mix well and then add the cooked mushroom and onion mixture. Stir to combine. In a separate bowl, mix the chicken broth, sage, parsley, onion powder, garlic powder, salt, and pepper to combine. Add this slowly to the bread mixture, combining well. Fill a lightly greased baking pan with the mixture. Cut the remaining butter into cubes and dot it over the top of the bread mixture. Cover the pan with foil and bake for 45 minutes. Remove the foil and bake for an additional 15 minutes. Serves 8–10.

Journeying with the Hermit

The Hermit card shows us the joy and power that can come from solitude. This journey will help you access this in every way. You may wish to record the following and play it back while you complete the journey work.

Find a comfortable seat. Sit down and close your eyes. Take a long, deep breath. Exhale. Imagine yourself at the top of a small staircase. The steps are numbered in descending order. You are standing at the top step, number ten. See both of your feet on the step. See the number written there. When you feel ready, step down to step number nine. See the number written there. Do you see letters or numbers? Really look at what is in front of you. When you see it clearly, step down to number eight. Continue stepping down through numbers seven, six, and five. See the numbers and your feet going down to number four, number three, then number two, and finally down to number one. When you get to the bottom of the stairs, you see a large and heavy gray door. Turn the doorknob and step into the world of the Hermit.

The sky is overcast. In front of you there is a lantern. It is glowing. Examine it. Pick it up if you like. Is it heavy? What color is the light shining from it? Is it an actual flame or possibly electric? Do you feel warmth from it? Where does its light shine? What is it illuminating? When you are done looking at it, place it safely on the ground. Also on the ground is a staff. Pick that up if you like. What is it made from? Is it wooden or made from something else? It will help to answer these questions out loud even if you are alone. Hold the staff in your hand. Does it feel heavy or light? You are the only person in this space. How does it feel to be alone? What thoughts come to you? Do your best to remember these thoughts and feelings. When you have learned all you can from this place, turn and walk toward the door you came through earlier. Turn the knob and walk back through.

In front of you are the same numbered steps you came down earlier. This time you are going to slowly walk back up these stairs. See your feet climbing up the first step to the second one. Then on to the third step, the fourth, going higher and higher up. Up to the fifth step, the sixth one, the seventh. Continue on up to the eighth step, the ninth one, and finally the tenth step. Now you are back at the top step. You can now open your eyes.

It may help to write down the things you discovered during this working in a tarot journal or notebook. You can repeat this whenever the Hermit card comes up in a prominent place in your reading.

Meditation Bath Spell

Many days the world is too much for us and we need to still our mind in order to have adequate rest and clarity to continue moving forward. This bath will help you do just that. It can be taken before or after meditating, or you can even meditate in the bath if you want to.

Ingredients

½ cup sea salt

¼ cup Epsom salt

Large jar

3 drops rose oil

3 drops sandalwood oil

3 drops myrrh oil

6 drops lavender oil

Directions

Gather all ingredients together on your tarot altar or shrine. If you don't have one, please check out the instructions in chapter 30. Place the sea salt and Epsom salt in the jar. Mix well. Then add the rose, sandalwood, myrrh, and lavender oils. Close the jar and shake well. Next take the jar and bury it in the dirt. If you don't have a yard or somewhere you can do this, consider getting a flowerpot and some soil and burying it there. Leave the jar in the ground for 24 hours and then dig it up. It is now ready for use.

Chapter Twelve
Wheel of Fortune

X - FORTUNE

WHEEL of FORTUNE.

In the Wheel of Fortune card, we see the cosmic, spinning wheel of fate. It can bring about great success or great misfortune depending on where you are in the complicated cycle. The classic tarot deck uses the Wheel of Fortune to again focus our attention on an object as opposed to a person. The wheel spins and no one is sure where it may land. In readings, I find that it more often means luck and changes are on the way, because it is the cruel twists of fate that often prompt someone to get a reading to begin with.

Certain decks also feature a lion and a bull. If you recall, we've seen the lion before as a symbol on the Strength card, implying fortitude and courage. It carries the same weight here. In some decks, the bull represents determination, patience, and power. The eagle is also another feature in many tarot decks, and so is the snake. The snake is evocative of the Ouroboros, going round and round in an eternal cycle of becoming. The deck featured on the previous page is the Millennium Thoth tarot. It shows different creatures all along the wheel: a monkey, a sphynx, and a crocodile. It is almost as if we can see possible blessings and misfortunes in every turn of the wheel. The Wheel reminds us that this constant cycle is a necessary part of life for all living things.

The Wheel of Fortune is often equated with the Roman goddess Fortuna. Roman emperors were said to keep gold statues of her in their homes to bring them great success and wealth.[12] So a healthy dose of success and financial reward accompanies this card.

If this card appears in your reading, a twist of fate is at hand. In that light, it can mean either struggles or successes are at hand depending on your current circumstances. Change on every level is the watchword here; embrace it and hold on tight.

This card may also hold a special appeal for those who practice faery magic. The energy here is very similar: things are not always what they seem and can change in an instant with a turn of the wheel or chance meeting with a faery.

Meanings and Correspondences

Popular meanings for the Wheel of Fortune include success, wealth, change in fortune, luck, destiny, and prosperity. Here are a few more correspondences and other associations for use in magic.

---

12.   Anna Francesa Bonnell-Freiden, "Fortuna and Risk: Embodied Chance in the Roman Empire," Society for Classical Studies, accessed August 5, 2023, https://classicalstudies.org/fortuna-and-risk-embodied -chance-roman-empire.

Crystal Correspondences

Pyrite—Pyrite is a stone of both protection and power. Witches of all types can use this to shield and also give themselves a boost of confidence and faith when necessary.

Moss Agate—This semiprecious stone is said to bring balance, which makes it a perfect choice to pair with the Wheel of Fortune card. It is also known to bring healing, calm, and happiness.

Staurolite—This mineral is colored reddish black, and it develops into the shape of a cross. Actually, another name for it is faery cross. It also has associations with Christ, as some devotees say it formed from the tears cried when he died. Staurolite helps narrow the gaps between the spiritual and physical planes.

Topaz—Topaz helps with truth telling and spiritual development. Keep a piece with your cards to assist with confidence and your ability to problem solve for your clients.

Herbal Correspondences

Lilac (*Syringa vulgaris*)

Four-Leaf Clover (*Trifolium repens*)

Spearmint (*Mentha spicata*)

Pine (*Pinus* spp.)

Other Correspondences

Animal—Lion, bull, eagle, snake

Astrological—Jupiter

Musical Note—A#

Magical and Culinary Recipes

Enhancing your readings by making magical concoctions and feasts allows for a greater understanding of what the cards are trying to share with you. Black pepper and mushroom are the foods most associated with this card, and they are featured in the appetizer recipe on the next page.

Magical: Lucky Gold and Silver Oil
This oil is used to bring luck, success, and a quick change in fortune.

Ingredients

Glass bottle

½ ounce sweet almond oil

6 drops sunflower oil

6 drops lemongrass oil

3 drops ginger oil

Gold glitter

Silver glitter

Directions
Gather all your ingredients together on your working altar or tarot shrine. If you don't have one, please check out the instructions in chapter 30. Place the sweet almond oil in the glass bottle. Next, add the sunflower, lemongrass, and ginger oils. Finally, add a pinch of gold and silver glitter. Cover the bottle. Shake well until the mixture is thoroughly blended. Rub the bottle quickly between your hands to charge it, and then it is ready for use.

Culinary: Nutty Mushroom Bites
The obvious reason mushrooms are associated with the Wheel of Fortune card is that they have the power to turn your world upside down and allow you to see things in a new way. This recipe uses baby bella mushrooms, not the really transformative ones, but it is delicious just the same. It is very easy to make using a prepared all-purpose baking mix. You can buy your own or make one from an online recipe.

Ingredients

1 tbsp extra virgin olive oil

3 cups sliced baby bella
    mushrooms

¾ cup chopped red onion

1 clove garlic, minced

½ cup water

1 lb fresh spinach, chopped

1 cup shredded swiss cheese

1 cup shredded cheddar cheese

1½ cups chopped walnuts

¾ cup all-purpose baking mix

1 tsp dried parsley

1 tsp onion powder

1 tsp salt

½ tsp black pepper   3 eggs, beaten

1⅓ cups sour milk

Directions

Preheat the oven to 400 degrees Fahrenheit. Lightly grease and flour a 13-by-9-inch baking pan. Heat a large skillet over medium heat. Add the olive oil. Place the mushrooms and onions in the pan. Cook until the onions begin to turn translucent. Add the garlic. Cook for 1–2 minutes more until the garlic begins to brown. Remove from heat. Next, take a large saucepan and add the water and spinach. Cover the pan and heat on low. Cook for 3–4 minutes and then remove the cover, stir, and check. If the spinach has begun to change color, remove it from the heat. If it is still firm, cook for 2–3 minutes more until done. Drain the spinach and spread it over the bottom of the baking pan. Sprinkle the mushroom mixture over the top, along with the two cheeses and walnuts. Then add the baking mix, parsley, onion powder, salt, and pepper to a large bowl. Whisk in the milk and eggs. When it is thoroughly combined, pour the mixture over the vegetables in the pan. Bake for 30 minutes or until a toothpick inserted into the center comes out clean. Cool to room temperature, then cut into squares and serve. Makes 16–24 bites, depending on the size.

Journeying with the Wheel of Fortune

The Wheel of Fortune card in the tarot shows us that the world, and everyone in it, is constantly turning. This journey is designed to help you discover which direction you should turn to find your true fortune. For this meditation you may use the traditional imagery detailed in the following, or choose a Wheel of Fortune card from your favorite deck and use that image as your focus. If you choose your own specific deck, you will need to alter the following instructions for the unique imagery presented in that card. You may wish to record the following and play it back while you complete the journey work.

Sit down and get comfortable. Close your eyes. Take a deep breath. Exhale. Repeat. When you feel comfortable and ready, imagine yourself at the top of a staircase. The steps before you are numbered in descending order. You are at the top step; the number ten is clearly written on it. See your feet on this topmost step. Clearly look at the number written there. When you are ready, slowly step down to step number nine. See the number written there. Look carefully at what is in front of you. When you see it clearly, step down to number eight. Continue stepping down through the numbers seven, six, five. See the numbers and your feet going down to step number four, the third step, then the second, and then last down to step number one. When you get to the bottom of the stairs, you see a large multicolored door. Turn the handle and step into the world of the Wheel of Fortune.

This is a land of activity and opportunity. All is possible here. In front of you there is a large wheel. The wheel is colorful and beautifully carved. Watch it as it spins. Watch it as it slows. Does it stop spinning? What symbol does it land on? What does this symbol mean for you? It will help to answer these questions out loud even if you are alone. Do you see any animals or people around the wheel? Are there birds flying above? Maybe you see an eagle, or is it nighttime and an owl has taken to the skies? Can you spin the wheel yourself? Where does it stop this time? Examine every part of your surroundings and do your best to remember what you see here. Explore as much or as little as you like. When you feel ready to return, begin walking back toward the door to the stairway that you came down earlier.

When you come to the multicolored door, open it and step through. In front of you are the same numbered steps you came down when you started your journey. This time you are going to walk up these stairs. See your feet climbing up the first step to the second one. Continue on to the third step, the fourth, going higher and higher up. Up the fifth, the sixth, the seventh step. Climb on up to the eighth one, the ninth, and finally the tenth. Now you are back at the top step. You can now open your eyes.

It may help to write down the things you discovered during this working in a tarot journal or notebook. You can repeat this whenever the Wheel of Fortune card comes up in a prominent place in your reading or when you are unsure what message it holds for you at this time.

Success Sprinkling Spell

This spell utilizes a sprinkling powder. Sprinkling powders are similar to gris-gris, except the herbal mixture is sprinkled about instead of being contained in a bag. Use this powder in situations where you need success. Be sure to sprinkle it on thresholds, on windowsills, and in corners around the room in small amounts. Be careful with your sprinkling if you have children or pets, as the mixture should not be eaten. If this is the circumstance you find yourself in, consider only sprinkling the mix outdoors.

Ingredients

¼ cup dried basil

¼ cup dried lavender

¼ cup dried patchouli

Gold glitter

Pieces of a dollar bill

Small bowl

Directions

Gather all ingredients on your ritual altar or shrine. If you don't have one, please check out the instructions in chapter 30. Place the basil, lavender, and patchouli in the bowl. Mix well. Add the gold glitter and dollar bill pieces. Mix again. Next, take a long, deep breath. Exhale onto the mixture. Repeat two more times. This will charge the mixture with your energy. Then it is ready to use.

Chapter Thirteen
Justice

The Justice card speaks of a concept rather than an individual: justice in the material world. The card means fairness, equity, and honesty. There is a cosmic rebalancing at work here. Very often in a reading, this manifests as the quest for justice, rather than the result. This is the time to proceed as your best self. Make sure everything is in order both personally and professionally. This is a card of law and order and the collective consequences of all your actions.

Most decks assign this card number eleven. This is represented by two ones. Even the number itself reminds one that there are two sides to every situation. Occasionally, decks will shift this card and have it as number eight, although it still carries the same meaning.

Like many of the other cards in the deck, this one also speaks of the issue of balance, such as a balancing of one's affairs both personally and professionally. The two sides of Justice's scale are rarely equal. Adjustment to these rules is a constant issue. When we know this, however, we can work to shift things back toward equilibrium. Sometimes what is needed is the help of a higher power, be it judges, juries, or even the ancestors.

Meanings and Correspondences

Popular meanings for Justice include court cases, laws, fairness, balance, adjustment, and order. Here are a few more of those important associations.

Crystal Correspondences

Jet—Jet is a stone of spiritual power that helps you accurately express your psychic abilities. It gives strength and deflects negative energy for all who use it. Jet can help with all forms of divination, including tarot and even mediumship.

Black Tourmaline—Black tourmaline can be helpful with clearing and releasing energy after a tarot reading. It is said to purify, protect, and help with concentration. Some people even use black tourmaline for scrying.

Malachite—This is a classic stone. It is great for removing negativity from past trauma and for healing on every level. When used with your tarot cards, it will help you with confidence and accuracy.

Opal—Opal is a stunning stone that is said to promote clarity and a harmonious connection to the higher realms. It is known to expand consciousness on every level.

Herbal Correspondences

Basil (*Ocimum basilicum*)

Dill (*Anethum graveolens*)

Holly (*Ilex aquifolium*)

Honeysuckle (*Lonicera periclymenum*)

Rosemary (*Salvia rosmarinus*)

Other Correspondences

Animal—Lion, camel, owl

Astrological—Libra, Venus

Musical Note—F#

Magical and Culinary Recipes

Expanding on your readings by making magical formulas and feasts allows for a greater understanding of what the cards are trying to tell you.

Magical: Court Case Oil

Use this oil to deal with court cases and legal matters when you need to ensure that justice is done. Anoint your hands and place a drop in each of your shoes before going to court.

Ingredients

Small glass bottle

½ ounce sweet almond oil

3 drops anise oil

3 drops rosemary oil

3 drops nutmeg oil

Pinch of dirt from outside a courthouse

Directions

Gather all ingredients together on your ritual altar or shrine. If you don't have one, please check out the instructions in chapter 30. Add the sweet almond oil to the bottle. Next, add the anise, rosemary, and nutmeg oils to the bottle. Last, add the pinch of dirt. Close the bottle and rub it back and forth between your hands to charge it with your energy. Leave it overnight on your altar or shrine space until morning when it will be ready to use.

Culinary: Garlic Chicken

Garlic is the food most often used to represent the Justice card, and this recipe uses a lot of it. It is one of my favorites. Most people will probably recognize the flavors here, as they are classic and combine beautifully.

Ingredients

½ cup flour

1 tsp onion powder

Salt

Pepper

6 pieces of chicken (legs, thighs, breasts, whatever you like)

Extra virgin olive oil

3 cloves garlic, minced

1 cup white wine

1 cup quartered cherry peppers

1 tbsp minced fresh basil

1 tbsp minced fresh parsley

1 tsp minced fresh oregano

1 cup chicken stock

Juice of 1 lemon

Directions

Place flour, onion powder, and a dash of salt and pepper into a large plastic bag. Shake well to combine. Add 2 pieces of chicken to the bag at a time, shaking well after each addition to coat. Heat a large saucepan over medium heat. Add approximately 1 inch of olive oil. When the oil is hot enough to brown a cube of bread, add the chicken. Fry just until golden brown on both sides. Remove from pan. Drain remaining oil and add 3 tablespoons of new oil back into the pan. Add the garlic and cook 1–2 minutes until it starts to brown. Add the wine and cook for 5 minutes. Then add the peppers, fried chicken, basil, parsley, oregano, and the chicken stock. Cook on low heat for 30–35 minutes, adding additional water and wine if necessary. The dish is done when the juice from all the pieces of chicken is running clear. Then add lemon juice and additional salt and pepper to taste. Serves 6.

Culinary: Herbal Delight Pea Soup

There are lots of herbs you can use in this soup, including garlic. It is hearty and fortifying. Make it ahead and freeze to serve for holidays and events.

Ingredients

2 cups green split peas

1 tsp salt

5 cups water

1 tbsp olive oil

¼ cup finely diced salt pork

1 red onion, minced

3 cloves garlic, minced

½ cup diced carrots

1 cup chopped spinach

1 bay leaf

1 tsp minced fresh rosemary

1 tsp minced fresh basil

1 tsp minced fresh parsley

2 cups chicken broth

Directions

In a large saucepan, place split peas, salt, and 4 cups of water. Bring to a boil. Turn the heat down to low and simmer for 60–90 minutes until the peas are tender. In a separate saucepan, heat the olive oil and add the salt pork. Cook until the pork begins to brown, then add the onion, garlic, carrots, spinach, and herbs. Cook for 3 minutes, then add this mixture to the split peas along with the leftover 1 cup of water and the chicken broth. Simmer for 1 hour or until the carrots are tender, stirring frequently. Add additional salt and pepper to taste. At this point, you can strain the soup if you like, blend it, or just eat it as is. Makes 8 servings.

Journeying with Justice

Fairness and equity are the watchwords for this tarot card. In this journey working, these principles are explored in real time. For this working, you can use the traditional imagery detailed in the following, or choose a Justice card from your favorite deck and use that image as your focus. If you choose your own specific deck, you will need to alter the following instructions for the unique imagery presented in that card before you. You may wish to record the following and play it back while you complete the journey work.

Find a comfortable place to sit. Relax and close your eyes. Take a deep breath. Exhale. Repeat. When you feel comfortable and ready, picture yourself at the top of a small staircase. The steps before you are numbered from highest to lowest. You are at the top step, on it is the number ten. See both of your feet on this topmost step. Clearly look at the number written there. When you are ready, slowly step down to step number nine. See the number written there. Look carefully at what is in front of you. When you see it clearly, step down to number eight. Continue stepping down through numbers seven, six, and five. See the numbers and your feet going down to step number four, number three, then number two, and then last down to step number one. When you get to the bottom of the stairs, you see a large gray door. Turn the handle and step into the Justice card.

This is a land of balance, of fairness, of equity. Look around. What do you see here? Is there a scale? What metal is it made of? Brass? Copper? Silver? Is it full of anything? Are there columns? What are they made of? Can you see a throne? What does it look like? It will help to answer these questions out loud even if you are alone. Is it balanced or unbalanced? Take a closer look. Try to remember what you see. Do you hear anything? Voices? Music? How do you feel when you are here? After you have taken it all in, turn and walk toward the door you entered through. Walk through and close the door behind you. In front of you are the same numbered steps you came down earlier. This time you are going to slowly walk up these stairs. See your feet climbing up the first step to the second one. Then on to the third step, the fourth, going higher and higher up. Up to the fifth step, the sixth step, the seventh. Continue on up to the eighth, the ninth, the tenth. Now you are all the way back at the top step. You can now open your eyes.

It may help to write down the things you discovered during this working in a tarot journal or notebook. You can repeat this whenever the Justice card comes up in a prominent place in your reading.

Justice Jar Spell

Jar spells are all the rage these days. You can make them for lots of different reasons. People use them for love, success, revenge, and lots of other things. This particular jar spell is to help you get justice in a situation.

Ingredients

Justice card from your deck

Glass jar

1 tsp dirt from near a courthouse

1 tsp dried lavender

1 tsp dried dill

1 piece galangal root

1 tsp grains of paradise

Piece of paper

Piece of person's hair

1 bottle High John oil

Small candleholder

7 tea light candles

Directions

Gather all ingredients together on your tarot altar or shrine. If you don't have one, please check out the instructions in chapter 30. Place the Justice card in the center of the space. Next, place the dirt, lavender, dill, galangal, and grains of paradise in the jar. Then write the name of the person seeking justice on the piece of paper. If possible, and only with their permission, add a piece of that person's hair. Next, pour the oil all over the contents of the jar. Close the jar and shake well. Place the candleholder on top of the jar. Add a tea light to the holder. Light the tea light and visualize the desired outcome in the situation. Remember to never leave a burning candle unattended. Light another tea light and meditate each night for the next 6 nights. On the last night after the candle is done burning, you are finished with the working. Dispose of the contents of the jar in the trash and recycle the jar.

Chapter Fourteen
The Hanged Man

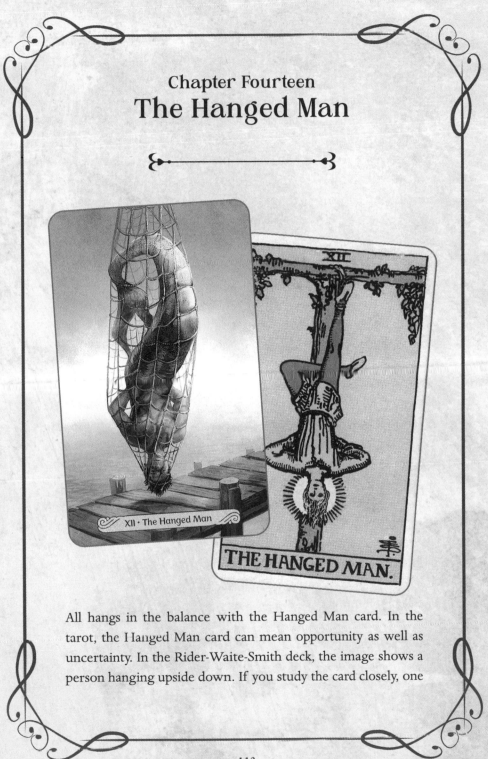

XII · The Hanged Man

THE HANGED MAN.

All hangs in the balance with the Hanged Man card. In the tarot, the Hanged Man card can mean opportunity as well as uncertainty. In the Rider-Waite-Smith deck, the image shows a person hanging upside down. If you study the card closely, one of his legs is bent and crossing at the knee. It is almost a yoga pose for balance; a pendulum of personal possibility lies ahead.

Some attribute a negative meaning to this card, but that is only one way of looking at it. If I am being honest, I don't really believe that there are any "bad" cards, just necessary steps on the journey of life. This card shows us a universe where everything is upside down. This upside-down perspective, which we see in the image from the Mermaid Tarot on the previous page, is one of the most important aspects of this card. I once had a conversation with a man about how in Australia they call redheads "bluey." He explained lots of slang in this place known as "down under" embraces opposites, such as a redhead being called a bluey. My immediate response was, "That's because it's an upside-down world." Because the primary figure of this card is hanging upside down, this reverse thinking is what is celebrated. Creative solutions and unusual thinking are sometimes necessary to travel effectively through the unknown.

Another interpretation of this card is a condemned individual, one who is sentenced to death. This can be either literal or figurative. It can manifest as a spiritual transformation or a physical and emotional one. A course of action or series of events has unfolded so that the person is being given the ultimate sentence of punishment. This could be warranted or unwarranted; many have been sentenced unjustly. This could be escapable or inescapable. When is a death sentence not a death sentence? One of my favorite parables speaks to this situation. An individual is given the message to place themselves in a coffin and float down the river. This could most certainly be considered an ending, yet they comply. As they float down the river, they are soon discovered by those in a neighboring town, these people had received a message through divination that the next ruler of their town would be found floating down the river in a coffin. The individual is removed and given all the benefits, power, and accolades the people there have to offer. This tale speaks to not only the issue of faith but also that of hope.

Some decks feature the central figure either supported by or entwined with a snake. Snakes know all about balance. They masterfully move their way through all types of situations with both grace and precision. While the figure in the Mermaid Tarot isn't entwined with a snake, they are found to be entwined or caught up in a fishing net. However, they look as though they remain relatively calm, given their situation. In many ways, this card is about both restriction and restraint, but also conservation and patience. The time to act may not be today, but it is coming and you must be ready in an instant. All these elements come into perfect alignment in this card.

Meanings and Correspondences

Popular meanings for the Hanged Man include indecision, uncertainty, inaction, suspension, stillness, and meditation. Here are a few other important associations for this card.

Crystal Correspondences

Aquamarine—This beautiful greenish-blue stone can be used to grant both courage and protection. Traditionally, it has been used to keep away the forces of darkness and attract the light.[13]

Selenite—This stone helps with internal and external transformation. Selenite grants clarity and access to the otherworldly. It is especially helpful in crystal grids to amplify energy, and it can also be used for scrying by itself or in conjunction with your tarot cards.

Garnet—Garnet is known to help with energy and courage. It can be useful in combination with your cards, as it will help to give you clarity and insight into the people you are reading for.

Herbal Correspondences

Ivy (*Hedera helix*)

Seaweed (*Rhodophyta*, *Phaeophyta*, and *Chlorophyta* spp.)

Lemon Balm (*Melissa officinalis*)

Other Correspondences

Animal—Snake, crow

Astrological—Pisces

Musical Note—G#

---

13.   Judy Hall, *The Crystal Bible* (Iola, WI: Krause Publications, 2003), 68.

Magical and Culinary Recipes

Enhancing your readings by making magical concoctions and feasts allows for a greater understanding of what the cards are trying to tell you. Grapes and basil are two foods associated with the Hanged Man card, and they are featured in the culinary recipes that follow.

Magical: Rebalancing Oil

For me, the Hanged Man is about balance at its core. Use this oil when you are having difficulties balancing the various aspects your life, like work and family or public and private.

Ingredients

Small glass bottle

½ ounce sweet almond oil

6 drops sandalwood oil

6 drops myrrh oil

6 drops jasmine oil

3 drops galangal oil

3 drops lemon oil

Pinch of dried seaweed

Directions

Gather all ingredients together on your tarot altar or shrine. If you don't have one, please check out the instructions in chapter 30. Place the sweet almond oil into the bottle. Then add the sandalwood, myrrh, jasmine, galangal, and lemon oils. Finally, add the seaweed. Cap the bottle, throw it gently in the air, and catch it. This will send it into the hands of the invisible world, if only for a second, to bless and charge it with energy. Now it is ready for you to use.

Culinary: Traditional Pesto

This traditional pesto contains all the good things: basil, garlic, and pignoli nuts. These are all blended together to make a healthy sauce for pasta or whatever you choose to put it on. It is both quick and easy. This recipe makes 3 cups, but you can halve it if you wish.

Ingredients

3 cups fresh basil leaves (without stems)

3 tbsp toasted pine nuts

3 cloves garlic, minced

¾ cup extra virgin olive oil

¼ cup freshly grated romano
cheese

½ cup freshly grated parmesan
cheese

Directions

Place the basil, pine nuts, and garlic into your blender or food processor. Mix until combined. While the machine is running, slowly add the olive oil. Most blenders and food processors have an access top where you can do this successfully without splattering the mixture everywhere. Finally, add the cheeses and process again, briefly, just until combined. Store refrigerated. Makes 3 cups.

Culinary: Roasted Red Grapes

If you have never tried roasted grapes, I suggest you try them right away. This recipe looks at grapes in a whole new way by drenching them in balsamic vinegar and roasting them with a variety of herbs. This is another great dish to make and share with your witchy friends.

Ingredients

3 cups red grapes

1 tbsp fresh parsley, chopped

1 tbsp fresh thyme

2 tbsp extra virgin olive oil

Juice of ½ orange

1 tbsp balsamic vinegar

Salt and pepper to taste

Directions

Preheat the oven to 375 degrees Fahrenheit. Place the grapes in a large bowl and sprinkle the parsley and thyme over them. Drizzle the oil over the grapes. Stir well to combine. Place the grapes on a cookie sheet and bake for 15–20 minutes or until the grapes start to wrinkle and split. Check on them every few minutes as the end time draws near, as these should not be overcooked. Remove the sheet from the oven and drizzle with the orange juice and balsamic vinegar. Add salt and pepper to taste. Serves 5–6.

Journeying with the Hanged Man

The card of the Hanged Man is a space of ultimate equilibrium and potential. While this card also references opposites, remember that opposites are an equal distance from the center. In this journey, we see ways in which we may be off balance or even upside down. In this meditation, you may use the traditional imagery detailed in the following paragraphs, or choose a Hanged Man card from your favorite deck and use that image as your focus. If you choose your own specific deck, you will need to alter the following instructions for the unique imagery presented in that card. Because the traditional imagery of this card includes someone bound, some readers may find this working triggering. In that case, some of you may wish to skip it altogether. If you do choose to move forward, you may wish to record the following and play it back while you complete the journey work.

> Sit down, get comfortable, and close your eyes. Take a deep breath. Exhale. Repeat. When you feel comfortable and ready, imagine yourself at the top of a staircase. The steps before you are numbered in descending order. You are at the top step; on it is written clearly the number ten. See your feet on this topmost step. Clearly look at the number written there. When you are ready, slowly step down to step number nine. See the number written there. Look carefully at what is in front of you. When you see it clearly, step down to number eight. Continue stepping down through numbers seven, six, and five. See the numbers and your feet going down to step number four, number three, then number two, and then finally number one. When you get to the bottom of the stairs, you see a large red and yellow door. Turn the handle and step into the space of the Hanged Man.
>
> Walk slowly into the space. What do you see there? Are there trees? Are there vines? Do you know what kind they are? It will help to answer these questions out loud even if you are alone. Look around completely. Is anyone there? Are they bound? Are they hanging? What are they hanging from? Can they free themselves? Do they have anything to share with you? Do your best to learn what you can in the space. When you feel you are finished, turn and walk back toward the door you came in.

Open the door slowly and walk over the threshold. In front of you are the same numbered steps you came down earlier. This time you are going to slowly walk up these stairs. See your feet climbing up the first step to the second one. Then on to the third step, the fourth, going higher and higher up. Up to the fifth step, the sixth, the seventh. Continue on up to the eighth, the ninth, the tenth. Now you are back at the top step. You can now open your eyes.

It may help to write down the things you discovered during this working in a tarot journal or notebook. You can repeat this whenever the Hanged Man card comes up in a prominent place in your reading.

Hanging Balance Bath Spell

This spell is to help you get though challenging times when things are uncertain and a balance back to normalcy is needed. Take this bath during the full moon to capitalize on this powerful energy. You may also repeat it each month as often as necessary.

Ingredients

Glass jar

1 cup spring water

½ tsp cinnamon

6 drops myrrh oil

6 drops sandalwood oil

6 drops basil oil

Directions

Gather all ingredients together on your tarot altar or shrine. If you don't have one, please check out the instructions in chapter 30. Place the spring water into the jar. Next, add the cinnamon and the oils. Close the jar and shake well. Place the jar under your bed to charge it overnight. In the morning, remove the jar and shake it again. Then it is ready to use. Pour it into your ritual bath on the night of the full moon. Fill the rest of the bath up with tap water. Climb into the bath. Focus your mind on creative solutions to the challenges you are facing. Sit in the bath for as long as you like. When you get out and drain the water, imagine all your unnecessary challenges going down the drain.

Chapter Fifteen
Death

XIII · DEATH

DEATH.

Certain tarot decks feature a literal skeleton for the Death card. An actual representation of transformation, it shows us what remains behind, what was inside all along. While this card is called Death, in reality it represents so much more. Transformation, necessary change, and rejuvenation are also the meanings of this card. Some of us, myself included, have known more than our fair share of deaths. Unfortunately, or perhaps fortunately, this gives us a unique perspective on the process.

The Death card shows us how different parts of us are connected to make a functional whole. The same is true for tarot: different elements combine in the cards to tell a complete story. Thirteen is the number assigned to this card, adding to its reputation as unlucky or negative. Some Witches, however, have embraced the number. Its quirky reputation can now be reclaimed.

The right-side card image on the previous page comes from the Gustave Doré tarot. It shows a skeleton grim reaper against a starry night sky, a grim reminder that death watches over everyone. Ultimately, death is the closing of one passageway and the opening of another. Even though it can be difficult to accept, it is simply a transformation that occurs for every living thing.

Meanings and Correspondences

Popular meanings for the Death card include rebirth, renewal, and ancestral influence. Here are more correspondences and associations for this often difficult card of profound meaning.

Crystal Correspondences

Abalone—Abalone is technically a shell, but many magical practitioners use it in the same way as crystals. It is known to impart a calming feeling to all who use it. Abalone can also help in your readings by providing protection from unwanted outside energy.

Garnet—Garnet is a stone known to help with revitalization and courage. It can be useful in combination with your cards, as it will help to give you clarity and a deeper understanding of the people you are reading for.

Obsidian—This is a stone of transformation. It will help with tarot by removing negativity from a situation and allowing you to focus on what needs to get done. Obsidian is dedicated to both truth and healing blockages from the past.

Black Tourmaline—Black tourmaline can be used to clear and release energy after a psychic reading. It is said to purify, protect, and help with focus. Some even use larger pieces of this stone for scrying.

Herbal Correspondences

Rue (*Ruta graveolens*)

Cypress (*Cupressus* spp.)

Lily (*Lilium* spp.)

Lavender (*Lavandula angustifolia*)

Parsley (*Petroselinum crispum*)

White Rose (*Rosa* spp.)

Elder (*Sambucus* spp.)

Other Correspondences

Animal—Caterpillar, butterfly

Astrological—Saturn, Pluto, Scorpio

Musical Note—G

Magical and Culinary Recipes

Enhancing your readings by making magical concoctions and feasts allows for a greater understanding of what the cards are trying to tell you. There are a few foods associated with this card, including chocolate cake, wake cake, and poppy seeds.

Magical: Ashes and Earth Oil

Use this oil to help remember the dead and the lessons they have left behind.

Ingredients

Small glass bottle

½ ounce sweet almond oil

6 drops vetiver oil

6 drops patchouli oil

6 drops frankincense oil

Directions

Gather all ingredients together on your tarot altar or shrine. If you don't have one, please check out the instructions in chapter 30. Put the sweet almond oil into the bottle. Then add the vetiver, patchouli, and frankincense oils. Place the cap on the bottle and shake well to combine. Bury the bottle overnight in the dirt to charge it. In the morning, it is ready to use.

Culinary: Vanilla Poppy Seed Cake

There are many different foods eaten when we are mourning or honoring the dead. Each culture has its own unique manifestations. Some societies associate dark foods like chocolate with funerals and death rites, while others celebrate the color white. This white cake is another of my treasured family recipes that I grew up with. We had it on our table every holiday without fail. It takes a while to prepare, but the delightful flavor of vanilla combining with poppy seed is well worth it.

Ingredients

2 cups sifted cake flour	½ cup unsalted butter
2 tsp baking powder	1 cup milk
⅛ tsp salt	6 egg whites
1½ cups vanilla sugar[14]	½ cup poppy seeds

Directions

Preheat the oven to 350 degrees Fahrenheit. In a large bowl, whisk together the flour, baking powder, and salt. In a different bowl, gradually cream together 1¼ cups of the vanilla sugar with the butter, combining well after each addition. Stir in ¼ cup of the milk. Add the flour mixture, alternating with remaining milk. Stir well after each addition. Beat the egg whites until they form stiff peaks. Beat the remaining vanilla sugar into whites. Fold the whites into the cake batter, followed by the poppy seeds. Pour the batter into a lightly greased and floured 9-inch tube or Bundt pan. Bake for 45–50 minutes or until a toothpick inserted into the center comes out clean. Let the cake cool in the pan for 10 minutes, then turn over and remove.

Journeying with Death

I recently read about a university in the Netherlands that has an open grave you can lie in to ponder your life. For a lot of people, this could be a bit extreme. The following meditation journey will accomplish many of the same things and allow you to process your thoughts and feelings surrounding the card and

---

14. To make vanilla sugar, mix 1½ cups white sugar with 2 tsp vanilla extract. Alternatively, you can place a vanilla bean in with the sugar and leave it for 2–3 days to infuse the taste (remove bean before using).

the concept of death. The meditation contains images that may be triggering. Feel free to modify the journey, or chose to skip it altogether if you like. As with other journeys, you can use the traditional imagery detailed in the following, or choose a Death card from your favorite deck and use that image as your focus. If you choose your own specific deck, you will need to change the following instructions for the unique imagery presented in that card before you. You may wish to record the following and play it back while you complete the journey work.

Sit down in a comfortable place. Close your eyes. Take a deep breath. Exhale. Repeat. When you feel completely comfortable and ready, begin to imagine yourself at the top of a staircase. The steps before you are numbered in descending order. You stand at the top step; on it is written the number ten. See your feet on this top step. Look at the number written there. When you are ready, slowly step down to step number nine. See the number. Look carefully at what is in front of you. When you see it clearly, step down to number eight. Continue stepping down through the numbers: seven, down to six, down further to five. See the numbers and your feet going down to step number four, number three, then number two, and then finally number one. When you get to the bottom of the stairs, you see a large black door. Turn the handle and step into the space of the Death card.

Here the sky is gray. There is a field in front of you. It is a graveyard, or soon will be. What do you see around you? It will help to answer these questions out loud even if you are alone. Are there bones? Are there bodies? Is anyone still living there? What else do you see? Many decks feature a grim reaper mounted on a horse. Do you see this figure? What does it look like? What does the horse look like? Are there any other animals there? What else is in this space? Are there flowers? What kind are they? What color are they? Can you hear anything here?

When you have learned all you wish from this place, turn and walk across the field toward the door you came through. You are leaving this place behind. Turn the doorknob and walk through. Close the door behind you. In front of you are the exact same numbered steps you came down earlier. This time you are going to slowly walk up these stairs. See your feet climbing up the first step to the second one. Then on to the third step, the fourth one, traveling higher and higher up away from that space and back to the present. Up to the fifth step, the sixth step, the seventh one. Continue on up to the eighth step, the ninth step, the tenth. Now you are all the way back at the top step. You can now open your eyes.

It may help to write down the things you discovered during this working in a tarot journal or notebook. You can repeat this whenever the Death card comes up in a prominent place in your reading.

Death Becomes Us Water Spell

This ritual water is used to honor our ancestors and our beloved dead. Cemetery water is easily obtained from any cemetery from the faucets found there for watering the plants left on the graves. If your local cemetery doesn't have one of these, ask if there is a restroom and get the water from the sink there.

Ingredients

Glass bottle

½ cup cemetery water

½ cup rose water

6 drops rose absolute oil

6 drops vetiver oil

6 drops lavender oil

3 drops myrrh oil

3 drops violet oil

Directions

Gather all ingredients on your working altar or shrine. If you don't have one, please check out the instructions in chapter 30. Combine all ingredients in the glass bottle. Shake well to combine. Bury the bottle in the ground overnight on the eve of the full moon. Dig it up in the morning and it will be ready to use. It can be used to bless your home or place of business or as an offering water for your ancestors on their altar or shrine.

Chapter Sixteen
Temperance

XIV - ART

In the traditional tarot deck Temperance, or Art as it is also called, is numbered fourteen. The word "temperance" means moderation and self-restraint. But the Temperance card has many meanings. Many decks depict Temperance as an angel with two chalices. This is said to represent divine virtue. Even in the Millennium Thoth tarot shown on the right on the previous page, which is titled "Art," we can still see the pouring of two substances from the figure's hands. One is watery and the other fiery, implying both heating and cooling, just like the alchemical process of tempering. Here is the gift of true balance, knowing and understanding the process and the rewards that will be gathered from it. The trick is to use the minimum amount of effort to produce the maximum effect.

Because some decks have named this card "Art," the card is also connected to creativity and artistic endeavors. Art can come from inspiration, it can come from madness, it can come from beauty—the possibilities are endless. The drive is to create. Where does creation come from? How do we create beauty? How do we create ourselves and craft our own personal journey? These are the questions this card begs.

This card also brings to mind the process of tempering, as you do with steel or even chocolate. This heating and cooling process both strengthens and improves the material you are working with. The card helps us understand our place in this process.

Meanings and Correspondences

Popular meanings for Temperance include discernment, patience, assistance, healing, and creativity. Here are more associations for your magical use.

Crystal Correspondences

Jasper—This supportive stone comes in a variety of colors: brown, red, yellow, green, purple, or blue. It helps with mental processes, and problem-solving. Jasper also helps to align people with higher realms.

Sapphire—Traditionally, sapphire was referred to as the wisdom stone. It is useful in any situations needing intuition and psychic power, which makes it the perfect stone to use with tarot.

Topaz—Topaz helps with truth and spiritual knowledge. It can also assist with your confidence and problem-solving. There are many different color manifestations of topaz; please find the one that resonates best with you.

Herbal Correspondences

Valerian root (*Valeriana officinalis*)

Freesia (*Freesia corymbosa*)

Peppermint (*Mentha ×piperita*)

Ginger (*Zingiber officinale*)

Other Correspondences

Animal—Horse, dog

Astrological—Sagittarius, Jupiter

Musical Note—G#

Magical and Culinary Recipes

Enhancing your readings by making magical concoctions and feasts allows for a greater understanding of what the cards are trying to tell you. Peppermint and ginger are frequently associated with this card and feature in the formulas here.

Magical: Fire and Ice Oil

This formula blends the two elements used when tempering: hot and cold. Use this oil when you feel like you are "going through it" and need to come out the other side stronger and wiser.

Ingredients

Small glass bottle

½ ounce sweet almond oil

3 drops peppermint oil

3 drops ginger oil

3 drops helianthus oil

3 drops eucalyptus oil

Directions

Gather all ingredients together on your tarot altar or shrine. If you don't have one, please check out the instructions in chapter 30. Place the sweet almond oil into the glass bottle. Next, add the peppermint, ginger, helianthus, and eucalyptus oils. Cap the bottle. Shake well to combine. Take a deep breath and exhale slowly onto the bottle to charge it with your energy. Now it is ready to use.

Culinary: Ginger Pecan Spread

The following recipe was given to me by a Witch friend who is sadly no longer with us. She shared this spread one sunny morning at a gathering, and I quickly asked for the recipe.

Ingredients

8-ounce package cream cheese, softened

¼ tsp cinnamon, ground

2 tbsp finely chopped candied ginger

½ cup finely chopped dried apricots

½ cup chopped pecans

Directions

Place the softened cream cheese in a medium bowl. Sprinkle with cinnamon. Then mix in the ginger, apricots, and pecans. Serve at room temperature with apple slices, crackers, bagels, or bread. Makes 8 servings.

Journeying with Temperance

In this meditation, you may use the traditional imagery detailed in the following, or choose a Temperance or Art card from your favorite deck and use that image as your focus. If you choose your own specific deck, you will need to alter the following instructions for the unique imagery presented in that card. You may wish to record the following and play it back while you complete the journey work.

Sit down and get comfortable. Close your eyes. Take a deep breath. Exhale. Repeat. When you feel comfortable and ready, picture yourself at the top of a staircase. The steps before you are numbered in descending order. You are at the top step; on it is written clearly the number ten. See your feet on this topmost step. Clearly look at the number written there. When you are ready, slowly step down to step number nine. See the number written there. Look carefully at what is in front of you. When you see it clearly, step down to number eight. Continue stepping down through the numbers, down to seven, six, five. See the numbers and your feet going down to step number four, further down to number three, then number two, and then finally number one. When you get to the bottom of the stairs, you see a large steel door. Turn the handle and step into the Temperance card.

You are in a grassy field. There are flowers. What color are they? Walk up close to them. What do they smell like? What else do you see there? Up ahead is a lake. Walk toward it. The water is clear. Look into it. Can you see your own reflection? What do you look like? What else do you see? It will help to answer these questions out loud even if you are alone. In front of you there may be two cups. Can you see them? What are they made of? Are they made of gold? Silver? Or something else? Pick them up. Walk down to the water's edge and fill one of the cups with water. Slowly pour the water back and forth between the cups. Try to develop a rhythm, pouring back and forth from cup to cup. How does this motion feel? What does it create? Do your best to remember everything you see and feel there. Is there anyone there? Do you hear anything? When you have explored this space as much as you wish, place the cups back at the water's edge and turn, walking back toward the door you came through earlier.

When you come to the door, open it and walk through. In front of you are the same numbered steps you came down earlier. This time you are going to walk up these stairs. See your feet climbing up the first step to the second. Then on to the third, fourth, going higher and higher up. Up the fifth, the sixth, the seventh. Continue on up to the eighth, the ninth, the tenth. Now you are back at the top step. You can now open your eyes.

It may help to write down the things you discovered during this working in a tarot journal or notebook. You can repeat this whenever the Temperance card comes up in a prominent place in your reading or when you are having trouble understanding what it means in your specific situation.

Temperance Gris-Gris Bag Spell

This spell is contained in a magical bag that can bring inspiration and assistance in all situations. Crafting this bag may be a real treat for artistic Witches out there because they can let all their creative impulses flow.

Ingredients

3 tbsp dried lavender flowers

3 tbsp dried mugwort

1 tbsp dried parsley

Small bowl

3 drops myrrh oil

6-inch square of fabric of your choosing

1 small piece amethyst

6-inch pieces of ribbon of your choosing

Directions

Gather all items together on your working altar or shrine. If you don't have one, please check out the instructions in chapter 30. Place the lavender, mugwort, and parsley into the bowl. Mix well. Sprinkle the myrrh oil over the top. Next, lay the fabric out in front of you. Put the amethyst in the center of the fabric. Place as much of the herbal mix as possible in the center of the fabric. Gather up the corners of the fabric and tie it up with the ribbon.

Now you can really let your artistic talent flow. Decorate the bag however you like. You can add beads, fabric paint, or whatever you want. When you are done with your creation, you are now ready to use it. Carry it with you or place it under your pillow to grant creative inspiration whenever you need it.

Chapter Seventeen
The Devil

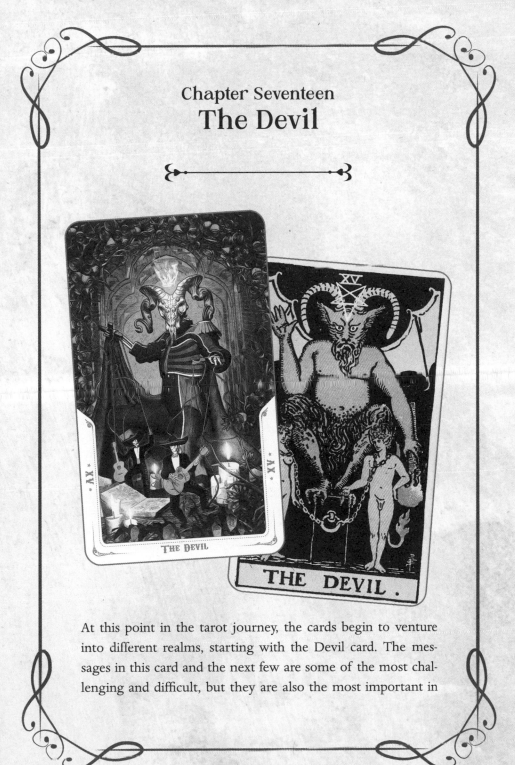

THE DEVIL

THE DEVIL.

At this point in the tarot journey, the cards begin to venture into different realms, starting with the Devil card. The messages in this card and the next few are some of the most challenging and difficult, but they are also the most important in the deck. This particular card, the Devil, shows us the attachments and connections that are deep, strong, and not always to our benefit.

Like so many cards in the tarot deck, the Devil is not always as it seems. It would be easy to associate this card with the popular image of a Christian-inspired Satan, full of temptation and evil. Most popular decks, however, take a more sophisticated approach to what this nuanced card truly represents.

The card is numbered fifteen. Images often feature a beastly creature with goat horns or an actual goat itself. Baphomet, Bacchus, and other dark and debaucherous figures party on this card.

In many decks, including the popular Rider-Waite-Smith, two figures are shown naked and chained to this devil. They are, however, loosely chained. They have the ability to free themselves, yet they are not free. If this card appears prominently in a spread, what is the seeker chained to? This could present itself as an addiction to drugs, alcohol, or sex or as unhealthy behaviors in any form, for example. The figures are weighed down by these behaviors and their connection to the "devil," however that may manifest for them.

The deck featured here from the Santa Muerte Tarot shows us a Baphomet-headed devil controlling two puppets of Mariachi band members. Here the chains are puppet strings, easily broken but still controlling the performers in every way. It raises the question of who controls our strings and why.

It is curious that among the remaining early decks extant in modern times, this card is conspicuously absent.[15] It may have been that no one wanted to hear the problematic messages that this card speaks to in depth. When it appears in a reading, consider any unnecessary and harmful attachments the seeker may have. Try to discover what it is that is holding them back, even if it might be themselves.

Meanings and Correspondences

Popular meanings for the Devil include boundaries, subconscious influences, addiction, taboos, inhibitions, oppression, blocks, restrictions, and our shadow selves. Here are some more correspondences for this powerful card.

---

15.   Giles, *The Tarot*, 17–18.

Crystal Correspondences

Hematite—This is a great stone to use for both divination and journey work. Hematite will help unite all aspects of your mind, body, and spirit. Hematite can also be used to improve concentration, allowing you to focus on the matter at hand. Take caution when purchasing hematite, however, as there are often fakes sold on the market. Real hematite is magnetic, and that is part of its magical power.

Jet—Jet is actually a form of coal. It activates spiritual power and will help you accurately express your psychic abilities. This crystal gives strength and deflects negative energy for all who use it. Jet can help with all forms of divination, including tarot and even mediumship.

Malachite—This is a classic stone. It is great for removing negativity from past trauma, and for healing on every level. Malachite has been in use for over six thousand years and is associated with the Goddess in all her forms.

Obsidian—As a child, obsidian was one of my favorite stones. I loved the fact that it is molten lava that has cooled and become solid. It is a stone of both truth and growth. It can transform what is unwanted into something useful. Anthropologically speaking, it was one of the first substances used for both tools and weapons. This shows us how we can use this stone to evolve and protect what is ours. Although not every-one thinks of it this way, it is also a stone of healing.

Black Tourmaline—Black tourmaline can be used to clear out and let go of unnecessary energy after a tarot reading. It is said to purify, protect, and also help with focus and concentration. Larger pieces or spheres of black tourmaline can also be used for scrying.

Other Correspondences

Animal—Goats, nutria

Astrological—Scorpio, Saturn

Musical Note—A

Herbal Correspondences

Devil's Shoestring Root (*Nolina lindheimeriana*)

Patchouli (*Pogostemon cablin*)

Fig Leaf (*Ficus carica*)

Magical and Culinary Recipes

Enhancing your readings by making magical concoctions and feasts allows for a greater understanding of what the cards are trying to help you with. The Devil card is connected to figs and black cherries, which are featured in the recipes here.

Magical: Down and Dirty Devil Oil

This is one of my few oil recipes that uses musk. Most musk that you can purchase commercially these days is synthetic and doesn't need to be derived from animals. This is lucky for animal lovers like me who still want that earthy, powerful blend while knowing no sentient beings suffered in the process.

Ingredients

Glass bottle

½ ounce sweet almond oil

6 drops musk oil

6 drops patchouli oil

3 drops cinnamon oil

3 drops ylang-ylang oil

1 small piece devil's shoestring root

Directions

Gather all ingredients on your tarot altar or shrine. If you don't have one, please check out the instructions in chapter 30. Place the sweet almond oil into the bottle. Next, add the musk, patchouli, cinnamon, and ylang-ylang oils. Then put the devil's shoestring root into the bottle and close it. Shake well to combine. Leave the oil outside overnight during the full moon to charge it. If you don't have a spot to place it outside, you can leave it on your windowsill where the moon's rays will touch it. Then it is ready to use.

Culinary: Black Cherry Jello Shot

When I first started pairing recipes with cards, I struggled a bit trying to figure out exactly what would be a perfect pairing for this card. Then it came to me: jello shots. Anyone who has indulged in too many knows they are in fact tools of the devil. If you choose not to imbibe for any reason, you can add a little Devil energy to regular jello by adding a pinch or two of black pepper.

Ingredients

1 package black cherry jello

1 cup tequila

Water

12 shot glasses

Directions

Make the jello according to the package directions, substituting the tequila for part of the water. Fill the shot glasses or similar shot-sized cups, and place them in the refrigerator for 5 or more hours. Enjoy in moderation.

Culinary: Lil Devil Cupcake

This is a recipe I have been making for decades. These tiny devil's food cupcakes are delicious, almost addictive. It follows logic that devil's food cake would be a good culinary matchup for this card.

Cupcake Batter

2¼ cups unbleached white flour

¾ tsp baking soda

¾ tsp baking powder

⅓ cup cocoa powder

1½ cup sugar

¾ tsp salt

1½ cup water

2 tsp vanilla extract

½ cup vegetable oil

Filling

6 ounces cream cheese, softened

3 tbsp beaten egg

¼ tsp ground cinnamon

½ cup sugar

¾ cup mini chocolate chips

Directions

Preheat the oven to 350 degrees Fahrenheit. In a large bowl, mix all the dry ingredients for the cupcakes. In a small bowl, mix the water, vanilla, and vegetable oil. Gradually add the contents of the dry mixture to the large bowl; stir well to combine after each addition. Prepare a muffin pan with paper cup liners. Fill each cup ⅔ full. In another bowl, combine all the filling ingredients and mix well. Spoon a tablespoon of filling into the middle of each cupcake. Bake the cupcakes for 15–20 minutes, until a toothpick inserted in the batter comes out clean. Remove from the oven and take the cupcakes out of the pan. Cool thoroughly. Makes 18–24 cupcakes.

Journeying with the Devil

The Devil represents a walk on the dark and wild side, through things we may or may not need to be connected with. In this journey, we will walk through this space and see what it really holds. For this working, you can use the traditional imagery detailed in the following, or choose a Devil card from your favorite deck and use that image as your focus. If you choose your own specific deck, you will need to alter the following instructions for the unique imagery presented in that card before you. As with a few of the other cards, this one contains images that may be triggering. Feel free to modify this or chose not to do it at all if you like. If you do move forward, you may wish to record the following and play it back while you complete the journey work.

Find a comfortable seat and begin to relax. Close your eyes. Take a deep breath. Exhale slowly. Repeat as often as you need. When you are ready, imagine yourself at the top of a staircase. The steps are numbered clearly in descending order. You are at the top step, number ten. See your feet on the step. See the number that is written there. When you are ready, slowly step down to step number nine. See the number written there. Do you see letters or numbers? Really look at what is in front of you. When you see it clearly, step down to number eight. Continue stepping down through numbers seven, six, and five. See the numbers and your feet going down to number four, number, three, then number two, and finally down to number one. When you get to the bottom of the stairs, you see a large red and black door. Turn the handle and step into the world of the Devil card.

When you walk through the door, you realize it is nighttime. What do you see there? It will help to answer these questions out loud even if you are alone. Are there people? Do they have clothes on? Are there chains? Is there music? Are there animals? How do you feel there? Remember you can choose to leave at any time. Take from the space what you need to discover. When you are done, return to the red and black door you came in.

In front of you are the same numbered steps you came down earlier. This time you are going to slowly walk up these stairs. See your feet climbing up the first step to the second one. Then on to the third step, the fourth, going higher and higher up. Up to the fifth step, the sixth, the seventh. Your body is leaving that other space behind. Continue on up to the eighth step, the ninth, the tenth. Now you are back at the top step. You can now open your eyes.

You are now back in the present realm. It may help to write down the things you discovered during this working in a tarot journal or notebook. You can repeat this whenever the Devil card comes up in an important place in your reading.

Devil Walks Spell

This working is for making a sprinkling powder that you can add to your shoes to make sure you are going in the right direction. Place a pinch in each of your shoes when you feel like you have a trying day ahead and need to stay on course.

Ingredients

1 tbsp dried basil

1 tbsp dried rosemary

1 tbsp dried patchouli

1 tbsp grains of paradise

Mortar and pestle

Directions

Gather all ingredients together on your tarot altar or shrine. If you don't have one, please check out the instructions in chapter 30. Place the basil, rosemary, patchouli, and grains of paradise into the mortar. Grind them up well with the pestle. Next, take the mortar in both hands and raise it up to the sky. Bend down and let the mortar touch the ground. Move the mortar to the right as far as you can reach. Move it to the left as far as you can reach. Now it is charged with the energy of the four directions. It is ready to use.

Chapter Eighteen
The Tower

XVI · THE TOWER

THE TOWER.

The Tower shows us the establishment crumbling to the ground. Established ways, established institutions, established buildings will not survive this serious transformation. An obvious reference for the Tower card is the Tower of Babel, which is depicted in the image on the right from the Gustave Doré tarot.

The Tower card is one of the most challenging cards in the tarot deck. Quite literally, things are falling apart. The situation cannot continue in the same way moving forward. This doesn't mean, however, that things can't improve. I remember one time early on in my tarot reading when I received this card in a spread. I immediately began to panic. Worried disaster and tragedy were around every corner, I worked myself into a frenzy. Since I was unsure where the problem was going to arise, I decided to be productive and do some laundry. As soon as I opened the cellar door, I saw the problem. My basement had flooded, my water heater had burst, and now everything down there was soaked with a few inches of water. In a way I was almost relieved. While the temporary flooding was a huge pain, the Tower card was telling me of a household issue, as opposed to a bigger problem with the health or safety of my loved ones.

An easy corollary for the Tower card is the Tower of Babel. For those unfamiliar with the biblical tale, the story comes from the book of Genesis. It speaks of a giant tower rising high up into the heavens. God was displeased with the people and their creation, so he made the workers building it all speak different languages. This made completing the work on the tower impossible. This tale is supposed to explain the variations of language in our modern world. So what does this evoke for us as a tarot card? To me, it is a tower with many tongues licking desperately at the edges of meaning. Another level of comprehension is needed, as normal communication has failed us terribly. Like the Bible story, the virtues of humility and cooperation are highlighted here. In many decks, we see the image of a tower crumbling. It is clear that the situations you have built up around work, relationships, home, or whatever the subject of your question will not stand. There is no doubt that this card presents a challenge, but the trick is knowing and being prepared to pivot into something even better.

Meanings and Correspondences

Popular meanings for the Tower include unexpected changes, difficulties, obstacles, challenges, and miscommunication. Here are more associations for you to use when working with this card.

Crystal Correspondences

Bloodstone—Bloodstone is a kind of chalcedony colored dark green with red flecks or inclusions. It is known for its healing and protective properties.

Red Jasper—This fiery-colored jasper can help discover problems that you may need to examine in the tarot reading. It also helps with recalling your dreams and could be useful when using tarot in concert with dreamwork.

Herbal Correspondences

Licorice (*Glycyrrhiza glabra*)

Yarrow (*Achillea millefolium*)

Other Correspondences

Animal—Dire wolf, wild boar, raven

Astrological—Mars

Musical Note—C

Magical and Culinary Recipes

Enhancing your readings by making magical concoctions and feasts allows for a greater understanding of what the cards are trying to tell you. Licorice is the food most associated with this card.

Magical: Taking Down the Tower Oil

Use this oil to remove things in your life that are unnecessary and poorly functioning. It calls for a swift solution to your problems. Be prepared.

Ingredients

Tower card from your deck

Tap water

Glass candleholder

Small black candle

Small glass bottle

½ ounce sweet almond oil

3 drops sandalwood oil

3 drops rosemary oil

1 small piece licorice root

Directions

Gather all ingredients together on your working altar or shrine. If you don't have one, please check out the instructions in chapter 30. Place the Tower card in the center of your space. Place a few drops of tap water in the candleholder. Put the candle in the holder and light it. Next, fill the bottle with the sweet almond oil. Add the sandalwood and rosemary oils to the bottle. Next, put the licorice into the bottle. Cap the bottle and throw it up into the air gently and catch it. Now leave the bottle on the table until the candle has burned down. If you have to leave or go to sleep, snuff it out and light it again as soon as you have time to devote to it. Remember to never leave a candle burning unattended. When the candle has burned down, the oil is ready to use.

Culinary: Licorice Brownies

In the US, we mostly think of licorice as only a candy. People decorate cupcakes with it for Halloween. But in other parts of the world, it is a prized flavor. This recipe calls for licorice powder. You will probably need to hunt for it online or in specialty shops, but if you love licorice, it is well worth the effort. This recipe pairs it with chocolate, and once you taste it, you will see why.

Ingredients

1 cup flour	1 cup white sugar
½ cup cocoa powder	3 eggs
¼ tsp salt	2 tsp vanilla extract
1 tbsp licorice root powder	¼ cup semisweet chocolate chips
12 tbsp butter, softened	¼ cup finely chopped soft black
1 cup brown sugar	licorice candy

Directions

Preheat the oven to 350 degrees Fahrenheit. Grease and flour a 9-inch square pan. In a large bowl, add the flour, cocoa powder, salt, and licorice powder. Whisk together until combined. In a separate bowl, mix the butter and sugar. After that is combined, add the eggs, one at a time, beating after each addition. Then add the vanilla and beat again. Next, gently fold in the chocolate chips and licorice candy. Bake for 35–40 minutes or until a toothpick inserted into the center comes out clean. Cool for at least 1 hour. Remove the brownies from the pan and enjoy.

Journeying with the Tower

This is a card of restructuring and change. This journey is crafted to help one discover when a drastic change is needed in their world. This journey may be too triggering for some, in which case, feel free to skip it. For this working, you can use the traditional imagery detailed in the following, or choose a Tower card from your chosen deck and use that image as your focus. If you choose your own specific deck, you will need to change the following instructions for the unique imagery presented in that card before you. You may wish to record the following and play it back while you complete the journey work.

Get comfortable and sit down. Close your eyes. Take a deep breath. Exhale. Repeat. Begin by imagining yourself at the top of a staircase. The steps before you are numbered in descending order. You are at the top step; on it is written clearly the number ten. See your feet on this topmost step. Clearly look at the number written there. When you are ready, slowly step down to step number nine. See the number written there. Look carefully at what is in front of you. When you see it clearly, step down to number eight. Continue stepping down through the numbers seven, six, and five. See the numbers and your feet going down to step number four, number three, then number two, and then finally number one. When you get to the bottom of the stairs, you see a large black metallic door. Turn the handle and step into the space of the Tower.

Step through the door and into the space. It is the dark of night. No moon is shining and a thick mist surrounds you. Up ahead in the distance is a stone tower. Walk toward it. Stop at a safe distance away and see what you can see. What kind of stone is it? Marble with thick veins running throughout? Granite with flecks? It will help to answer these questions out loud even if you are alone. Look at the color. Look at the overall structure itself. Maybe it's crumbling. Maybe there is smoke or flames coming out of its cracks. From a safe distance, do your best to see what is actually happening.

In the distance, you hear whispers. They are speaking many languages you do not know. They seem foreign, confusing, and they are growing louder. When you have seen and heard enough, turn and walk back toward the black door you used to enter. Turn the doorknob and walk through.

In front of you are the same numbered steps you came down when you started your journey. This time you are going to walk up these stairs back to the world of the present. See your feet climbing up the first step to the second one. Continue on to the third step, fourth, going higher and higher up. Up the fifth step, the sixth, the seventh. Climb on up to the eighth one, the ninth, and finally the tenth. Now you are back at the top step. You can now open your eyes.

It may help to write down the things you discovered during this working in a tarot journal or notebook. You can repeat this whenever the Tower card comes up in a confusing place in your reading or when you need more clarity about what message it holds for you at this time.

Tower Truth Candle Spell

This spell candle is designed to silence the nonsense and lies and help you discover the truth of what is happening in the situation.

Ingredients

1 tsp tap water

Candleholder

Pinch of dried lemon balm

Pinch of mustard seed

Pinch of dried rosemary

Mortar and pestle

3 drops lemongrass oil

3 drops orange oil

Yellow votive candle

Directions

Gather all ingredients together on your working altar or shrine, If you don't have one, please check out the instructions in chapter 30. Place the tap water in the bottom of the candleholder. Next, place the lemon balm, mustard seed, and rosemary in the mortar. Sprinkle the lemongrass and orange oil over this mixture.

Crush with the pestle until it is thoroughly mixed. Take the candle and cover the sides with the ground mixture. Place the candle into the holder and light. It is best to perform this spell on the waning moon. As the candle burns, focus on the flame and concentrate on the necessary truths coming toward you. When the candle has burned down, the spell is finished and you can expect to have some revelations coming to you quickly about people and things that are not as they seem. Remember to never leave a burning candle unattended.

Chapter Nineteen
The Star

XVII - THE STAR

THE STAR.

The Star shines above many of the cards that come before it. In my humble opinion, this is one of the most beautiful cards in the deck, both the meaning and imagery are glorious. It signifies the cosmic alignment when all is right in the universe, as it should be on every level. Both the message and the card evoke great calm and successful outcomes.

Very often, actual water is depicted in this tarot card. We see an individual lifting a chalice above their head, as if pouring water over themself. The other hand holds an additional chalice that appears to be scooping up water. This ebb and flow of one chalice emptying and another filling represents the ebb and flow of life, showing us that the stars we see nourish us and everything else around us, either in the sea or on the land. Things are finally turning our way. The Star guides us and rewards us simultaneously.

One of the main meanings of this card is destiny. The Star shows us who we are and what we were born to do. Cosmic Witches may have a special connection to this card, as it references astrology and how the stars above determine our character and our destiny.

The number seventeen is assigned to the Star card. Very often, decks feature seven stars in the sky. The Millennium Thoth tarot card featured on the left on page 149 shows three stars, the largest one seeming to illuminate the whole image and the smallest seeming to pour from one of the figure's chalices.

Meanings and Correspondences

Popular meanings for the Star include destiny, inspiration, healing, calm, transcendence, and hope. Here are more correspondences as you explore this card.

Crystal Correspondences

Amethyst—Amethyst is a stone of clarity, spirituality, joy, and self-awareness. When we talk about stones, amethyst is one of the most popular. It can help heal both physical and emotional pain. This is one of the best stones to use in conjunction with tarot because it can be very valuable when doing spiritual journey work. Amethyst will help you connect with higher realms and also grant you insight in all situations.

Staurolite—This mineral is colored reddish black and is known to develop in the shape of a cross. Some people call this the faery cross. It also has associations with Christianity, with some believers saying it formed from tears cried when Christ died. It is used to bridge the gaps between spiritual and physical planes.

Celestite—This light blue stone is also said to be connected to space and the stars. Years ago, a dear friend gifted me a large piece, and it has been on one of my bedroom shrines ever since. Not only helpful in dreamwork and astral travel, this stone also helps with all spiritual communication. Art Witches may find it helpful with inspiring creativity.

Tektite—A tektite is a mineral that comes from a meteorite as it enters Earth's atmosphere. It is connected directly to space and the messages the stars there have for us. The mineral is black in color and, magically, can help us discern what we need to know from our astrology chart and other planetary influences on us. It is said to help with spiritual growth and insight on every level.

Sapphire—Sapphire is called the wisdom stone and is useful with concentration and promoting calm.

Sugilite—This is a beautiful stone with purple and lavender hues. It is one of my favorites and is said to help with your connection to spirit and communicating with other worlds.[16]

Herbal Correspondences

Apple Blossom (*Malus domestica*)

Ginger (*Zingiber officinale*)

Myrrh (*Commiphora myrrha*)

Rosemary (*Salvia rosmarinus*)

Violet (*Viola* spp.)

Other Correspondences

Animal—Peacock

Astrological—Aquarius, Uranus

Musical Note—A#

---

16.   Hall, *The Crystal Bible*, 279–80.

Magical and Culinary Recipes

Enhancing your readings by making magical concoctions and feasts allows for a greater understanding of what the cards are trying to tell you. The two foods connected to this card are apple and ginger, which feature heavily in the recipes here.

Magical: Star-Crossed Oil

Use this oil to help cleanse your troubles and place you back on the proper path toward your destiny.

Ingredients

Small glass bottle

½ ounce sweet almond oil

6 drops rosemary oil

3 drops ginger oil

3 drops myrrh oil

Directions

Gather all your ingredients together on your tarot shrine or altar. If you don't have one, please check out the instructions in chapter 30. Put the sweet almond oil in the bottle. Next, add the rosemary, ginger, and myrrh oils. Close the bottle and rub it back and forth between your palms. Leave it on your windowsill overnight, where it will be blessed by the light of the stars. In the morning, it will be ready to use.

Culinary: Apple Cranberry Chutney

This is a great make-ahead recipe that is great for sharing with your fellow Witches.

Ingredients

½ cup honey

½ cup apple cider vinegar

2 tsp minced ginger root

3 whole cloves, crushed

½ tsp ground cinnamon

¼ cup diced dried apricot

½ cup chopped fresh apple

2 cups fresh cranberries

½ cup minced red onion

Pinch of salt

Directions

Warm the honey over low heat on the stove or briefly in the microwave on low power. Combine it in a large bowl with the vinegar, ginger, cloves, and cinnamon. Next, place a saucepan on the stove over low heat. Add the apricot, apple, cranberries, and onion. Add the honey spice mixture. Finally, add a pinch of salt. Continue to cook over low heat for 60 minutes or until the fruit has begun to break down into a jam-like consistency. Let it cool and store it in the refrigerator for up to 2 weeks. Serves 6–8 people.

Journeying with the Star

Dreams and destiny are the watchwords of the Star card. In this journey meditation, the seeker will go to the stars and back to find what their destiny holds. For this working, you can use the traditional imagery detailed in the following, or choose a Star card from your favorite deck and use that image as your focus. If you choose your own specific deck, you will need to change around the following instructions for the unique imagery presented in that card before you. Once you get familiar with this method, feel free to use it whenever and wherever you like. It may be easier to record the following and play it back while you complete the journey work or, alternatively, have a friend read it out loud to you.

Get comfortable and sit down. Close your eyes. Take a deep breath. Exhale. Repeat. When you are completely ready, picture yourself at the top of a staircase. The steps before you are numbered in descending order. You are at the top step; on it is written clearly the number ten. See both your feet on this topmost step. Clearly look at the number written there. When you are ready, slowly step down to step number nine. See the number written there. Look carefully at what is in front of you. When you see it clearly, step down to number eight. Continue stepping down through the numbers, down to seven, six, five. See the numbers and your feet going down to step number four, further down to number three, then number two, and then last down to number one. When you get to the bottom of the stairs, you see a large dark blue door. Turn the handle and step into the universe of the Star card.

When you walk through the door, you are entering into a universe of both light and life. The distance you have experienced until now is changed into a glorious presence. Here you are not bound by gravity. Here you float effortlessly through the stars, through space. In this realm, you see one star that is brighter than all the others. It sings to you as you move closer to it. You see it radiate the spectrum of all colors. Red, orange, yellow, green, blue, indigo, and violet are all present here. How do you feel basking it its light? It will help to answer these questions out loud even if you are alone. Why did this star call you to it? Your fingers and toes begin to tingle as you uncover its secrets and powerful beauty. Take it all in. Breathe and take it all in some more. When you are done bathing in its light, travel back to the door you originally traveled through. Remember you can return here anytime you like. When you return to the blue door, turn the handle and step through.

Directly in front of you are the same numbered steps you came down earlier. Now you are going to slowly walk up these stairs, back to the world of the present you left before. See your feet climbing up the first step to the second one. Then on to the third step, the fourth, going higher and higher up. Up to the fifth step, the sixth, the seventh. Continue on up to the eighth, the ninth, the tenth. Now you are all the way back at the top step. You can now open your eyes.

It may help to write down the things you discovered during this working in a tarot journal or notebook. You can repeat this whenever the Star card comes up in a prominent place in your reading.

Star Uncrossed Candle Spell

So much of magic these days is wrapped up in bringing things to you. This could be money, great sex, a new house, or whatever. What people tend to forget, however, is that magic operates on a principle of balance. You can't attract great things to yourself if there are blocks and obstacles standing in the way. This candle is about getting those roadblocks to success in all areas out of your way. This working may have extra appeal for the Cosmic Witches out there. One of the best astrologers I ever consulted told me, "You might have a chal-

lenging star chart, but that doesn't mean you can't hack it into a better one."
That thought in and of itself was a revelation. Light this candle whenever you
feel like something unnecessary is standing in your way.

Ingredients

Toothpick

1 small white candle in glass

3 drops rosemary oil

3 drops myrrh oil

Silver glitter

Directions

Gather all the items together on your tarot altar or shrine. If you don't have
one, please check out the instructions in chapter 30. Using the toothpick, carve
a pentagram, or five-pointed star, on the top of the candle. Make sure the wick
is in the center of the star. Next, add the rosemary and myrrh oil to the top
of the candle. Gently swirl the candle around to get the oil into all the cracks.
Next, sprinkle a small amount of the glitter on the top. Gently hold the candle
between your palms and rub them back and forth to charge it with your own
energy. The candle is ready to light. Remember to never leave a burning candle
unattended. You have a choice to light it for a short time every night and snuff it
out before you go to sleep or to spend a longer time with it, meditating on the
obstacles you wish to have removed.

Chapter Twenty
The Moon

As the cards progress through this epic hero's journey, the next card is the Moon. It gives us external guidance from the forces that be. The Moon means so many things to so many different people, and this tarot card references every single one of them.

Astrologically, the Moon is seen to be representative of deep emotions and hidden forces.

The card I chose to illustrate this entry is from the Santa Muerte Tarot by Fabio Listrani, on the right on page 157. The imagery on this card features a moon shining above a body of water and someone on the edge of this body of water looking in. Looking back at this person is their skeletal reflection. Some decks feature either a dog or a jackal, representing both our dreams and our nightmares. Also in attendance is either a crab or a scorpion, depending on which deck you are using. These represent the depths of what lies within. This card quite literally shows the liminal space, a place of in-between. Here in this location of neither land nor sea, anything is possible.

To us here on Earth, the moon appears to go through phases, and each one interacts with us differently. People tend to blame their behavior on the moon, for it can indeed make us do mysterious things. It goes from waxing to waning and everything in between. Because of these transitions and transformations, this card represents timing. The Moon card urges us to use that timing to our ultimate advantage.

The Moon card also speaks to faith. This is a faith born of the cosmos and things we can barely see, let alone touch. Yet somehow we know they are there. Some readers consider this a negative card, but for me, it represents things hidden from view, things to be sought after, things to discover.

This moon is the dwelling place of the Triple Goddess, the Maiden, the Mother, and the Crone responsible for bringing life into existence. These are spiritual beings that continue to guide us even if we cannot always see them in the light of day.

Meanings and Correspondences

Popular meanings for the Moon include secrets, changes, hidden meaning, occult knowledge, and power. Here are a few more.

Crystal Correspondences

Emerald—This popular gemstone is said to help with memory and intelligence. It is said that even Cleopatra wore one as a display of her power.

Moonstone—This stone can help with all levels of psychic ability and accessing the unknown. It is a stone of honesty.

Selenite—Selenite is said to help with inner and outer transformations on all levels. The stone grants clarity and access to higher realms. It is especially useful for crystal grids and can be used for scrying by itself or in conjunction with your tarot cards.

Labradorite—This stone shines in a way others don't. Its iridescent beauty is like no other. It is said to help with spiritual awareness and knowledge.

Blue Kyanite—Kyanite is a stone of extremely high vibrations. This crystal creates bridges and pathways where none were to be found before. Unlike other stones, it does not take on negative energy. Thus, you may perform rites or rituals to bless or consecrate it, but none for cleansing will ever be needed.

Pearl—Pearls are formed in the ocean by oysters or in fresh water by mussels. They can also be man-made. These shimmery gifts have been connected, in many cultures at many times, with femininity and the Goddess. Pearls are really helpful with full moon readings and workings. Water Witches may find these helpful because they are born of water.

Unakite—This is a stone that can grant great vision and guidance. Having the ability to unite body, mind, and soul, it is a great addition to any tarot-inspired collection. Also referred to as unakite jasper, this stone is pistachio green in color with accents of pink or bright peach.

Herbal Correspondences

Eucalyptus (*Eucalyptus globulus*)

Hibiscus (*Hibiscus* spp.)

Hyssop (*Hyssopus officinalis*)

Ginger (*Zingiber officinale*)

Moonwort (*Botrychium lunaria*)

Lettuce (*Lactuca sativa*)

Lily (*Lilium* spp.)

Lotus (*Nelumbo nucifera*)

Rose (*Rosa* spp.)

Violet (*Viola* spp.)

Other Correspondences

Animal—Dog, jackal, crab, scorpion

Astrological—The Moon, Cancer, Pisces

Musical Note—B

Magical and Culinary Recipes

Enhancing your readings by making magical concoctions and feasts allows for a greater understanding of what the cards are trying to tell you. The foods most often connected to this card are mangoes, poppy seeds, and tangerines, some of which are featured in the recipes that follow.

Magical: Full Moon Magic Oil

The full moon is a great time to do magic, whatever type of Witch you are. As you may have noticed, several of the oils in this book get charged and blessed under the light of the full moon. This recipe is specifically for the moon and is one I have relied on for some time to boost my magic during this moon phase. One of the great things about this oil is that it is like having the power of the full moon in a little bottle to bust out whenever you need it.

Ingredients

Small glass bottle

½ ounce sweet almond oil

3 drops rose oil

3 drops violet oil

3 drops myrrh oil

3 drops hyssop oil

3 drops sandalwood oil

Directions

Gather all your ingredients together on your tarot altar or shrine. If you don't have one, please check out the instructions in chapter 30. Place the sweet almond oil into the bottle. Then add the rose, violet, myrrh, hyssop, and sandalwood oils. Place the cap on the bottle and shake well. Leave the oil blend outside overnight during the full moon to charge it. If you don't have a spot to place it outside, you can leave it on your windowsill where the moon's rays will touch it. Then it is ready to use.

Culinary: Mango Muffins

These muffins are a delight to serve for holidays, sabbats, coven meetings, or whenever you want to enjoy them, whether the moon is full or not.

For the Topping Crumble

¼ cup chopped walnuts

¼ cup dark brown sugar, packed

¼ cup oats

¼ cup unbleached flour

¼ tsp ground cinnamon

¼ tsp ground nutmeg

Pinch of salt

3 tbsp unsalted butter, melted

For the Muffins

½ cup sour cream

½ cup milk

1 cup oats

1¼ cup unbleached flour

1 tsp baking powder

¾ tsp baking soda

½ tsp salt

½ tsp ground cinnamon

1 large egg, beaten and at room temperature

¼ cup light brown sugar, packed

2 tsp vanilla extract

5 tbsp unsalted butter, melted and cooled

1 large mango, finely diced

Directions

In a small bowl, stir together the walnuts, brown sugar, oats, flour, cinnamon, nutmeg, and salt. Pour the melted butter over the top and mix well to combine. The mixture should resemble a crumble. Set this aside and work on the muffin bottoms. Preheat the oven to 400 degrees Fahrenheit. Grease a 12-muffin pan or insert paper cups. In a large bowl, whisk together the sour cream and milk until combined. Add the oats and let them soak in the mixture for 20 minutes. In a separate bowl, stir together the flour, baking powder, baking soda, salt, and cinnamon. When the oat mixture is done soaking, add the egg, brown sugar, vanilla, and butter to it. Next, gently add the flour mixture, stirring only to combine. Fold in the mango. Fill the muffin cups with the batter, then sprinkle with the crumble topping. Bake for 20–25 minutes, until the tops are browned and a toothpick inserted into the center comes out clean. Cool for 5–10 minutes and serve warm. Makes 12 muffins.

Journeying with the Moon

On the night of the full moon, prepare a space on the floor in your bedroom or another space where you can carry out the meditation undisturbed. Take the Moon card from one or more tarot decks to use in your meditation. Wash a circular space on the floor approximately one yard in circumference with the moon water from the spell on the next page. Take the tarot card and place it on the edge of this circle and then sit in the center of the circle and get comfortable. It may be easier to record the following and play it back while you complete the journey work or, alternatively, have a friend read it out to you.

> Say the following aloud: "I gaze upon the moon, and I look within, my journey is wondrous, I'm ready to begin." Once inside the circle, continue to repeat the above as you use the moon water to wash your hands, your feet, and the back of your neck.
>
> Next close your eyes and imagine a thin silver cord connecting you to the moon. See it shine in the moonlight. See what appears on either side of it as you take this trip. Once the cord has reached the moon, know that you are connected and can travel back and forth on it safely and securely. In your mind's eye, imagine yourself traveling along this silver cord to the moon to find the answers you need. When you arrive at the moon, you will find a silver box containing the answers you need about your situation. Open the box. When you see what lies there, close the box and travel safely back down this silver cord to your safe moon circle space on your floor.

Open your eyes. Wash your hands, your feet, and the back of your neck again with the moon water in the recipe that follows. Pick up the tarot card and put it back with your deck. Your journey ritual meditation is now complete.

Moon Card Spell

The Moon card is one of the few in the deck that features actual water. This ritual takes a bit of time, but it will help you access the mystery and the magic that the Moon has to offer you.

Ingredients

1 cup spring water	6 drops myrrh oil
½ cup rainwater	6 drops sandalwood oil
½ cup white rose petals	Large glass jar

Directions

Place all the ingredients into the glass jar. Shake well to combine. On the night before the full moon, leave the jar outside or on a windowsill where the moon's rays will touch and bless it. The following night it will be ready to use.

Chapter Twenty-One
The Sun

XIX - THE SUN

THE SUN.

The Sun card represents the glorious, shining moments of life. This is a card of both harmony and energy, and it is one of the most glorious cards. The Sun is a card of happiness, rejoicing, success, and bliss. It is number nineteen in the deck, which breaks down to a ten in numerology (1 + 9 = 10). Ten is seen as a number of wholeness, potential, and beginning. In contrast to the previous card, here everything is out in the open. Nothing is hidden; everything is out in the sunshine. In the Millennium Thoth Tarot card pictured on the left of the previous page, we see two winged twins dancing under the twelve rays of the sun. In this representation, all twelve zodiac signs are present. They symbolize all possibilities.

Some associate this card with the sun gods and goddesses—Adonis, Apollo, Amun, Arinna, Eos, Helios, Hathor, Huitzilopochtli, Inti, Lugh, Mithra, Ra, Sol, Surya, and others. Each one carries with it its own blessings and burdens. The sun gives us life, and as you see, so many different cultures knew that and represented it in their own cosmology in different and beautiful ways. What different and beautiful ways will the sun help you manifest your own growth?

Meanings and Correspondences

Popular meanings for the Sun include success, vitality, birth, marriage, creativity, happiness, and joy. Here are a few more associations for this bright and cheerful card.

Crystal Correspondences

Amber—Technically, amber is not a crystal at all; it is a solidified form of tree resin. The resin hardens over time and becomes fossilized. It can be of particular interest to Earth Witches and Green Witches, as it comes directly from plants. It is known to help with motivation and intelligence. When used with your tarot reading, it can assist with decision-making and messages from both the ancestors and the higher realms.

Sunstone—This crystal is obviously connected to the sun. It can bring luck and encourage optimism in all situations. It is also helpful in giving a boost to self-confidence.

Carnelian—Carnelian is a stone not only of the sun but of fire. If you are a Fire Witch, you might want to place this on your ritual shrine or use it in a piece of power jewelry.

Citrine—This yellow crystal is actually a variation of quartz. It can be great for doing tarot readings about love or healing. Citrine can clear your mind, helping improve psychic awareness and spiritual growth.

Topaz—Topaz helps with truth telling and advancing your spiritual development. Used in combination with your cards, it can also assist with your confidence, connections, and problem-solving.

Yellow Calcite—Also called honey calcite, this stone is great for opening up your mind to the sacredness of the Divine. It can grant both intelligence and mental focus, making it helpful when reading tarot for yourself or others.

Herbal Correspondences

Sunflowers (*Helianthus* spp.)

Heliotrope (*Heliotropium arborescens*)

Marigold (*Tagetes erecta*)

Cinnamon (*Cinnamomum verum*)

Frankincense (*Boswellia serrata*)

Other Correspondences

Animal—Lizard, salamander, turtle, meerkat

Astrological—Sun

Musical Note—D

Magical and Culinary Recipes

Enhancing your readings by making magical concoctions and feasts allows for a greater understanding of what the cards are trying to tell you. Sunflower seeds, oranges, and tangerines are all associated with this card.

Magical: Sun and Success Oil

Use this oil to bring glorious success to the matter at hand.

Ingredients

Small glass bottle

½ ounce sweet almond oil

3 drops helianthus oil

3 drops cinnamon oil

3 drops frankincense oil

3 drops amber oil

Directions

Gather all ingredients together on your working altar or tarot shrine. If you don't have one, please check out the instructions in chapter 30. Add the almond oil to the bottle. Next, add the helianthus, cinnamon, frankincense, and amber oils. Close the bottle and shake well. Leave it outside or on a sunny windowsill for 24 hours, where the sun's rays will have a chance to bless and charge it with energy. After the time has passed, the oil is ready for use.

Culinary: Sunshine Salsa

This edible concoction embodies summertime and sunshine with every bite. It contains either oranges or tangerines—or both, if you like—using these sun-loving citrus fruits to help bring joy.

Ingredients

¼ cup diced red onion

3 cups diced and deseeded plum tomatoes

2 tsp minced jalapeño pepper

¼ cup diced and deseeded yellow pepper

2 tsp orange juice or tangerine juice

1 tbsp minced cilantro

½ tsp onion powder

¼ tsp ground pepper

¾ tsp salt

2 cloves minced garlic

Directions

Combine all ingredients in a glass bowl. Mix well. Chill for 1 hour or more. Serve with corn tortilla chips. Makes approximately 3½ cups salsa.

Journey Working with the Sun

For this working, you can use the traditional imagery detailed in the following paragraphs, or choose a Sun card from a less conventional deck and use that image as your focus. If you choose your own deck, you will need to change the instructions for the unique imagery presented in that card before you. It may be easier to record the following and play it back while you complete the journey work or, alternatively, have a friend read it out to you.

Sit down. Get comfortable. Close your eyes. Take a deep breath. Exhale slowly. Repeat. Envision yourself at the top of a staircase. The stairs in front of you are numbered in descending order. You are at the top step, number ten. See your shoes standing on that step. Look at the number written there. Slowly step down to step number nine. See the number written there. Do you see letters or numbers? Really look at what is in front of you. When you see it clearly, step down to number eight. Continue stepping down through the numbers, down to seven, six, five. See the numbers and your feet going down to number four, number three, then down to number two, and finally all the way down to number one. When you get to the bottom of the stairs, you see a large golden door. Turn the handle and step into the world of the Sun card.

Here your entire being is bathed in sunlight. It feels warm on your face. Take a breath. You smell sunflowers. There are sunflowers all around. Mammoth ones towering over your head. Small ones tickling at your ankles. The smell is intoxicating. What do they smell like? Off in the distance you see a child riding a horse. Maybe there are two children. They are laughing. Walk toward them. What do they look like? It will help to answer these questions out loud even if you are alone. Ask them if they have anything they would like to tell you. Pay attention to their response. Ask them anything else you would like to know about this card. When you are done and have received the answers you seek, turn and walk back through the field to the golden door. Take your time and really feel every step.

Open the door. Directly in front of you, you see the exact same numbered steps you came down when you began. This time, you are going to slowly walk back up these stairs. See your feet climbing up the first step to the second one. Then on to the third step, the fourth, going higher and higher up. Up to the fifth step, the sixth, the seventh. Continue on up to the eighth, the ninth, the tenth. Now you are back at the top step. You can now open your eyes.

It can help to write down the things you discovered during this process in a tarot journal or notebook. You may repeat this whenever the Sun card comes up during a reading and you need more insight.

Sunshine Day Bath Spell

For over a decade, I lived in an apartment with a shower and no bath. So now every chance I get, I take a long, transformational ritual bath. The Sunshine Day ritual bath is a little unorthodox; pairing the sun, which is associated with fire, with a bath of water is unusual. However, this bath will give you a feeling of joy and happiness. Who does not want to immerse themselves in that?

Ingredients

Large glass jar

1 cup sea salt

1 cup Epsom salt

6 drops frankincense oil

6 drops helianthus oil

12 drops orange oil

1 tsp ground calendula flowers[17]

Directions

Gather all ingredients together on your tarot altar or shrine. If you don't have one, please check out the instructions in chapter 30. To the jar, add the Epsom salt and sea salt. Add the frankincense, helianthus, and orange oils one at a time. Shake well after each addition. Finally, add the calendula flowers. Close the jar and shake again. Leave the jar outside on a sunny day where the sun's rays will bless it and charge it with energy. After this, it will be ready to use. Take ½ cup of the mix and add it to your warm bath. Makes enough for 4 baths.

---

17.   To make ground calendula flowers, grind up dried flowers in a coffee grinder or with a mortar and pestle.

Chapter Twenty-Two
Judgement

XX · JUDGEMENT

The Judgement card is numbered twenty. Our epic journey through the tarot major arcana is almost complete. This is a card in which the individual is at the mercy of external forces, the decisions handed down are set in stone, and little can be done to change this at this point.

The Judgement card represents concepts that are grounded both in religion and practicality. There is the final judgment that is said to come after death, when all our deeds, good and bad, are weighed up to determine the course of our afterlife. From a Christian perspective, this is said to determine your entry into heaven, hell, or somewhere in between. The Gustave Doré tarot card pictured on the right on the previous page references this biblical judgment, ripe with angels and souls waiting to be judged. There are also legal judgments of the corporeal world, which can determine your fate in regard to the matter at hand. In some ways, this card represents payment for the work, or lack thereof, that you have done to ensure a favorable outcome.

This is a card of Anubis, a card of Ma'at, a card of Minerva, a card of Maman Brigitte and all the divinities who represent the ultimate judgment. When this card appears in a reading, it may help to think objectively about all your actions in a situation and what the likely consequences are, either good or bad.

Meanings and Correspondences

Popular meanings for Judgement include decisions, final judgment, completion, truth, and karmic justice. Here are a few more of the correspondences for this card.

Crystal Correspondences

Fire Opal—This beautiful crystal will help align you with higher realms and help improve your psychic perception. It held special significance for ancient Maya and Aztec cultures and was said to provide both joy and luck.

Kyanite—There are many different colors of kyanite: black, blue, green, and orange. It is a stone of meditation. It will help connect you to your personal deities and spirit guides. Kyanite is also particularly useful in conjunction with dreamwork and journey work, as it helps with recall and understanding of these different realms.

Herbal Correspondences

Basil (*Ocimum basilicum*)

Hyssop (*Hyssopus officinalis*)

Rosemary (*Salvia rosmarinus*)

Other Correspondences

Animal—Raven

Astrological—Pluto

Musical Note—C

Magical and Culinary Recipes

Enhancing your readings by making magical concoctions and feasts allows for a greater understanding of what the cards are trying to tell you. Divinity candy is the food frequently connected to this card.

Magical: Maman Brigitte Oil

Maman Brigitte is the representation of all the sacred foremothers in the Haitian tradition. She is represented as a grandmother to us all. She is all grandmothers across time. We are all connected to her. This oil will help you when you are seeking to be treated fairly and rewarded for your efforts. Be sure you realize the distinction here that you are not commanding this energy, the same way you would not command a great-grandmother who should be treated with deference and respect. It is better to conceive of this oil as just creating the proper conditions so the right things will occur in the situation.

Ingredients

Small glass bottle

½ ounce sweet almond oil

3 drops violet oil

3 drops lavender oil

3 drops orange oil

3 drops orange blossom oil

Pinch of graveyard dirt

Small bowl

Cotton balls

Directions

Gather all ingredients on your tarot altar or shrine. If you don't have one, please check out the instructions in chapter 30. Add the sweet almond oil to the bottle. Add the violet, lavender, orange, and orange blossom oils. Next, add the graveyard dirt. Close the bottle and shake well. Place the bottle into the bowl. Cover it with cotton balls and leave it overnight. In the morning, dispose of the cotton balls in the trash and remove the bottle. It is now ready for use.

Culinary: Divinity

This delightful candy has been a favorite for a long time. Recipes for it started to appear in the 1900s, and it is still a popular holiday treat today. You will need a candy thermometer for this recipe.

Ingredients

⅔ cup light corn syrup

2⅔ cup white sugar

½ cup water

2 egg whites

1½ tsp vanilla extract

⅔ cup chopped pecans

Directions

Heat the corn syrup, sugar, and water in a saucepan over low heat. Stir constantly until the sugar is dissolved. Stop stirring but keep cooking until the temperature of the mix reaches 260 degrees Fahrenheit. In a medium bowl, beat the egg whites until they form stiff peaks. Pour in the hot syrup mixture in a thin stream while continuing to beat. Please be careful and use a stand mixer if at all possible or enlist the help of a friend. Then add the vanilla. Continue beating for 10 minutes or until the mixture begins to hold its shape and the color turns slightly dull. Stir in the nuts. Remove the mix from heat and drop spoonfuls from a buttered wooden spoon onto wax paper. Let stand at room temperature for 12 or more hours. Turn them over once about halfway during the process. Eventually, the candies will begin to firm up, and then you can store them in an airtight container. Makes roughly 36 candies.

Journeying with Judgement

In this working, you can use the traditional imagery detailed in the following paragraphs, or choose a Judgement card from your favorite deck and use that image as your focus. If you choose your own deck, you will need to change the following instructions to correspond with the unique imagery presented in that card before you. Once you get familiar with this method, feel free to use it whenever and wherever you like. It may be easier to record these words and play them back while you complete the journey work or, alternatively, have a helper read it out to you.

Get comfortable. Sit down and close your eyes. Take a deep breath. Exhale. Repeat. Imagine yourself at the top of a staircase. The steps before you are numbered in descending order. You are at the top step; on it is written the number ten. See your feet on the step. Clearly look at the number written there. When you are ready, slowly step down to step number nine. See the number written there. Look carefully at what is in front of you. When you see it clearly, step down to number eight. Continue stepping down through the numbers seven, then six, then five. See the numbers clearly and your feet going down to number four, number three, then number two, and then last, down to the bottom, number one. When you get to the bottom of the stairs, you see a large blue and white door. Turn the handle and step into the world of the Judgement card.

In the distance you see water and mountains. Walk toward them. The sky above is peaceful. The water ahead is calm. This is a space of confidence. Here all the rewards will be given. Pay attention to how you feel as you move through this space. You travel across the land with ease. It is almost as if your feet barely touch the ground. It feels like you are floating. You hear horns coming from above. They are playing the sweetest melody. Can you hear it? Do you recognize it? Above you are clouds. Do you see shapes in the clouds? What do they look like? Do your best to remember every detail. It will help to answer these questions out loud even if you are alone. Do your best to remember how you feel. Soak it all in. Breathe deeply. Look around; it is almost as if you are seeing with new eyes. When you feel you have explored the space as much as you want, turn and return to the door you entered through.

Walk through and close the door behind you. In front of you are the same numbered steps you came down earlier. This time you are going to slowly walk up these stairs. See your feet climbing up the first step to the second one. Then on to the third step, the fourth, going higher and higher up. Up to the fifth step, the sixth step, the seventh. Continue on up to the eighth, the ninth, the tenth. Now you are all the way back at the top step. Open your eyes.

It may help to write down the things you discovered during this working in a tarot journal or notebook. You can repeat this whenever the Judgement card comes up in a confusing place in your reading and you need more clarity.

Judgement Clarity Candle Spell

The following candle spell will give you clarity in a situation where you need to find answers and understanding. This candle will operate quickly to help you uncover the truth about a situation, so be prepared for whatever it is you may discover.

Ingredients

1 small tea light candle

Candleholder

1 drop basil oil

1 drop frankincense oil

1 drop neroli oil

Pinch of silver glitter

Directions

Gather all ingredients together on your tarot altar or shrine. If you don't have one, please check out the instructions in chapter 30. Place the tea light in the candleholder. Add the oils. Then sprinkle with glitter. Light the candle. Concentrate on the situations you need clarity about. Take a deep breath. Focus on the light radiating out from the candle and covering you. When the candle is done burning, dispose of the remnants in the trash. Remember to never leave a burning candle unattended. Then pay attention for the next 24 hours; the truth may come to you in a dream or through waking clues that appear throughout your day.

Chapter Twenty-Three
The World

XXI · THE WORLD

THE WORLD.

The World is the final card of the major arcana. The hero has completed their journey. The World card is the fulfillment and acceptance of all we have learned on our tarot journey. There have been ups and downs along the way. Hopefully, there have been some important lessons learned and now the real fun can begin. This is the revelation of everything, everywhere, and all at once. Celebrate this joyous time in every possible way.

The Gustave Doré Tarot card on the previous page used to illustrate this entry shows us a full world of possibility. There are angel-like beings circling around, perhaps moving toward, a singularity of light, the "light at the end of the tunnel." This image reminds us of the beginning of our tarot journey, which we saw in the Fool card. We have reached the end, but in this world, or possibly the next, it is all getting ready to begin again.

Some envision this as the best card in the tarot deck. Rewards, joy, and successes have arrived. Welcome them and rejoice.

Meanings and Correspondences

Popular meanings for the World include balance, success, rewards, attunement, achievement, and joy.

Crystal Correspondences

Black Tourmaline—Black tourmaline is a great choice for clearing and releasing energy after a tarot reading. It is said to purify, protect, and assist with concentration. Black tourmaline can also be used for scrying.

Lapis Lazuli—This highly prized stone is said to boost psychic connection and also protection in all realms physical and spiritual. Lapis is a stone of great power and is known to have been associated with the goddess Isis.

Sapphire—Another name for sapphire is wisdom stone. It is useful with intuition and psychic power.

Smoky Quartz—This cloudy gray type of quartz is great for all types of psychic work. It cleanses, focuses, and centers your energy on the situation at hand. It is also a stone of protection and energy.

Herbal Correspondences

Oak (*Quercus* spp.)

Sandalwood (*Santalum album*)

Other Correspondences

Animal—All animals

Astrological—Earth

Musical Note—A

Magical and Culinary Recipes

Enhancing your readings by making magical concoctions and feasts allows for a greater understanding of what the cards are trying to tell you. All flowers and herbs are said to be connected to this card.

Magical: Wider World Oil

This formula is designed to help you receive the gifts and bounty that are available to you. It will help you know that you are both worthy and deserving.

Ingredients

Glass bottle

½ ounce sweet almond oil

3 drops sandalwood oil

3 drops jasmine oil

3 drops rose oil

3 drops violet oil

3 drops lemon oil

3 drops vanilla oil

Directions

Gather all ingredients together on your tarot altar or shrine. If you don't have one, please check out the instructions in chapter 30. Take the bottle and add the sweet almond oil. Then add the sandalwood, jasmine, rose, violet, and lemon oils and the vanilla extract. Close the bottle. Throw it gently up into the air to bless it and place it in the hands of the invisible forces of the universe. Catch it. Now it is ready to use.

Culinary: Magic Herb Bread

This is a quick recipe that celebrates the bounty of nature. If you are lucky, you can customize this recipe to include the herbs that are readily available in your own garden. Here we use a ready-made, all-purpose baking mix to simplify things; you can purchase this or make your own from a recipe you find on the internet. All flowers and herbs are connected to this card as they are bounty directly from the earth. This recipe uses several herbs, but feel free to add more if you like.

Ingredients

2¼ cups all-purpose baking mix

2 large eggs, beaten

2 tbsp extra virgin olive oil

½ cup sour cream

1 cup buttermilk or sour milk

3 tbsp minced fresh basil

1 tbsp finely snipped fresh rosemary

3 tbsp minced fresh parsley

1 tbsp finely snipped fresh chives

Directions

Preheat the oven to 350 degrees Fahrenheit. In a large bowl, combine the baking mix, eggs, and olive oil. Mix well. Then add the sour cream and buttermilk gradually, stirring well after each addition. Stir in the herbs until they are distributed throughout the mix. Pour the batter into a greased loaf pan and bake for 55–60 minutes or until a skewer inserted into the center comes out clean. Makes 6–8 servings.

Journeying with the World

In many ways, this card means the entire world is at your fingertips. This journey working allows you to walk around and explore the full universe of worldly possibility. For this working, you can use the traditional imagery detailed in the following, or choose a World card from your favorite deck and use that image as your focus. If you choose your own specific deck, you will need to change the following instructions for the unique imagery presented in that card before you. It may be easier to record these words and play them back while you complete the journey work or, alternatively, have someone read it out to you. Once you get familiar with this method, feel free to use it whenever and wherever you like.

Sit down and get comfortable. Close your eyes. Take a deep breath. Exhale. Repeat. When you are completely ready, picture yourself at the top of a staircase. The steps before you are numbered in descending order. You are at the top step; on it is written clearly the number ten. See your feet on this topmost step. Clearly look at the number written there. When you are ready, slowly step down to step number nine. See the number written there. Look carefully at what is in front of you. When you see it clearly, step down to number eight. Continue stepping down through the numbers, down to seven, six, five. See the numbers and your feet going down to step number four, further down to number three, then number two, and then last down to number one. When you get to the bottom of the stairs, you see a large dark blue door. On it is painted a globe. Turn the handle and step into the universe of the World card.

Walk out into this wide World. Where are you? Is it a forest? A city? It will help to answer these questions out loud even if you are alone. Are you by the beach or on a mountaintop? Is it daytime or nighttime? Breathe deeply. The smell is delightful. Does it remind you of anything? Look around. Are there any animals there? What kind? Perhaps you see a lion or a bull. Are there birds in the sky? Maybe you see an eagle or a peacock. Are there flowers there? Do you know what kind they are? You hear music in the distance. You recognize the song. What is it? Look around again. Are there people there? If so, walk toward them. Ask them if they have anything to tell you. Explore as much as you like here. When you have seen and done all that you like, turn and walk back toward the door you entered through. Turn the handle and walk back in over the threshold.

In front of you are the same numbered steps you came down earlier. This time you are going to slowly walk up these stairs. See your feet climbing up the first step to the second one. Then on to the third step, the fourth, going higher and higher up. Up to the fifth step, the sixth, the seventh. Continue on up to the eighth, the ninth, the tenth. Now you are back at the top step. You can now open your eyes.

It may help to write down the things you discovered during this working in a tarot journal or notebook. You can repeat this whenever the World card comes up in an important place in your reading.

Spell for the World

This spell working incorporates elemental ingredients as well as herbs and plants gathered from around your home to manifest some powerful and transformative magic directed wherever you like.

Ingredients

1 tbsp mugwort

1 cup fresh herbs gathered
   from around your home
   or property

1 cup spring water

Cheesecloth

Large glass bowl

1 rainbow 7-day candle in glass

1 small piece amethyst

3 drops myrrh oil

3 drops frankincense oil

3 drops ylang-ylang oil

Directions

Gather all ingredients together on your tarot altar or shrine. If you don't have one, please check out the instructions in chapter 30. Combine the mugwort and fresh herbs from around your home in a saucepan with the spring water. Simmer them over low heat for 15–20 minutes. Remove from the stove. Let the mixture cool and strain it through the cheesecloth into the bowl. Place the candle into the center of the bowl. Make sure it is sitting securely; remove some water if necessary and discard. Next, add the amethyst to the water. Add the oils to the top of the candle. Light the candle. Concentrate your energy on the flame. Focus your thoughts on all the wonderful things that are manifesting in your life. Sit for 30 minutes or more, then extinguish the candle. Remember to never leave a burning candle unattended. Repeat every night until the candle is burned down. When it is finished, dispose of the water out on the earth, and throw the candle glass into your recycling bin. Now the spell is done. Repeat as often as you like.

Chapter Twenty-Four
Wands

ACE OF WANDS

ACE of WANDS.

Wands are traditionally thought of as representing fire, although there are some decks that assign them the element of earth or air. The suit of wands is also called batons, scepters, staves, rods, or clubs. They are symbolic of profound growth and energy. As with all of the minor arcana, the aces up to number ten signify a progression for sublime beginnings to intense endings and everything in between.

If we look at the symbolism in the Rider-Waite-Smith deck, we can see the obvious phallic imagery. This represents passion, fertility in all realms, and exuberance. With all the wands cards, we can see the spark of a new beginning and the seeds of a new endeavor. These are cards not only of sacred fire but also of desire on every level. Wands push through boundaries, burn bridges, and burst forth into new realms.

Early in my tarot career, I taught beginning tarot to a group of delightful sisters ranging from ages nine to thirteen who were being homeschooled. We had some interesting discussions about the cards; what I remember, however, is when we talked about the nature of wands. The sisters were used to their traditional meanings, most likely learned from literature and popular culture. For them, wands were something magical and external, crafted from specially selected wood and adorned with crystals. I think I shook them a bit when I asked, "What if your fingers are magic wands?" There is definitely something to think about here: manifestation, energy, and power are literally right at your fingertips. It is only a question of perspective.

The downside to this fire energy is that it can sometimes feed anger, ego, and impulsive behavior. Fire can rage, and it does not appreciate attempts to contain it.

Fire Witches may feel a particular affinity for these cards. They are at their core cards of swift and appropriate action. Better understanding of them may come with use of candle magic or ritual campfires.

The Numbered Cards

The numbered cards in tarot range from ace to ten. Sometimes they are referred to as pip cards, as they frequently feature minimal illustrations and instead just use symbols to differentiate between the cards. Tarot readers often incorporate numerological meanings to these cards; for example, twos are said to represent balance, which can be applied to each of the suits in a unique way.

Ace of Wands

Aces are the start of creation and therefore the beginning of the suit. The Ace of Wands represents the explosive seed of creation. It can be an idea that paves the way for something truly inspired. If it appears in your reading, it could be a sign of new starts in business or life; possibly, an actual birth is on the way.

Two of Wands

The number two is representative of partnership and balance. Here in the Two of Wands, it is representative of both balance and alliance. The Two of Wands is the first steps toward manifestation and realization of the seeker's personal power.

Three of Wands

This card has to do with plans, study, and work beginning to come to fruition. What was thought of in the ace, and acted upon in the two, is now starting to pay off. This is the beginnings of success and rewards.

Four of Wands

Very often the minor arcana cards numbered four have to do with stability; this card is no different. The Four of Wands is a card of establishing a foundation. The wands here are roots that reach deep into the earth to anchor you for whatever is to come.

Five of Wands

In this card we see confusion, strife, squabbles, and struggles. The stability of the preceding Four of Wands has been turned upside down and sideways. Here everyone has an opinion, and they are hell-bent on forcing it on all around them.

Six of Wands

This is a card of victory and success. The seeker is secure in their position. After much hard work, achievement has been won.

Seven of Wands

Here we see challenges arise from those who may feel envy or jealousy. The seeker is in a good position to defend themselves against these attacks, and they must remember this at all costs. They have both the wisdom and the skill to succeed.

Eight of Wands

This is a card of love and success. It is a satisfactory conclusion to whatever struggles the seeker has been facing. The Eight of Wands can be actual falling in love and the feeling of being swept away by a new lover.

Nine of Wands

Problems and difficulties from the past may be about to return. Be cautious about who you trust. Be patient before taking any serious action.

Ten of Wands

Continue fighting despite whatever challenges arise. Be cautious not to overburden yourself or take on too many projects at once.

The Court Cards

For some readers, understanding the court cards can be one of the most challenging aspects of interpreting the cards. In the book *Holistic Tarot*, Benebell Wen, writes about how these specific cards have a unique voice.[18] I agree with this wholeheartedly. I might even take a step further and say that the court cards have not only a voice but also a song—a song that harmonizes with all the cards that surround it in a reading. When we think about a court in the traditional royal way, it consisted of individuals that surrounded the ruler to give them both support and good counsel. This is how these cards function too; they show you who and what is around you giving you counsel. In many ways the court cards of the tarot are designed to represent specific individuals or situations that may be around the seeker. Because of their correlation with fire, the individuals represented here may have Aries, Leo, or Sagittarius as their Sun sign. Some decks say that physically the wands court cards could represent someone with red or light brown hair and green eyes.

---

18. Benebell Wen, *Holistic Tarot: An Integrative Approach to Using Tarot for Personal Growth* (Berkeley, CA: North Atlantic Books, 2015).

Princess or Page of Wands

This card may represent a fire sign, a child or young person, or someone with red or light-brown hair and green eyes. It can also mean a message from a person like this.

Knight of Wands

This knight may be representative of a teen or young adult. When looking at their astrological profile, they could be a fire sign Sun, meaning an Aries, Leo, or Sagittarius. Some believe knights represents written communication such as contracts or agreements.

Queen of Wands

This card traditionally represents a kind and energetic woman who may be helpful in the situation. It can mean compassion and the drive to succeed despite obstacles. She knows how to triumph by remaining calm and in control.

King of Wands

The King of Wands represents a mature man who is an optimistic leader commanding respect. They have a charm and enthusiasm that can be infectious.

Wands Incense

This incense is designed to be burned on charcoal disks. All charcoal-burned incense can get smoky, so please consider opening doors and windows or even perhaps burning it outside.

Ingredients

1 tbsp marigold	1 tbsp sassafras
1 tbsp ginger	Glass jar
1 tbsp copal	Charcoal disk
1 tbsp carnation	Firesafe bowl or incense burner

Directions

Combine all the botanical ingredients in the glass jar. Shake well to combine. Leave it outside overnight on the evening of the full moon. In the morning, it will be charged and ready to use. Put the charcoal in a firesafe bowl or incense burner, light it, and place a tablespoon of the mix on top to burn.

Fire Crystals for Wands

The tarot suit of wands can light up any situation with its fire. This list of crystals is a good starting point for using crystals to better utilize the messages the wonderful wands are trying to tell you. Individuals who identify as Crystal or Earth Witches may find extra benefits when using crystals in combination with their cards.

Sunstone

This crystal is obviously connected to the fire and the sun. It can bring great luck and encourage optimism in all situations. It is also used to boost self-confidence.

Carnelian

Carnelian is a stone of fire. If you are a Fire Witch, consider using this on your ritual shrine, or use it in a piece of jewelry that you wear for your next fire ritual or when doing readings.

Red Jasper

This fiery-colored jasper can help uncover hidden problems concerning the situations that arise in the tarot reading. Any time you have a wand card that you are confused about, try holding a piece of red jasper and meditating on what you need to know about the situation.

Chapter Twenty-Five
Cups

Cups are believed to represent the element of water and all that comes with it. Also called chalices, in a tarot spread they may symbolize love, emotions, feelings, and abundance. Some Witches view this suit not as cups but cauldrons, holding and cooking up great magic for all the world to utilize.

Sea Witches and other Water Witches may feel drawn to these cards. It may help with gaining a greater understanding of them by making magical baths and floor washes or by spending time near a favorite body of water.

Ritual stylized cups also known as chalices are frequently pictured in this suit. Sometimes it's a Holy Grail holding the power of healing or eternal life. The Santa Muerte Tarot pictured on the previous page shows skulls as cups, a practice that has been in place for thousands of years.

The Numbered Cards

The numbered cups cards start with the ace, full of watery feeling and potential. As the cards progress, the reader can see the full range of emotions play out. Here we find joy, love, happiness, delusion, laziness, and bliss.

Ace of Cups

The Ace of Cups can mean marriage, birth, new relationships, and feelings of love. It is the beginning of water, and the seeker is just starting to "catch feelings" in the situation. Some believe the cup or chalice featured in this card represents the Holy Grail, which some equate with the last cup used by Jesus at the Last Supper, while others associate this with King Arthur and his quest for the cup that could grant both miraculous healing and eternal youth. All of that is referenced here.

Two of Cups

This is a card of deep and abiding love it all its forms. It can mean actual marriage or proposals, or simply friendship, partnership, or strong unions. The Two of Cups can also mean passion or ecstasy. Because this card is numbered two, there is also a nod toward balance or equilibrium between individuals.

Three of Cups

Very often the image shown on this card is of three muses, granting creative inspiration to all who seek it. It is a card of joy, affection, happiness, and celebration with loved ones.

Four of Cups

This is a card of luxury and also of promise. Help is there for the seeker if they are willing to see it. It also cautions against boredom or complacency.

Five of Cups

In the Rider-Waite-Smith deck, this shows a caped individual looking at three spilled cups while two standing cups remain behind them. If we take this image literally, it points to loss, but with some resources still remaining. In a reading this card can mean sadness or grieving and also possibly divorce or inheritance. The loss seen here could be emotional or financial. But possibly, the seeker is ignoring what they still have.

Six of Cups

This is a card of the past, past memories, childhood, or children. It can point to the need for shadow work or re-parenting of one's inner child. I have also seen this come up as a need to take pleasure in simplicity.

Seven of Cups

The Seven of Cups can mean insight, fantasy, debauchery, dreams, and visions. This card points out the difference between positive visualization and living in the realms of fantasy. Interpretation and nuance are key. It is possible that all is not what it seems.

Eight of Cups

This is a card of stillness and possible loss. There is little to no progress happening here. It can be a time of abandoning what is unproductive and moving forward into the unknown for the chance at something better.

Nine of Cups

The Nine of Cups in a reading can mean that your dreams, wishes, and hopes are going to be fulfilled. This is a joyous card full of satisfaction and enjoying great pleasure.

Ten of Cups

This card can mean harmony, stability, happiness, family, emotional content-ment, love, and marriage. Some readers even give this card the meaning of fairy-tale endings.

The Court Cards

In many ways, the court cards of the tarot are designed to represent specific individuals or situations. Because of their correlation with the element of water, the individuals represented here may have Pisces, Cancer, or Scorpio as their Sun sign. Some decks say that the cups court cards could represent some-one with fair hair and blue eyes.

Princess or Page of Cups

This can mean a young person full of gentleness and simplicity. It can also mean news about marriage or birth.

Knight of Cups

This is a card of daydreams and romance and people who love that. There is a tendency toward frivolity and a lack of commitment in exchange for great fun.

Queen of Cups

The queen here is a mature woman who is loving and sensitive. She is nurtur-ing and in tune with her emotions and her psychic ability.

King of Cups

Customarily, this is seen as meaning a man with great kindness who can also get carried away by his emotions. He can be intuitive and passionate, but he may also have a tendency toward manipulation. He can remain calm in even the most tumultuous of circumstances.

Cups Incense

This incense is designed to be burned on charcoal disks. All charcoal-burned incense can get smoky, so please consider opening doors and windows or even perhaps burning it outside.

Ingredients

3 tbsp dried rose petals

1 tbsp dried jasmine flowers

1 tbsp dried orris root

1 tbsp ground seaweed

3 drops ylang-ylang oil

Glass jar

Charcoal disks for burning

Firesafe bowl or incense burner

Directions

Combine all the botanical ingredients in the glass jar. Shake well to combine. Leave the jar outside overnight on the evening of the full moon. In the morning, it will be charged and ready to use. Put the charcoal in a firesafe bowl or incense burner, light it, and place a tablespoon of the mix on top to burn.

Water Crystals for Cups

What is a cup if not a vessel for water? The following crystals are great to use with the suit of cups. Those who relate to Water Witchcraft or Crystal Witchcraft may find using these particularly helpful. It might be beneficial to wear a piece of jewelry containing these stones when you are doing tarot readings for yourself or others.

Turquoise

This powerful blue-green stone is one of protection, success, and luck. It was particularly prized by certain Indigenous North American peoples and used in their jewelry and art.

Lapis Lazuli

This valuable crystal is said to amplify psychic connection and also provide protection in all realms physical and spiritual.

Rose Quartz

This variety of quartz is said to help with love in all its forms. It was used in ancient Persia, in ancient Egypt, and in Asian beauty spells, and you can certainly utilize its great benefits in modern times. This wonderful crystal is prized by many goddesses and is ultimately used as a vehicle for the divine feminine.

Chapter Twenty-Six
Swords

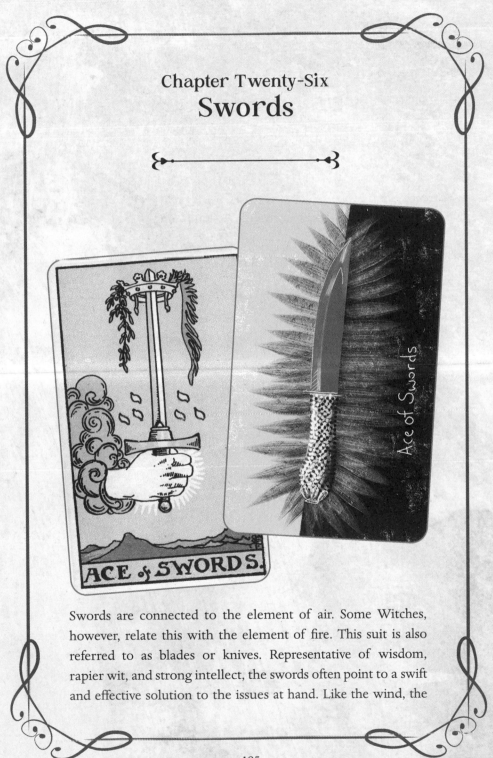

Ace of Swords

Swords are connected to the element of air. Some Witches, however, relate this with the element of fire. This suit is also referred to as blades or knives. Representative of wisdom, rapier wit, and strong intellect, the swords often point to a swift and effective solution to the issues at hand. Like the wind, the air energy found here can be unpredictable and unreliable. In its negative manifestations, it can be anxiety ridden and argumentative.

Air Witches can gain particular insight from these cards. Magical incense and sacred songs or chants may aid in processing the lessons found in these cards. The image pictured on the previous page is from the Orisha Tarot and shows a knife on a green and black background with some leafy imagery.

The Numbered Cards

Swords are both weapons and tools. The minor arcana swords cards show both the knowledge and the change that this suit can bring.

Ace of Swords

In the Rider-Waite-Smith deck, this card shows a hand reaching through the clouds and holding out a sword. It represents the birth of air, the start of logic, reason, knowledge, and intellect. In a reading this can mean a breakthrough or necessary communication is on the way. Alternatively, it can also signify that justice and fairness will prevail. The unnecessary situations are in the past, and new directions are available finally.

Two of Swords

This card represents a time for balance, meditation, and careful thought.

Three of Swords

The Three of Swords can mean pain or heartache. It is almost as if the hurt is coming from every direction. The Rider-Waite-Smith deck features a heart in the center of the card being stabbed by three different swords. Often when this appears in a client's spread, there is an extra person in their situation causing sorrow or difficulty.

Four of Swords

In this card, rest, seclusion, and meditation are the watchwords. The seeker needs to take time to remove themselves from difficult situations to discover themselves and what is actually happening around them.

Five of Swords

One of the most challenging cards in the deck, the Five of Swords indicates disagreements and conflict. Issues of oppression and inequality have come to the fore, and someone in the fight may have an unfair advantage.

Six of Swords

This is a card of transition through difficulty. Wisdom and intelligence must be applied to the matter at hand, as well as an awareness that changes are ahead.

Seven of Swords

In the Rider-Waite-Smith deck, this card shows an individual fleeing from an encampment carrying five swords, while two remain behind. If we interpret this quite literally, it can mean that deception and dishonesty are at hand. Look to the individual motives and the actions that follow in the situation if this comes up in a reading. Arrogance and trust issues can also be a motivator here.

Eight of Swords

In the Rider-Waite-Smith deck, we see this card as a figure blindfolded and bound, surrounded by eight swords. This is a challenging card. The seeker cannot see clearly or take any action at this time. Do your best not to initiate any changes or even hope progress can be made at this time. There are lots of obstacles and much interference on this path.

Nine of Swords

This card represents sorrow, loss, and grieving. It can mean nightmares and cruelty being experienced at this time. These unfortunate circumstances can be self-inflicted or brought about by others. The seeker should attempt to focus on the next best tasks at hand and look for possible solutions.

Ten of Swords

Undoubtedly, this is one of the most challenging cards in the deck. Like it or not, there are struggles and difficulty ahead. Pain and even possible betrayal may have led the seeker to this point.

The Court Cards

The court cards of the tarot can be viewed as representing specific individuals or situations. Because of their correlation with the element of air, the individuals represented here may have Aquarius, Gemini, or Libra as their Sun sign. Some decks say that the swords court cards could represent someone with light brown hair and eyes.

Princess or Page of Swords

This can represent an individual who is rooted in truth and justice. There is also, however, a tendency toward impulsivity and vengeful thinking that must be examined.

Knight of Swords

The Knight of Swords favors skill and bravery. Take notice of tendencies toward impatience and carelessness. Fixation on there being only one right solution should be avoided.

Queen of Swords

This queen knows sorrow but also the knowledge and wisdom that comes from having survived difficulties. When this shows up in a reading, it very often points to the power of the intellect and knowing how to tackle problems with a rational mind and logical solutions.

King of Swords

Here we have an individual with power who sits in judgment. This could be an actual judge or lawyer; or an author, teacher, preacher, or politician; or another prominent individual. This is a time of reckoning.

Swords Incense

This incense is designed to be burned on charcoal disks. All charcoal-burned incense can get smoky, so please consider opening doors and windows or even perhaps burning it outside.

Ingredients

3 tbsp frankincense tears	1 tbsp dried marjoram
3 tbsp myrrh tears	6 drops lavender oil
3 tbsp powdered white sandalwood	Glass jar
1 tbsp benzoin	Charcoal disks for burning
	Firesafe bowl or incense burner

Directions

Combine all the botanical ingredients in the glass jar. Shake well to combine. Leave outside overnight on the evening of the full moon. In the morning, it will be charged and ready to use. Put the charcoal in a firesafe bowl or incense burner, light it, and place a tablespoon of the mix on top to burn.

Air Crystals for Swords

Strong and wise, the suit of swords is very often associated with the element of air. Any or all of the following crystals can be helpful with the tarot suit of swords. Individuals who identify as Crystal or Earth Witches may find extra benefits when using crystals in combination with their cards. It might be helpful to wear a piece of jewelry containing these stones when you are doing tarot readings for yourself or others.

Staurolite

This mineral is colored reddish black, and it develops into the shape of a cross. Alternatively, it is called faery cross. Staurolite helps narrow the gaps between the spiritual and physical planes. It can be used to take the airy energy of swords and bring it down to a concrete and manageable space.

Howlite

This interesting crystal is said to help one gain access to spiritual realms. Howlite grants knowledge and sharp insight into problems. It is especially useful for all types of divination as well as journey working.

Labradorite

This iridescent stone shines in a way others don't, and it is one of my favorites. Its brilliant beauty is like no other. Use it to assist with spiritual awareness and knowledge about the suit of swords.

Chapter Twenty-Seven
Coins

Ace of Pentacles

ACE of PENTACLES.

This suit is connected to the element of earth. It is also named pentacles, disks, stones, or stars. Coins are known to represent matters of money, stability, and the home. There is a tangible aspect to all things coins, as they relate to things that you can actually see and touch.

The Numbered Cards

The suit of coins shows the numbered cards exploring the connections between finances, home, stability, security, career, planning, and success. When these cards appear in your reading, pay careful attention to what you are growing and nurturing and where your roots are planted.

Ace of Coins

The Ace of Coins is the manifestation of earth. In a reading, it may mean the first steps toward stability. The seeker may be becoming financially stable by getting a new job or getting approved for a mortgage. This is a card of both earthy creation and opportunity. The image featured on the left on page 201 from Tarot of the Vampires, while nontraditional, does show an opportunity of sorts, a hand coming from a grave—an opportunity at new life.

Two of Coins

Like all the twos in the minor arcana, this card is about balance. The balance here usually has to do with earthly matters like home and finances. Does the seeker have an issue where they are trying to juggle too many things at once? Is there a fear that it may all come crashing down?

Three of Coins

In some interpretations, this is a card of learning or apprenticeship. Many traditional decks show someone working hard to learn a craft. In modern times apprenticeships are not as popular as they once were—everyone wants to run before they can walk. This card, however, shows us the value of learning from others, as someday we may be the master.

Four of Coins

As we saw in the cards numbered four in the other suits, this card is about stability and holding on to what you have gathered, learned, or created. Because the Rider-Waite-Smith deck depicts the figure in this card holding on to coins, some have given this the meaning of hoarding wealth or miserliness.

Five of Coins

This is very often a card of hardship, struggle, and adversity. It can quite literally mean homelessness or displacement, or simply that the seeker cannot find their spiritual or emotional home at this time.

Six of Coins

The Six of Coins is a card of both giving and receiving. It speaks to generosity, charity, and success.

Seven of Coins

This can be a card of success and getting ready to reap the benefits of hard work. The situation is yet undetermined, and failure can also be an option. With this card, it is very important to look to the surrounding cards to find exactly how the situation will play out. In some decks, this card shows an individual looking at their garden. As all good gardeners know, success depends on a variety of factors sometimes beyond your control.

Eight of Coins

Eight of Coins is a card of wisdom but also cautiousness and careful planning. It is also a card connected to the seeker's work and employment. Patience and discipline are needed to ensure success at this time.

Nine of Coins

This card can mean money, happiness, and financial security. The Nine of Coins cautions against greed or gluttony. Now is a time of harvest and productivity.

Ten of Coins

This card can mean both legacy and the culmination of success. In the Rider-Waite-Smith deck, there are dogs pictured in this card, representative of both faithfulness and loyalty.

The Court Cards

The court cards of the tarot can be seen as representing specific individuals or situations. Because of their correlation with the element of earth, the individuals represented here may have Capricorn, Taurus, or Virgo as their Sun sign.

Some decks say that the coins court cards could represent someone with dark hair and eyes.

Princess or Page of Coins

The page or princess very often represents a young or youthful person. In this instance, it is a young person with great drive and ability to succeed. It can also mean that there will be messages concerning money or finance coming your way.

Knight of Coins

This card can represent an actual person with the qualities of maturity and stability or just the need for the qualities themselves in your life. It can also mean issues of money and responsibility and the need for both.

Queen of Coins

This card usually represents a mature woman who takes pleasure in the simple things in life, like home and family. She may be fond of gardening and nature. Her Sun sign may be Virgo, Taurus, or Capricorn.

King of Coins

This card most often represents a mature man who is successful in business. He may be an earth Sun sign—Virgo, Taurus, or Capricorn. He is a hard worker, and home and family life are very important to him. He can be both kind and generous to others.

Coins Incense

Use this incense for all things relating to the suit of coins: earth magic, home and garden spells, and so on.

Ingredients

1 tbsp dried patchouli leaf

1 tbsp powdered myrrh

1 tbsp dried five-finger grass

1 tbsp dried marjoram

Pieces of a paper bill ($1, €5, or whatever you have)

Glass jar

Charcoal disks

Firesafe bowl or incense burner

Directions

Combine the patchouli, myrrh, five-finger grass, marjoram, and money in the glass jar. Shake well to combine. Leave outside overnight on the evening of the full moon. In the morning, it will be charged and ready to use. Put the charcoal in a firesafe bowl or incense burner, light it, and place a tablespoon of the mix on top to burn.

Earth Crystals for Coins

The suit of coins or pentacles becomes associated with earth probably because it is representative of the material world. Crystals themselves are of the earth, so this is a lovely way to connect with the suit of coins. Earth Witches may feel particularly drawn to these stones and may wish to use them on their tarot altar or in their tarot bag.

Malachite

This green stone is connected to the earth and financial success. Malachite is wonderful for removing negativity from past trauma and for healing on every level. When used with your cards, particularly the suit of coins, it can bring both confidence and accuracy to the table.

Tiger's Eye

Tiger's eye is said to enhance psychic awareness and ability. In conjunction with your tarot readings, it can assist in bringing clarity and differentiating between wishes and reality. It has a grounding influence that is especially well matched with the suit of coins.

Pyrite

Pyrite is a stone of both protection and power. Witches of all types can use this to shield and also give themselves a boost of confidence and faith. Because it is also called fool's gold, people use this for workings concerning money and success.

Chapter Twenty-Eight
Choosing a Deck

There are lots of factors that go into choosing a deck. You could choose one that you like or one that has been recommended by a friend. Some Witches believe they have to find a deck or have it gifted to them. Whatever deck you pick, be sure to realize that there are practical concerns, like how it fits in your hands and if it is aesthetically pleasing to you.

Fortunately, there are several different decks included as illustrations in this book. There are modern ones, like Starman Tarot, TV Series Tarot, and Millennium Thoth Tarot. Alternatively, there are ones that are classically inspired, like Tarot of Tales and Legends, Gustave Doré Tarot, and Mermaid Tarot. There are even a few that incorporate images from Black, Latinx, and Indigenous traditions, such as the Orisha Tarot and Santa Muerte Tarot. Hopefully, these will inspire you to explore the wide range of possibilities that are present when choosing a deck.

Things to consider when choosing a deck:

- What type of deck do you want? Do you want one with traditional images like the Rider-Waite-Smith? Or one like the Thoth? Maybe you want one with nontraditional imagery, or even plants, animals, TV characters, rockstars, etc. The possibilities are vast.
- How are you going to use this deck? Some Witches like to use different decks for different readings, such as readings done for the self or those done for the public.

- Trust your intuition. Is there a deck that you feel speaks to you? This could be a love you have for the images or just the way it feels when you hold it in your hand.
- What size and shape do you want? The average size tarot deck is rectangular, measuring 2.75 inches by 4.75 inches. There are, however, mini decks, oversize decks, and even round decks.
- If you can, preview your potential deck online or in person to see if it's really for you before you make a purchase.

Recommended Tarot Decks

I have read with a lot of different decks over the years. Actually, there are so many decks in existence these days, you could probably read with a different one every day for a year and never use the same deck twice. In fact, such a multitude of decks exists that it could be overwhelming. The following deck choices are a good place to start if you are thinking about getting a new set of tarot cards or just replacing an old one. Remember to try out lots of different decks in a variety of situations until you find out what works exactly best for you.

New Orleans Voodoo Tarot by Sallie Ann Glassman and Louis Martinié. This is one of my favorite decks in existence. I use it every day. It features New Orleans icons like Marie Laveau and the original Dr. John, as well as a variety of both Loa and Orisha.

Dust II Onyx by Courtney Alexander. This is a beautiful and powerful deck created by the amazing Courtney Alexander. It features seventy-eight mixed-media collage paintings that feature Black symbolism, cultural myths, and history.

Dalí Tarot by Salvador Dalí. Most people reading this are probably unaware that one of the most famous artists of our time, Salvador Dalí, created his own tarot deck. It was published with a limited run in 1984 and quickly went out of print. Luckily, it is available again. It may be of particular interest to Art Witches out there to see this deck created by one of the great masters.

The True Heart Intuitive Tarot by Rachel True and Stephanie Singleton. This deck is inclusive and representational on every level. The beautifully illustrated deck is wonderfully complemented by the highly informative book. This deck allows you to expand your own thoughts on the tarot and make meaning highlighted by your own insight.

The Hoodoo Tarot by Tayannah Lee McQuillar. McQuillar created the deck in 2020, and it was a welcome addition to the list of tarot choices available. For so long, decks representing Black people and also created by Black people were nonexistent, so it made me delightfully happy to see this.

Miss Cleo's Tarot Power Deck by Miss Cleo. Many of us grew up with Miss Cleo as the face of TV psychics everywhere. Her story was a difficult one and something not many people know. In many ways she was viewed by the general public as a caricature of what a psychic person is. The reality of the situation could not have been further from the truth. Because Miss Cleo was an accomplished psychic and initiated priestess, I was proud to get to interview her shortly before her death and even more proud to call her a friend. These cards are a variation on the Rider-Waite-Smith deck.

The Way Jodorowsky Explained Tarot to His Cat by Alejandro Jodorowsky and Kazan. This is probably the only deck cowritten by a cat. Even though I have my trusty Boston terrier Queenie by my side trying so hard to help as I write this book, I appreciate the feline nature of this deck. The best thing I can tell you about this deck is that there is a reason people call Jodorowsky the master. His epic tarot film *Holy Mountain* premiered in 1973, probably before many of those reading this were even born. His understanding of tarot, based on decades of experience, resonates almost on a visceral level. It is so sublime even a cat can understand it.

TV Series Tarot by Davide Corsi and Gero Giglio. This deck incorporates pop culture into the world of tarot. It uses the medium of television to help illustrate the sacred journeys we all find ourselves on during this thing called life. With references to everything from *Twin Peaks* to *Little House on the Prairie*, this deck gives us meaning in a modern context.

Thoth Tarot Deck by Aleister Crowley and Lady Frieda Harris. One of the most popular decks out there, these tarot images are sublime and beautiful. Many choose to use this deck as a beginner one, especially as an alternative to the Rider-Waite-Smith deck. It gives a more esoteric interpretation than the other decks on the market, but many find it invaluable.

Millennium Thoth Tarot by Renata Lechner. This is a more modern take on the Thoth Tarot. It features vibrant colors and compelling characters. It may be a good alternative for Traditional Witches who prefer some of the classical imagery.

Starman Tarot by Davide De Angelis. This deck was born out of an artistic collaboration between the artist and David Bowie. It features the fantastic in this realm and the next. Incorporating phenomenal art and eloquent design, it helps push the boundaries of what is traditionally featured in most tarot decks.

Rider-Waite-Smith Tarot by Pamela Colman Smith and Arthur Waite. For many years, this was the most widely used deck in print. I'm not sure if that is because of availability or success rate, but this is certainly one that almost everyone is familiar with. It's recently become part of the public domain, so anyone can enjoy these images and build upon them in new and exciting ways. I think for a lot of readers, these are some of the most basic images that almost anyone can relate to in the context of a reading.

The Wild Unknown Tarot by Kim Krans. This beautiful deck very quickly became a bestseller, and it is well on its way to being a classic. The colors and the images are like no other, and I definitely suggest checking it out.

Birthing Your Tarot Cards into Existence

You could be a veteran tarot reader or one who just got their deck yesterday; in either case, from time to time you may wish to go through the process of birthing a new tarot deck. Most readers that I know have more than one deck, and some even have a collection numbering in the hundreds. Birthing a new deck is only the first step in a long life of caring for and feeding your cards, as I like to call it. The process can be as complex or as simple as you would like to make it. You can use any or all of the following methods as you birth your tarot deck into the world.

Candle Blessing Spell

This method uses a candle to help awaken your cards. The candle is charged with oils and herbs, and also your own personal energy. The following is a suggested method for doing this. If you would rather purchase a prepared candle for tarot or psychic knowledge, by all means, you can do that.

Ingredients

Large white cloth made of natural fiber (cotton, etc.)

1 small candleholder

1 small purple tea light candle

3 drops lavender oil

Small pinch of sandalwood   Your tarot cards
    powder

Directions

Gather all ingredients together on your table in a place where it and you will not be disturbed for the duration of the working. Spread the cloth on the table and place the candleholder in the center. Take the tea light and add the lavender oil and the pinch of sandalwood powder. Place it in the holder and light it. Place the cards on the table across from you, so that the candle sits between you and the cards. As the candle burns, tell it and the cards the names of your ancestors, tell them where you were born, tell them where you live now. Tell them whatever you think the cards need to know to understand who you are and why you need them to take this psychic journey with you. Speak them into existence. When you are done, sit there in silence until the candle has burned out. Dispose of the tea light remains in the trash. Pick up the cards, as they are now ready for use. Repeat this candle burning exercise as often as you need to help with reinforcing your bond with the cards.

First Food Blessing Spell

This blessing will most likely appeal to Kitchen Witches who love cooking up their magic. It is best done with your morning breakfast or brunch meal. It is best to do it the morning after you receive your new deck of tarot cards, but you can also complete it later on if necessary. For this ritual, you will be preparing food and drink for you and your deck. You will share this meal together, which will help familiarize you with the deck and vice versa.

Ingredients

2 cups   Breakfast of choice (toast, eggs, etc.)

2 plates   Your tarot deck

Beverage of choice (coffee, tea, etc.)

Directions

Gather all ingredients on your table. Lay the table with two cups and two plates. You will need to make your favorite morning beverage, such as coffee, tea, matcha, or whatever you prefer. Pour some in both cups. Then you will need to make your usual breakfast. If you have cereal or toast, make that. If you have eggs and bacon, make that. Place some of the food on each plate. Sit behind one plate and place the cards on the table behind the other plate. As you eat the food, think about the cards as another sentient being that is sharing this day and will share all the days to come with you. The first time I did this working, it helped to think of the cards as a new friend whom I was excited to get to know. When you are done, you may wish to save a small amount of the food for the Tarot Blessing Jar Spell outlined below.

Tarot Blessing Jar Spell

Connecting with your new cards is one of the most valuable steps you can take in the journey to understanding and insight. This spell working helps bond you to your new deck and any decks you might acquire from this point forward.

Ingredients

Small portion of food (see First Food Blessing Spell on page 211)

Small clipping of your hair

Small clippings from your fingernails

Small piece of fabric cut from an old garment

1 tsp dirt from outside your home

1 newly minted coin (try to find one with the current year's date)

Small glass jar

Your tarot deck

Directions

You will need to do the First Food Blessing Spell and save a small spoonful of the meal you shared and prepared. Place the food, hair, fingernail clippings, fabric, dirt, and coin and in a small glass jar. Close the jar and shake well. Place your cards under the jar and leave them overnight on the night of the full moon. In the morning, the cards will be activated and ready to use. Save the jar and place it on your tarot altar or shrine. Whenever you get a new deck, you can use this jar to awaken that deck too. Just place the new cards under the jar and leave them on the windowsill again overnight during the new moon.

Tarot Bag Working

Another great idea for containing your cards is a tarot bag. I used to make my own. You can make one too. This could be in your favorite color or fabric and can be decorated with beads, charms, or whatever you like. I have had ones made in purple velvet, black astrology fabric, and even skull fabric to honor my ancestors. Some people recommend using a natural fabric, and I think this is wise, as synthetics tend to carry a fake and manufactured energy. The only limits are your own imagination and creativity. Even if you're not a Stitch Witch and sewing isn't your thing, you can buy a premade bag and add your own patches or beads or even paint it with fabric paint. Making a bag like this is a great way to connect with the energy of this particular deck of cards. You can keep things inside the bag too; this will help your cards gain power and connect with your energy.

Ingredients

Ready-made bag large enough to fit your tarot deck

Fabric paint, beads, or ribbons for decoration

Herbs and crystals to place inside the bag

Your tarot deck

Directions

This working is guided by your own creativity and imagination. You can choose a bag in a neutral color and paint it with your favorite power symbols from astrology or your own witchy practice. Alternatively, you can buy a bag in a color that appeals to you personally and magically. You will need to choose which crystals and herbs you are going to place into the bag. Right now, I have crystals, stones from sacred places I have traveled, herbs, and even my pendulum inside my tarot bag. When I journey to events or even go on vacation, this bag comes with me, and it serves as my tarot travel kit for whatever I may encounter along the way. There are a few crystals and botanicals that I recommend adding to your bag, such as myrrh and amethyst, but really the items you put in here are designed to reflect you. Consider including your favorites, maybe your birthstone or a treasured stone given to you by a friend. Another idea, if you can find them, is to add crystal chips or dust to your bag. These smaller pieces of stone are a lot lighter, yet they still carry the same energy of their larger counterparts.

Chapter Twenty-Nine
Your Cards and You

—•—

If you are just getting started learning to read cards, you should begin your practice with the major arcana. Here you will find concepts and imagery you are most likely familiar with from other parts of your life. It may help to spread them out on a table in front of you. Look at the images, see which ones you are drawn to, and see which ones look ominous or confusing.

Another good idea is to lay the major arcana out in two rows in front of you in numeric order. Notice how the cards in the beginning of the deck feature individuals, which gradually shift to concepts as you go through the deck. Many people see the cards as an allegory for the journey we all take through life. What stories do you see unfolding here?

As you get more comfortable with tarot reading, see how these stories apply to the readings you pull for yourself and others. There are connections here: connections between you and the cards and connections between the cards themselves. With the help of seasoned practitioners, I offer some tips on getting started in your tarot practice.

Reversals

Often new readers try to simplify the reading process by reducing the meanings down to a single word. Over time, however, the process of reading tarot reveals itself to include that word and so much more. This brings me to the subject of reversals. These are different meanings that come into play when the cards show up upside down in your spread. The logic behind this system is that when cards are reversed, they carry a lesser or reversed meaning. Like everything concerning the tarot, the meaning as it presents itself during a reading is up to you. I personally don't read reversals, but I know several readers who do.

A system that I do adhere to, however, is the concept of ill-dignified cards. This, explained as simply as possible, means that even good cards can be lessened, diminished, or soured by the cards that surround them in your reading. Certain cards carry a difficult or challenging message; in general, these cards include but are not limited to the Tower, the Devil, Death, and the Three, Five, Seven, Eight, Nine, and Ten of Swords. If these cards present themselves in your reading, even if wonderful cards are present, the road to success will be more challenging. If you choose to read reversals, there's a good chance those meanings will be specific to the deck you are using. Please refer to any accompanying materials from that deck to learn more.

Shuffling

It may be helpful to explore different shuffling and cutting methods. Each tarot reader needs to uncover which shuffling and cutting methods work best for them. When I read for others, I usually ask them to shuffle and cut the deck whichever way they prefer. I used to be much more regimented about it, but then I had a few clients who accused me of arranging the cards into a special order before their reading, as if I had the time or would even know what to choose. I seriously wonder about people sometimes. Allowing people to shuffle in their own way both gives them a personal connection and control over their reading and also allows for those who may have limited mobility or dexterity challenges. Some may like to shuffle three times and cut three times to the left with their left hand. This is a traditional way to prepare the cards before each reading.

Daily Draw

Both new readers and veteran ones sometimes like to supplement their tarot practice by doing a daily draw. This simply involves pulling a card each day. Awo Robert Ogbe Di explains, "Daily readings for yourself will teach you what the indications mean (cards, astrological configurations, etc.) much more than sitting down once a month. Make the divination system a part of your life; identify life events and things you see in daily life as representations of the energies of the cards, stars, runes, whatever you use. For example, if you see an older woman looking sour and pensive, think *Ah, Queen of Swords*; if a friend describes a love triangle, try to imagine how that situation would be described by the cards in a reading. This type of engagement with the images and symbols will dramatically speed up your learning process and encourage your intuition to chime in more quickly and reliably."[19]

Tarot Journals

It doesn't matter if you are a tarot beginner or veteran, having a log of your readings in a journal or elsewhere should be a serious consideration. Creating a tarot journal is a great way to help chronicle all that you have learned about the tarot. If you are a Creative Witch, you may wish to use this space to keep your drawings or poems about tarot. If you are doing dreamwork with the cards, it is a great place to record those dreams. Even if the meanings of them aren't immediately clear, you will most certainly gain more insight into them over time. Tarot reader and priestess Bernadette Montana advises, "Keeping a journal is another great and helpful way to keep track of your experiences with the tarot and, of course, the readings that you have completed."[20] You can use a regular notebook, but there are several ready-made tarot journals you can use too.

One of my favorites is *Ancestral Illumination: A Guided Journal for Black Tarot* by Nyasha Williams. It includes places to record every reading, including date, moon phase, deck used, and, most importantly, moments of gratitude for the ancestors who helped guide you to the solutions in your reading. Author and tarot reader Andrieh Vitimus noted, "If you would like to grok your deck, really sit with each. Skim the book first, but only spend a little time on that. Clear your head, sit with the card, and write down your body sensations and the sensory qualities of your thoughts in a journal. Take a break and do a different card. Eventually, return to your notes and repeat the game with your card and add more to your journal. After you do that a couple of times with a card, go through your experiences and see if the experience has the vibe of the card. Add the experience in another section for your card to your journal. Ultimately, you'll have a great framework that links your experiences with the

---

19.   Awo Robert Ogbe Di, interview conducted by Lilith Dorsey, April 30, 2023.

20.   Bernadette Montana, interview conducted by Lilith Dorsey, March 26, 2014.

card. You could use that grimoire-like information for evocation, divination, and invocation."[21]

Practice

The next tip is simple and reminds me of that old joke "How do you get to Carnegie Hall?" The answer is "practice." In order to get to be a better tarot reader, the best thing you can do is practice. You know the adage: practice makes perfect. Practice with yourself. Practice with your friends and family. It may help to even do a daily card pull for a while using the instructions starting on page 216 so you can home in on what each specific card means for you.

I often do a daily card pull, and one of the funniest things happened to me when I did one during my early days as a reader. For most of my life, I lived in New York City, and like most New Yorkers, I rode the subway. That morning I had drawn the Two of Cups. Now for me, when this appears in a spread, it almost always means marriage and proposals. When I pulled the card, however, I was quite puzzled. I wasn't in a romantic relationship at the time, and a marriage proposal was the furthest thing from my mind. Who knew how it would play out? When I stepped onto the subway that day and found a seat—another New York miracle—a group of street performers got on the train. In the middle of their busking and singing, the lead singer got down on his knee, took my hand, and proposed. This was an obvious plea for donations, but I will never forget it. The Two of Cups might not always make you laugh, but it does not disappoint.

Practicing will help you to understand all the different ways these energies manifest in a reading by or for you. Awo Robert Ogbe Di, Ifa priest and psychic reader, adds, "The main advice is practice. Do it over and over until you are completely familiar with the process; it is almost impossible for the intuition to provide any insight when you are still completely focused on trying to remember what step or steps need to be done next. Once you have the process down, then you will start noticing that stray intuitions start popping in."[22] This fantastic advice is also vital for author and psychic Mat Auryn, who said, "Like any skill, divination requires practice and dedication to develop. By strengthening your psychic muscles through regular practice, you can gain more con-

---

21.   Andrieh Vitimus, interview conducted by Lilith Dorsey, April 28, 2023.

22.   Awo Robert Ogbe Di, interview conducted by Lilith Dorsey, April 30, 2023.

fidence in your abilities and develop a deeper understanding of the tools and techniques you are using."[23] Your tarot talent is a muscle too, and it needs to be flexed in order to grow strong.

To help your practice, you may want to find a tarot buddy. This is a friend who is also learning cards and with whom you will be able to exchange readings and share all the new knowledge you are learning. If you are unable to find someone to meet with face-to-face, consider going online and checking out some of the social media groups and hashtags for tarot and divination. Deborah Lipp, author and tarot scholar, said, "Learn your system, whatever it is, thoroughly. Memorize card meanings or rune meanings or what have you. This is like a music teacher telling you to practice your scales. There's simply no substitute."[24]

Tarot Vision Boards and Coloring Books

Consider making a tarot vision board. This tip may have extra appeal for the Creative Witches out there. It allows you to create a tarot collage that will inspire you. Place it somewhere you will be able to see it daily. Here you will include all the images relating to tarot that have special meaning to you. It can be actual cards or their representations, but feel free to think outside the box. Include images that feel like the card to you. Include images of animals or plants that have a connection to tarot. Consider even including words that will help expand your thinking around divination in general. I have one friend who included a picture of a beautiful person dancing around a fire. This was the vibe that they wanted to bring to their spiritual life. It turns out they ended up marrying that person a few years later. I'm not sure all vision boards can manage to manifest like this, but it is always important to keep your eyes on the prize.

Another creative idea is to consider getting a tarot coloring book. Artistic Witches and even nonartistic Witches will appreciate the joy of coloring in different cards. It is amazing how the character and feel of the cards can be changed drastically by using different colors and textures to complete them. Experiment and let your talent and intuition flow. One of my favorites is the *World Spirit Tarot Adult Coloring Book* by Lauren "Madame Onça" O'Leary. The

23. Mat Auryn, interview conducted by Lilith Dorsey, April 25, 2023.

24. Deborah Lipp, interview conducted by Lilith Dorsey, August 1, 2015.

images are delightful and will help anyone spark their imagination and creatively open the way to better understanding of the cards.

Readings for Self and Others

Most readers, professional or not, find it easier to read for others than to read for themselves. Diviner and Ifa priest Awo Robert Ogbe Di commented, "It is usual that your readings for other people will be more accurate sooner than the readings for yourself, so if you find that your readings for others are spot on but your readings for yourself aren't quite there yet, don't give up! Keep at it, and slowly you will come to realize that your readings are becoming startlingly accurate."[25]

A Word about Ethics

My soul wishes I didn't have to include a bit about ethics, but people are people so here we are. In some locations it is prohibited by law to give someone a reading that gives some awful prediction like death or disaster. Now, personally, I have never foretold that in a reading for anyone, not because I didn't see rough times ahead for any of them, but because my readings always focus on solutions and preparing for challenges ahead. Some readers I have spoken to refuse to predict pregnancies, understandably, as that can be complicated news to break to someone. Always evaluate what you think is ethical and best on a case-by-case basis.

Sometimes if you are reading for others, you may find that some clients are terrified of what the cards may hold. Because of this, I always recommend doing a special blessing for your cards when you first get them. Try something simple like lighting a small white candle and asking them not to reveal anything that you or your clients can't handle at this time. Share with your clients that they won't receive any information that is too much for them. This way you can get the most productive reading for all the people involved. As you navigate the beautiful world of tarot, you will be faced with challenges, but remember you will be faced with many blessings too if you can see them.

---

25.   Awo Robert Ogbe Di, interview conducted by Lilith Dorsey, April 30, 2023.

Bless the Cards Again

Another suggestion I have is to bless your cards often. Cleansing and blessing the cards is necessary between readings, especially if you are dealing with lots of different questions or clients. You can do this with your own special incense blend, by lighting a candle, by spraying magical water around the space, or with many of the other ways to bless that are talked about in this book. The simplest way, however, is to hold them in both hands and gently toss them into the air without this turning into a game of seventy-eight card pickup. When you toss them into the air like this and then catch them, it allows the cards to journey into the world of the invisible, if only for a second. It adds an extra blessing from the Divine, and I do it as part of every reading. Experiment with various kinds of blessing and cleansing methods to use both before and after a reading. Ultimately, you will need to discover whatever works best for you. Water Witches may prefer a water blessing, while Fire Witches may want to craft a candle to use while they are reading. Word Witches might like to craft a special chant or thank-you to their patron goddesses or gods. The possibilities are numerous. Also, be sure to remember that you can use as many blessing methods as you like.

Additional Tips and Tricks

Studying tarot is a lifelong process. It involves diligent learning and implementing that knowledge in a variety of circumstances. There are, however, some suggestions that may help to improve the process. The following tips and techniques come from me as well as some of the leading experts in the field. These individuals have the insight about tarot that only comes with time.

Sleep with the Cards

One unusual tip I often have for tarot readers who are just beginning is to sleep with the cards under your pillow for a night. It doesn't have to be an elaborate dreamworking, but it can be if you desire. The only sure thing I recommend is getting a bag or cloth to wrap them up in so you don't end up with cards all over the place. This is another useful tactic for helping you connect with the cards and vice versa. This technique works best when sleeping alone.

Character Interaction

Never forget the relationship between the individual cards is important. Author and tarot expert Dorothy Morrison says, "If you're using tarot cards, get rid of the accompanying book immediately! Instead, actually look at the characters in the cards you've laid out and pay attention to what they're doing. How are they interacting with the characters in the other cards on the table? Are they looking at each other? Are they turned away? Are they facing forward as if they're completely indifferent to the others? Just try reading them as if you're looking at a comic strip storyboard without the benefit of words—you'll be amazed at how easily the reading will flow."[26]

Too Many Readings?

There is such a thing as too many readings. Asking the same question over and over again will not grant you different results. Some readers even have cards that they believe mean "stop asking." This could be the Four of Swords saying "take a rest" or the Hermit telling you to spend some quiet, meditative time alone. I've heard it said that the High Priestess card or the Hierophant means the answer is in the realm of the Divine and cannot be known at this time. It is an easy trap to get stuck in, especially if you are reading for yourself and it is extra hard to be objective. Trust the process and remember even if the reading isn't what you want at this time, it may be exactly what you need.

Musical Inspirations

Think about what music, if any, helps you with your tarot readings. There are several tarot-themed songs online. Try them out. Musical Witches may even wish to compose something of their own. Personally, I like to listen to *The Holy Mountain* soundtrack, which reminds me of Jodorowsky and the most amazing tarot film ever. Even thinking about a reading as a piece of music may be helpful. Mat Auryn, occult author and tarot reader, explains that tarot "provides a structured approach to interpreting the information. It's like having a road map or a set of instructions that can help me to navigate through the information and gain a deeper understanding of it. If I were to compare psychic information to music, tarot would be like having the sheet music, providing a clear

---

26.   Dorothy Morrison, interview conducted by Lilith Dorsey, September 17, 2013.

timeline and organization to the information. The images and symbols on the cards help me make connections and associations that may not be immediately obvious."[27] Creative Witches may find that music helps with their readings on many different levels.

Tarot Walk

Consider going on a tarot walk. It's a magical journey in the real world. This can be done in an urban or rural setting. You can do it close to or far from home. Begin by choosing a major arcana card. You can pick it by doing a blind draw or by choosing a specific card you wish to consciously focus on. You are now going to go for a walk with this card both literally and figuratively. Place the card in your pocket or a bag that you will bring with you. Now begin your walk. Pay attention to anything that seems to stand out. Maybe you hear a bird singing. If so, try and find out what kind of bird (there are many apps to help with bird identification). Maybe you see a coin buried in the dirt. What is it made of? Where is it from? What is written on it? Perhaps someone drives by with music playing. What are the lyrics for that song? There are apps to help with that too. In what ways do these things speak to the card you have with you? Do you see anyone or anything on the walk? This is all important too. Take your time. This is an exercise in knowledge gained through observation. Each of these observations will give you a chance to make connections you may not have realized before.

Trust Your Intuition

Very often in readings, my psychic knowledge or "spidey senses" will go off, prompting me to say something unusual. Almost 100 percent of the time, these impulses are correct. When you receive interesting thoughts in a reading, always make sure to gently ask the client if they might connect to the reading; you never know what might happen. Deborah Lipp, author and tarot scholar, advised, "Trust yourself. If you know what you're doing and you work to improve your mind skills, it's easier to trust yourself. At that point, learn to let

---

27. Mat Auryn, interview conducted by Lilith Dorsey, April 25, 2023.

go, to keep going past uncertainty, to share your trust and confidence with your querent."[28]

Patience

Many of the cards speak to patience. They urge the seeker to be patient and always search for solutions. Tarot cards can be challenging at times. I've even heard them referred to as passive-aggressive aunties. But the truth can be hard to take, especially when it is staring you in the face. Remember that time and the cards move in mysterious ways. You can always find solutions. This rigorous patience is important not only for the answers you are seeking but the entire tarot process itself. Tarot reader and author Courtney Alexander urges the reader, "Be patient with yourself. Experiment. Remove the idea from your mind that divination has to look a certain way. There are no concrete rules. Learn how your spirit speaks and give it attention. You will always be way better at a method tailored to you than picking someone else's. You will also build trust in yourself that way, which will strengthen everything you do. Anything can be read and used for divination. Water, shells, cards, smoke, roadkill. *Anything*. Because divination methods are tools to draw out of you what is already there, honor and appreciate the gift you have."[29]

28.   Deborah Lipp, interview conducted by Lilith Dorsey, August 1, 2015.

29.   Courtney Alexander, interview conducted by Lilith Dorsey, October 16, 2016.

Chapter Thirty
Tarot Altars and Shrines

❧————————❧

Anyone who works regularly with the tarot should consider creating a tarot altar or shrine. An altar is a temporary setup that is designed to be used for a short period of time and then dismantled. Shrines are designed to be left in place permanently. Before you set up either of these, you might want to consider doing a birthing ritual for your deck. Instructions on doing that are in chapter twenty-eight. Tarot cards leave the factory numbered in order and wrapped in plastic, but they really only come to life in your hands. This is your deck and completing a birthing and blessing ritual only helps to strengthen that connection.

Crafting Tarot Altars

As stated earlier, altars are temporary creations designed to be used briefly and for a specific purpose. You can make one to help you with an important tarot reading: for example, one for the new year or a wedding. If you are reading at an event like a party or a festival where you will be consulting the tarot for others, it may help to set up an altar. Below are some examples of how you might put one together.

Working Tarot Altar

This is a simple tarot altar you can put together whenever necessary. Feel free to customize it with your favorite additions as needed. Pick a space where your altar will not be disturbed. Even though this creation is only going to be in place for a short time, you don't want it being interfered with by pets or anyone else. This is a sacred place for your cards and your magical energy. Start by wiping down the space with a small amount of spring water on a cloth. Next, you may wish to place an altar cloth. This should be a natural fabric such as cotton or silk. You can choose a cloth in the corresponding color that supports your witchy practice. For example, Fire Witches may wish to use a red cloth, Water Witches may choose a blue cloth, and so on. Then put your cards into the center of the space. If you like, surround them with your favorite crystals. Light a small candle; a votive or tea light will do. If you desire, you can also light some incense. Now your temporary working altar is ready to use.

Specialty Tarot Altars

These temporary but nonetheless serious creations can be made to help focus your energy and that of your cards in a specific direction. Maybe you're reading cards for a wedding party and want to set up an altar for love to help create a loving atmosphere for the couple and everyone getting their tarot read. Alternatively, you could be reading for a corporate event, which happens more often than you would think, and you want to focus on money and business in that atmosphere. The following instructions will help you figure out how to set these and other specialized spaces up for maximum positivity and effectiveness.

Tarot Altar for Love and Relationships

Pick a place where your altar will not be disturbed. Wipe down the space with a small amount of rose water on a cloth. Cover the spot with a pink or red cloth. Place your cards in the center of the space. Surround them with your favorite love crystals, such as azurite, desert rose, kyanite, rose quartz, selenite, turquoise, or unakite. If you like, you can add a red or pink candle. It is now ready for use.

Tarot Altar for Money and Success

Choose a place where your altar will not be disturbed. Wipe down the space with a small amount of spring water on a cloth. Cover the table with a green or gold cloth. In the corners, place four new coins with this year's date on them. Place a small green tea light in a holder in the center of the table. You may also choose to put a large crystal in the center; some good choices for attracting money are malachite and pyrite. Place your cards down between you and the candle. Now it is ready to use.

Tarot Altar for Healing

Locate this in a space where it will not be disturbed for the length of your working. Wipe down the space with a small amount of salt water on a cloth. Then cover the space with a yellow cloth. Place your cards in the center of the space. Light some lavender or myrrh incense. Get four small crystals to put in the corners of the space. Some good choices are rose quartz, carnelian, or tourmaline. It is now ready to use.

Tarot Altar for Protection

Set up this protection altar in a space where it will be undisturbed by humans or pets for as long as needed. Choose a white or black cloth to cover the area. Place your cards in the center of the space. Light some sage, sandalwood, or other protection incense. In the corners of the table, place four crystals. Consider using jet, obsidian, or amethyst. If you like, you can draw protection symbols on the crystals. This could be a rune, a veve, a sigil, or something from your own tradition. Place a black and white reversible candle in the center of the table. The altar is now ready for use. Light the candle when you are doing readings or workings, and remember to never leave a burning candle unattended.

Tarot Shrine

If you use your cards every day like I do, you might wish to set up a tarot shrine. This is a sacred location where your cards will rest and recharge when you are not actively using them. The first thing to do is choose a space that will be undisturbed by pets or the other people in your home. It could be a small table, a shelf, or anything large enough to hold the items that will be placed there. In some African traditional religions, shrines are created in cabinets with a door, so they can be closed and kept away from disapproving or prying eyes. The choice is up to you.

As with a tarot altar, you will need to start by making sure the space is physically and spiritually clean. After you perform the physical cleansing, then it is time for the spiritual one. Here are some ideas for shrine setup based on what type of Witch you might be.

Art Witch Tarot Shrine

The Art Witch tarot shrine is where the Art Witch can really shine. Here you can use your art to create a beautiful space that appeals to your eyes and your soul. Consider including sculptures, statuary, collages, or vision boards. You may also wish to take the time to include a carved candle. An embroidered cloth is another great idea. Expand your creativity and expand your magic.

Beginning Witch Tarot Shrine

As a Beginner Witch, looking at the sacred shrines of others can be a bit overwhelming, but creating your own doesn't have to be. The best advice is to use this spot for all the witchy things you love. If you have favorite rocks or crystals you have had since you were young, put them on the shrine. Are you trying to work with other divination tools besides cards, like runes or dowsing rods? Put them on the shrine. Do you have a beautiful feather you found on a nature walk? Put it on the shrine. When you are starting out, this doesn't have to be your only shrine. At one time, I counted twenty-eight different ones set up in my home. It may help, however, to use the tarot shrine as a place where you come to draw inspiration and psychic energy from your cards whenever you need to feel that. You should also store your cards here when you are not using them.

Chaos Witch Tarot Shrine

The Chaos Witch will create a tarot shrine that is truly inspired. Here they can include found items, gifted items, or anything else they choose to assemble together. I could try to include what should go here, but that logic defies the principle behind chaos magic. Go with what inspires you, mix things up if you like, and embrace the chaos.

Cosmic Witch Tarot Shrine

Cosmic Witches will be influenced by astrology and should highlight this in their creation of a tarot shrine. Because of the connection between psychic energy and the moon, the best time to create and magically charge this space is while the moon is full. You may also wish to correspond the exact times you are working it with the planetary hours. The Cosmic Witch may wish to choose a cloth that features stars or other astrological symbols as their tarot cloth. The first step is to lay that cloth down on the permanent area for your shrine. Alternatively, you may decide to choose a cloth corresponding to your moon sign. The fire signs Aries, Leo, and Sagittarius are traditionally represented by red. Green is the most common color for earth signs Virgo, Taurus, and Capricorn. Water signs Pisces, Cancer, and Scorpio are represented by blue, while yellow is the most common color used to represent the air signs Aquarius, Gemini, or Libra. These colors can also be used for the candles or other items used on your tarot altar. To represent the cosmos on your shrine, you might want to include gems from outer space. The stone moldavite is believed to have been formed when an asteroid hit earth around fifteen million years ago. Its beautiful green color can help influence and inspire your readings. Pallasite peridot is another gem from space; it comes with a hefty price tag, though, as it is one of the rarest gems on earth. A more affordable option may be to just include a piece of meteorite on your shrine.

Cottage Witch Tarot Shrine

This type of Witch centers their practice around the home. They might certainly want to set up a tarot shrine in their magical home. This shrine will gain extra benefits from its surroundings, and I would consider it almost a divine extension of your home itself.

Coven-Focused Witch Tarot Shrine

Coven-focused Witches do it together. That's a joke, or possibly even a bumper sticker. Seriously, however, if you are in a coven and you are setting up a tarot shrine, consider involving your coven-mates. Ask them what they keep on their tarot shrines. Plan a ritual with them to help bless and charge your shrine once it is set up. Even though I haven't been part of a coven in years, I still have many treasured pieces on my tarot shrine that have been gifted to me or made by my magical friends.

Crystal Witch Tarot Shrine

There's so much information about crystals and tarot that I dedicated a whole chapter to the subject. Crystals most definitely have a place on the tarot shrine for these Witches. Use big crystals, crystal points, crystal spheres, chips, tumbled stones; any and all of these are welcome here. Also remember you don't have to only limit yourself to the table space in front of you; you can hang crystals above the space too.

Elemental Witch Tarot Shrine

With an elemental tarot shrine, you will truly employ the sacred power of a particular element to help you get the most out of your readings and your cards.

Fire

For fire, start by choosing a cloth that represents this element for you. It could be red or maybe have actual flames as part of the print. Set this down on your sacred shrine space. In the center, you will put a red candle in a glass candleholder. If you can pull the candle out of the glass, you may wish to decorate it with fire symbols and red glitter. Then, consecrate it with a few drops of a fire oil such as basil, carnation, cedar, or frankincense. Always remember to burn with caution and never leave a burning candle unattended.

Next, prepare your incense. You can choose to burn dried herbs on charcoal. All charcoal-burned incense can get smoky, so please consider opening doors and windows, burning it outside, or using a prepared incense instead. Some fire-inspired ones to choose from are orange, frankincense, and sunflower.

When that is done, prepare a fiery drink offering. This can be something like peppermint tea, strong coffee, or even something stronger such as jalapeño-infused tequila.

Then, gather four fire crystals. They can be all the same, all different, or a combination. Some possible fire crystals are Botswana agate, fire agate, carnelian, citrine, fire opal, and raw ruby.

Once you have all these items assembled, take the crystals and place them in the four corners of your space. If you are using a round table, align the stones with the directions north, south, east, and west. Place the fiery drink to the left of your space, light the incense, and place the incense burner on the right side of your space. Say whichever words of power you choose or simply "Now my sacred shine is activated." It is now ready for tarot readings and other workings.

Water

Water Witches will be guided by intuition to create their sacred water tarot shrine. Begin by choosing a cloth that represents water to you. It could be blue or maybe even in an elaborate salt silk or batik design that speaks to the element. Use this to cover your sacred shrine space. Next, take a large glass bowl and put it in the center of the space along with a blue candle in a glass candleholder.

Gather together all the sacred waters you want to use to help charge and bless this shrine. You can start with tap water from your own home. This represents the water spirit of place. Sprinkle some gently on the cloth and then pour a splash into the bowl. Then you might add some different waters from other sources. Maybe you have gathered ancestral water from a cemetery spigot or sacred water from a holy well. Use your intuition and proceed accordingly. Repeat the sprinkling process. You can continue this with as many waters as you like.

Next, gather your water crystals and shells. You will need four of each. Some good crystal choices are lapis, turquoise, azurite, and blue topaz, to name a few. Place the crystals in the four corners of your shrine. If you are using a round table, align the stones with the directions north, south, east, and west. Place the shells on the shrine surrounding the glass bowl.

Get your incense ready. You can use a prepared incense for your patron, if you have one. Alternatively, you may wish to burn some water-ruled herbs on a small piece of charcoal in an incense burner. Some scents to choose from are bay, chamomile, jasmine, lemon, lilac, lotus, rose, thyme, and vanilla. Remember all charcoal-burned incense can get smoky, so open your doors and windows or even perhaps burn it outside.

Next, light the candle in the center and light the incense. Place your tarot cards on the shrine. You may also wish to put your other divination tools here to bless and keep. This would be a good place for dowsing rods or even your pendulum. Let the candle and incense burn out. Remember to never leave a burning candle unattended. Now your shrine is ready for use.

Air

Air is all around us. Setting up a shrine and using it to focus your airy energy for tarot workings might be a more tangible way to access the elemental power of air. The most common colors used to symbolize the element of air are yellow and silver. You may wish to keep these colors in mind for your cloth, or maybe choose a pattern that features clouds or birds. Once you pick a fabric, spread it out over your shrine space.

Next, take a yellow or silver candle and place it in a holder in the center of the table. If you wish, you can carve the symbol for air or the symbol for Jupiter, Mercury, or Uranus (all considered planets ruled by the air) onto the candle.

Then get some air incense. This can be a specific blend for air or one formulated for Gemini, Libra, or Aquarius, the air signs. You could also burn some air-ruled herbs on charcoal in an incense burner. Some possible herbs are bergamot, lavender, mastic, myrrh, and rosemary. You can also make a mist by placing five drops of any of these botanicals in essential oil form into a spray bottle along with a few ounces of tap water. You can use this to spray the shrine as needed and also your hands before you begin and end a reading.

Next, gather four crystals that are used in workings for air. The crystals can be alike, all different, or a combination. Consider using amethyst, quartz, mica, or selenite.

Now you are ready to activate your shrine. Light the candle in the center of the table. Place the four crystals in the corners of the shrine. Before you place each one down, hold it in your hands and exhale a long, slow breath onto the stones. This is your own personal blessing of air. Place your tarot deck on the shrine in front of the candle.

The next task is to light the incense. Pass its smoke all around the shrine, paying special attention to the cards themselves. As you do this, feel free to sing or say your favorite air chant. If you don't have anything in mind, you can simply say, "I consecrate this shrine with the elemental power of air." Now it is ready to use.

Earth

For Earth Witches, every day is Earth Day. They see the value and beauty of the earth and everything that grows in it. There are many ways that Earth Witches can utilize this to help craft a tarot shrine. As with the other elemental shrines, this shrine will need components that come from each elemental category but also have a unique earthbound vibe. The colors most often associated with the earth are brown and green. Pick an altar cloth made in one of these colors or one that features images of actual plants, leaves, or trees. Lay this cloth out on top of your shrine.

Next, place a spoonful of one or more special dirts in a small bowl. When gathering dirt from special places, please be respectful, be lawful, and remember to always leave a small offering and give thanks. For example, you may wish to add dirt from a crossroads, which is known to bring blessings of success and guidance. Similarly, you can add dirt from a cemetery to bring blessings and connection to your ancestors. Dirt from the river's edge is said to bring love. Use any or all of these in your bowl. Place the bowl in the center of your shrine. Either on top of this dirt or directly in front of it, place a green or brown candle in a candleholder.

Next, gather four coins dated with the year of your birth. Align these with the four directions on your shrine. Each direction will receive a coin.

Gather your crystals. Almost all crystals come from the earth. Some, however, are a bit more earthy than others. Good choices include moss agate, picture jasper, serpentine, staurolite, and vanadinite. You may use four different stones, four of the same, or a combination. Place your stones on the cross-quarter points directly between the coins you laid out earlier.

Next, you will leave out a glass of spring water or tap water, if you prefer. This will represent the earth in water; both of the choices come from inside the earth, by accident or design, respectively. Then it is time to ready your incense. This can be a prepared formula created with the earth energy in mind, or you can burn your own combination of herbs on charcoal to represent this aspect. Some acceptable choices would be mint, rose, and violet. Place your cards directly on the table in front of you and light the incense. Remember that charcoal-burned incense can get smoky, so open doors and windows or burn it outside.

First, raise the incense above the shrine, then move it below. Take the incense stick or burner and move it around the space. First, go in a counterclockwise direction to remove any unnecessary energy in the space. When that is finished, switch directions, moving clockwise to bless and charge the area with earth energy.

Light the candle in the center of the table. Remember never leave a burning candle unattended. If you wish, you may choose to say a blessing of your choice for the earth. Now your shrine is ready to use whenever you wish.

Eclectic Witch Tarot Shrine

By definition, the type of magic used by this type of Witch is a sacred blend of components that come together to create magic. My best suggestion if you are this type of Witch is to go through the other shrine instructions and see what resonates with you, what speaks to you, and incorporate that into your tarot shrine. Talk to your fellow practitioners and ask if you can visit their altar and shrine spaces to see if you can get inspiration. Another good resource for ideas is to go online and search for pictures of other tarot shrines that people have created. Try one idea and then another. Continue until you find a setup that works well for you.

Faery Witch Tarot Shrine

If you are in an established faery tradition, of which there are many, look to those time-honored ways for creating your shrine and follow those guidelines. However, if you are not part of one, you can still create your own sacred space for tarot inspired by the Fae and your own beliefs. Your tarot shrine could contain some of the herbs loved by the Fae, such as primrose, lavender, chamomile, basil, and others. You can place these on your shrine as live plant cuttings in a vase or use dried herbs and burn on charcoal as an incense. Another idea is to fill this shrine with items traditionally offered to the Fae; this could include things like acorns, shiny new coins, and pine cones. Food offerings are also acceptable and could include milk or cream, honey, bread, candy, or wine. When these offerings have sat on the space for twenty-four hours, feel free to remove them, take them outside, place them on the earth, and return to your space, replacing them whenever you feel the need.

Shiny crystals such as mica, pyrite, and green crystals like peridot can also be used. This is the one type of tarot shrine where I would recommend not leaving your cards permanently but instead placing them there only when you need to charge them with the shrine's energy or are ready to perform a reading. The reason for this is because you don't want the Fae to take a liking to your deck and decide it belongs to them. We all know how they are.

Green Witch Tarot Shrine

Green Witches can utilize the instructions for elemental Earth Witches given on page 232 for creating a shrine and expand on those. They may wish to take their connection to plants a bit further and even include cuttings of their favorite botanicals directly on the shrine in the quarters and cross-quarters.

Healing Witch Tarot Shrine

This type of Witch will use their tarot shrine as a space to heal themselves, others, and their actual cards. It is a space designed to rebalance and equalize that which may be causing illness on every level. When I first started out as a professional Witch, someone gave me the best advice. They said, "All magic is healing magic." Most people think of healing as something that occurs only with living beings. However, we can use healing energy to help fix any unwanted and unnecessary situation in our lives. If we are having financial issues, we can heal our bank account. If we are having love problems, we can heal our relationship. Healing is everywhere, and this type of Witch knows that deep down in their soul.

When creating a healing tarot shrine, start by choosing a cloth to cover your space. This can be green or yellow, the two colors frequently associated with healing. Alternatively, maybe you want to choose fabric with a caduceus on it, a commonly used symbol of medicine. Place the cloth on the table, covering your space. Next, you will find a small bowl and fill it with a few tablespoons of water. This can be water from a hospital or doctor's office, or it can be a different type of healing water, such as that from a sacred well like Lourdes. In New Orleans, we have a Healing Grotto as part of the International Shrine of St. Jude. Directly outside the space is a holy water font where visitors can fill up a bottle for themselves to take home. Donations are always appreciated, but this would be another great choice for a healing water to add to your bowl. Feel free to use a combination of waters, as this will only increase the healing power of your space exponentially. In the center of the water bowl, place a small white votive candle.

Next, choose healing crystals for this space. Crystals that are customarily used for healing are carnelian, lapis lazuli, sugilite, and rose quartz, to name a few. Gather a minimum of four crystals; you can use all the same, all different, or a combination. Place these in the directional points on your shrine. Use one or more each in the north, south, east, and west of your space. The next step is to make a healing herbal infusion. Take a teaspoon of each of the following dried herbs and place into a heat-safe bowl: chamomile, echinacea, ginger, and lavender. Pour a cup of very hot water over the herbs. Let it steep for twenty-five to thirty minutes and then strain through a piece of cheesecloth. Take the strained liquid and put it into a spray bottle with a pinch of sea salt. Use this to

spray down the space, your hands, and your feet both before and after a reading. Light the candle in the center of the table. Remember to never leave a
burning candle unattended. Place your cards on the space, along with whatever
other tools you use for healing. Now the space is ready to use.

Hedge Witch Tarot Shrine

A Hedge Witch will use many of the techniques we have discussed to create
their tarot shrine. They may wish to use treasured crystals to mark the cardinal
points on their shrine, or they may wish to use stones from their own property.
This Witch could choose any of the herbs we have mentioned in the descriptions thus far to create incense or sacred energy on their shrine, or they could
use plants and botanicals from their own backyard. Most Hedge Witches have
a connection to the Fae, so consider reading those instructions above to see if
you would like to incorporate any of it into your sacred shrine now. This type
of Witch very often likes to keep things simple, so feel free to use elemental
representations here or not; it is all up to you.

Hereditary Witch Tarot Shrine

This type of shrine will be influenced by the wisdom and teachings of your
ancestors. You may wish to combine this shrine with your general ancestor space.
Ancestor shrines are a part of many different world religions. They are found in
Christian homes, Buddhist homes, Pagan homes, and even in atheists' homes.
They can be as simple as a glass of spring water and a picture of Grandpa, or they
can be given an entire room to spread out in. Cleansing of the space before you
begin is highly recommended. The shrine should be both physically and spiritually clean. Here in New Orleans, anything and everything can be present on
an ancestor shrine. Like the Crescent City itself, shrines are a delicious spiritual
gumbo of elements mixing and combining to make something uniquely wonderful. I've seen anything and everything a person can hold dear from money to
jewelry placed here. Sometime petitions are placed beneath or around the wick
of a candle to send messages and requests to those who have passed on. Most
common are offerings of money, liquor, photos, medals, and mass cards.

Unlike a traditional ancestor altar, which will include items only for your
actual blood relations, this type of shrine can include those who have passed
with whom you had a magical connection. This could be things from your

magical teachers who are no longer living and also those who may have been in ritual with you while they were alive. Once you have assembled all your items, add your deck of cards to the space, and the shrine is ready for use.

Kitchen Witch Tarot Shrine
In this type of shrine, you will highlight the joy of cooking. If you have been paying attention as you go through this book, you have seen that each major arcana card is given its own special recipes. In some ways, just assembling the ingredients for each of these recipes can be seen as a temporary altar to that particular tarot card. Keep your cards close by, but in a place where they will not get dirty, when you are crafting these recipes to give them extra strength and energy. You may also think about placing a small tarot shrine in the kitchen if you have the space. Here you can include fresh fruit and herbs, changing them out as often a necessary.

Solitary Witch Tarot Shrine
Spaces like this tarot shrine will be invaluable for the Solitary Witch as one of the main locations to store their power and also draw strength from. Depending on their practice, they may wish to borrow from any of the other shrine creation ideas found here. Even if you live with friends or family, make sure you situate your shrine in a place where it will be undisturbed. If that is not possible, consider making a small shrine out of a cigar box or similar so that you can close it away from prying eyes when necessary.

Traditional Witch Tarot Shrine
For this type of shrine, the Traditional Witch will be guided by their own practices. Talk to your elders, and in turn ask them about their elders. Find out what they thought necessary to place on their shrine. Let the tradition guide you.

Chapter Thirty-One
Crystals, Herbs, and Gardens

—•—

There are lots of different ways to amplify and clarify your tarot readings. Using crystals, herbs, and even, on a larger scale, gardens are all some of these ways. Humans learn by doing, and simply giving readings and getting them is one way to learn, but incorporating some of the other tactics in this book will help open up lots of other levels of understanding.

Using Crystals with Your Cards

All of the major arcana cards examined in this book also come with corresponding crystals to help you better explore and understand them. There are several ways to utilize crystals in connection to your cards.

- Place crystals in your tarot bag along with your cards to help energize and strengthen them.
- Set up a crystal grid on your tarot altar before you set out your spread.
- Make your own crystal-based tarot set from the major arcana crystals. You can then keep them in a box or bag and pull one as needed.

Crystal Grids and Tarot

Whether they know it or not, almost everyone who utilizes crystals in their home is forming a type of crystal grid. Also called a crystal net, a grid is simply a layout where crystals are laid out in positions for maximum effectiveness. This technique maximizes the power of both geometry and crystals to strengthen and focus your magic and your tarot practice. Some believe that Stonehenge is evidence of an early crystal or stone grid. It was clearly created to align with the stars and the seasons and produce a site of maximum energy.

While setting up your grid, be sure to state your intention aloud before and after the grid is created. You can choose to purchase a ready-made grid to lay out your crystals. Some of these are very elaborate and based on established religious symbols, or you can make your own grid based on the following shapes. You can set these grids up in your tarot room or sacred space, even if it's just a temporary altar. Alternatively, you can set these up in the room before a tarot journey work or as part of a larger spell or ritual. Some Witches may even wish to use grids when they are meditating on tarot.

Square Grid

The simplest crystal grid is a square. You can set one up in your space by laying the crystals out in the four corners of a room, a bed, a table, or whatever other space you wish. Alternatively, you can lay the crystals out according to the four directions: north, south, east, and west. A square grid will help you set boundaries in this world and the others. A square is one of the most stable shapes in nature, and this will help to ground your readings in reality.

Star or Pentacle Grid

A pentacle grid is laid out according to the five points of a star. This shape is designed to bring rebirth, change, protection, and spiritual transformation. You may wish to use this grid when doing a reading about major changes that are happening in your life.

Hexagram or Star of David Grid

This type of grid is based on the number six. It forms a shield that is based in balance and alignment. There are similar shapes in Judaism and the religions of India or Tibet. It may also be familiar to those who practice Thelema and use it to symbolize cosmic forces.

Circle Grid

Circular crystal grids represent unity, wholeness, and completeness. To create this type of grid, simply place crystals in a circle on your altar or shrine and place your tarot cards or other sacred tools in the center.

Triangle Grid

A triangle represents the sacred power of three. For some, it may evoke the Triple Goddess, the Holy Trinity, or the unification of mind, body, and spirit. This type of grid is designed for manifestation, connection, and inspiration. It can be used in conjunction with your tarot readings to aid in receiving spiritual illumination and inspiration.

Choosing Your Crystals

So which types of crystals should you use in making your tarot-inspired grids? I've already detailed the different crystals that are associated with the cards, but what shape or type of crystal should you use? The truth of the matter is each different shape of crystal will focus its energy in slightly different ways. There are crystal points, either natural or cut. These work to direct energy toward a specific point. There are also double-terminated points. These will focus energy directly off each of the two points present. Crystal pyramids are typically four-sided and have a flat base on which to sit. They are manufactured this way and are helpful with increasing the overall power of your grid as a whole. Crystal balls or spheres are man-made balls. They need to sit in a base or holder. To some, they are a stereotypical tool used by Witches to foresee the future. That may be true, but they are also very successful tools to use in conjunction with your crystal grid. They help contain and protect the space you are crafting, while adding immense psychic energy. You can also get crystals shaped like hearts for love or skulls to honor your ancestors.

So which should you use? As mentioned, each one will carry its own unique energy and focus. Most people use tumbled stones or crystal points. My best advice is to try out a few different types in varying positions and see what works best for your unique set of circumstances.

Cleansing Your Crystals

Just like your tarot cards, your crystals will need to be cleansed. This can be done using incense such as sage, sandalwood, or myrrh. An alternate method would be to cleanse them using reiki, which requires specialized training. Others recommend burying crystals overnight in the yard or even in a flowerpot. Whatever method you use, crystals will probably need to be energetically cleansed at least every time you set up a new grid.

Gardens and Herbs

Each of the major arcana cards that I have explored in this book has its own corresponding herbs and plants that go along with it. Some of you, particularly the Green Witches, may wish to incorporate some of these herbs into your own garden, either inside or out. Working in partnership with nature is one of the best ways to explore your spiritual path, so I hope everyone reading this gives it a try.

The most famous tarot garden is in Tuscany, Italy. It is a series of large mosaic sculptures depicting each of the twenty-two major arcana cards. The project was officially begun in 1980 by Niki de Saint Phalle.

They began with the High Priestess. All the works were inspired by the artist's love of both tarot and the famous mosaic artist Gaudi. In this garden, plants are intermingled with sculpture. It works wonderfully in this instance and may be something you want to consider for yourself.

The gardens in Italy are on a grand scale, but obviously not everyone will have those types of resources at their disposal. Never fear—you can create your own tarot garden on a smaller scale. You can make one in your own backyard, and you can even make one in a flowerpot or window box. If you don't resonate with any of those ideas, you could even make a tarot-inspired seed mix to sprinkle in vacant lots and abandoned areas. You can do any or all of the things; the only real limitation is your own imagination.

Once your tarot garden or plants are established, you can use it to harvest botanicals to use in your tarot spells and working, or you can even use the site as a place to charge your cards and meditate on the readings you are doing to gain clarity and calm around the issue.

These gardens provide a space to truly experience tarot with all your senses, connecting with the plants, animals, and insects that will call your garden home. Tarot gardens aren't just for Green Witches. Earth Witches might relish the chance to get down and dirty creating a tarot garden. Hedge Witches might welcome another way to protect and bless their home, namely a tarot garden for protection. Love Witches might enjoy making a tarot of love garden. Don't limit yourself; you just might be surprised.

Tarot Garden for Psychic Awareness

The most basic garden you may wish to create is one for psychic awareness. The plants included here will help your readings get better in every way. Depending on your climate, you may need to make some adjustments. At the current moment, I live in New Orleans, Louisiana. We are growing zone 9b. We get a ton of rain (it is the swamp, after all), and in the summer the heat climbs over 110 degrees Fahrenheit daily. For many years, I lived in New England, which was almost the opposite climate. It was growing zone 5. We had snow on the ground for several months out of the year, and the temperatures rarely got over 90 degrees Fahrenheit. The plants I grew in these places were very different. The list of plants I'm including here offers a wide range of choices, and hopefully you can find something that will thrive in your own climate. It may turn out that you use some of these as houseplants or tender annuals if you live in a colder climate.

> **Bay** (*Laurus nobilis*) A lot of people are familiar with bay leaf as an herb used in cooking. It is a Mediterranean herb and is hardy to zone 8. Many people grow it in pots and bring it inside when cold hits. The plant requires full sun and well-draining soil.

> **Borage** (*Borago officinalis*) The tiny blue flowers that grace a borage plant are said to be beloved by faeries and otherworldly folk. The foliage can cause skin irritation, but the flowers are edible. You can add the flowers to your magical dishes as well as your ritual baths and washes. It may also help to put dried borage flowers in your tarot bag or on your altar. This plant is an annual but will readily self-seed in your garden. Plant it outside from starts or sow from seed after danger of all frost has passed. It prefers a sunny spot but only needs an average soil.

Chicory (*Cichorium intybus*) Chicory is associated with the sun and the element of air. It is useful for helping with divination, as it grants clarity and access to the ancestors. All parts of this plant can be used, including the root, leaves, and flowers. Folklore tells us it is best collected in silence to keep its power strong. Like most salad greens, it prefers temperatures between 45 to 70 degrees Fahrenheit. Keep it in a sunny location and harvest up until it is ready to go to seed.

Dandelion (*Taraxacum* spp.) Many think of dandelion as a common weed and an unwelcome addition to the garden. In actuality, these glorious yellow flowers are easy to grow and provide both magical and medicinal benefits. Also known as white endive, lion's tooth, blowball, Irish daisy, and other interesting names, this flower is said to be ruled by the element of air and makes a great herb to keep with your cards or on your tarot altar to help with psychic communication. Dandelion grows wild in a variety of locations but does best in full sun to partial shade.

Galangal (*Alpinia galanga*) The root of this plant is most often utilized in both magical formulas and cooking. It is native to China and does best when planted from rhizomes after all danger of frost has passed.

Ginger (*Zingiber officinale*) Ginger comes in both edible and ornamental form. In many different cultures, it is said to help connection with the dead and also the other realms. This plant thrives in tropical climates; if you live elsewhere, consider growing it in pots. It does best in full to partial shade with rich soil.

Juniper (*Juniperus* spp.) Juniper trees are conifers that are part of the cypress family. Very often you will see the berries, which are in fact seeds, used in magic for cleansing and purifying. Sometimes people also add the leaves to smoke-cleansing bundles or incense blends. It grows great in a variety of climates and needs full sun.

Lavender (*Lavandula angustifolia*) Lavender is a wonderful all-purpose plant that is suitable for many different environments. It promotes psychic connection on every level. It is especially effective when placed with your tarot cards or burned as an incense before a reading. This plant

grows well in a variety of climates, and chances are you can find
starts ready to go in your local garden center. Plant lavender in the
spring after all danger of frost has passed. It prefers a sunny location
and sandy soil.

Morning Glory (*Ipomoea* spp.) Morning glory is particularly effective when
used as an aid for psychic connection, astral travel, and journey
work. It is an easy-to-grow annual that can be started simply from
seed. It needs plenty of sun and a location that is sheltered. Give it
something to climb on and the vines will take off.

Poppy (*Papaver somniferum*) There are many different varieties of poppy
plant, and they came in many different colors. They grow in a whole
host of different climates, and it should be easy to find one suited
to your garden. They require full sun and thrive in a dry and warm
location. While this is the plant that our common poppy seeds come
from, it is also the one used to make narcotics, so as with all herbs,
use caution.

Thyme (*Thymus vulgaris*) This common kitchen herb is said to help with
psychic visions and prophecies. It grows easily in a variety of climates, and can be added to your ritual baths, floor washes, or even
your meals. Plant it in full to partial sun with good drainage, as it
hates standing in water. Thyme grows best from cutting, so either
buy transplants from your local garden center or get some cuttings
from friends who have established plants.

Wisteria (*Wisteria floribunda*) The magical properties of wisteria are
many. I recommend using the purple blooms very carefully in your
workings, as they are toxic to humans and animals. Unfortunately,
almost all commercial oil formulas for wisteria you can obtain are
synthetic. My favorite way to use it in divination rituals is to simply
place a bouquet on the tarot altar or shrine. Be careful when planting this in the garden because certain varieties can be very invasive.

Tarot Garden for Protection

Protection magic is something every Witch should be good at. If you are doing
readings for others, you should take extra care to make sure you are protected
from any energies you may pick up during these readings. Healing Witches

should also take extra care that they are safe and protected from the energies they come in contact with. Planting a protection tarot garden or even a flowerpot will help make sure you are safe and secure no matter what.

Dill (*Anethum graveolens*) You might have dill in your pickle jar, but hopefully you will have it in your sacred garden as well. Dill is a great plant for a tarot garden because it is useful for both communication and protection, two things you definitely need when doing tarot readings. It grows easily in well-draining and slightly acidic soils. Find a place that will be in full sun to partial shade, and it should grow quite well.

Marjoram (*Origanum majorana*) This plant will grow great in a pot but also makes a lovely ground cover. It should be in full sun and given well-draining soil. Magically, this plant is sacred to Mercury, which will help with psychic communication, and Venus, which will help with any readings you are doing about love. It is also an herb of protection. Kitchen Witches may recognize this as a normal ingredient in the herbes de Provence mix. Frequently used to flavor chicken and soups, it can be utilized in similar ways to oregano as it is botanically related.

Mint (*Mentha* spp.) Mint is probably the easiest to grow of all the plants listed here. It is so vigorous that oftentimes people plant it in a pot so it doesn't take over the rest of the garden. There are many different types of mint. Most people are familiar with peppermint and spearmint, but there is also chocolate mint, lavender mint, and many other cultivars. Visit your nearest garden center and see what appeals to you. It makes a wonderful herbal tea that can be drank as part of your tarot ritual when you are performing readings. All types of mint are used for cleansing and protection. You may wish to make an infusion to add to your floor washes or to add to a spray bottle for quick spiritual cleaning.

Mugwort (*Artemisia vulgaris*) For many, mugwort is the herb for psychics. It is said to impart access to other realms. It can be used with dreamworking, protection magics, and all types of divination, which makes it a glorious addition to the tarot garden. The plant thrives best in a sunny location with moist but well-draining soil. It can be used as an incense or added to mojo or medicine bags. (Pregnant women must not use mugwort.)

Primrose (*Primula vulgaris*) This delicate little flower is praised in folklore as beloved by faeries. It grows easily throughout most parts of North America and Europe. Plant it in a slightly shaded area and add some organic material to the site, and it should do quite well. An alternate name for this plant is St. Peter's keys, and it is said to unlock spiritual doorways that are normally closed to us. Primrose is said to bring success, protection, and blessings. Magically, it is said to be used as an offering for not only faeries but also the divine goddesses Freya, Flora, Diana, and Bast.

Rosemary (*Salvia rosmarinus*) Rosemary is another kitchen herb that we frequently see used in spells of protection. Easily obtained and easily cultivated, rosemary is a perfect addition to your magical bag of tricks. The herb, the wood, and the oil are all used. But as with most herbs, use caution with pregnant women and small children. Astrologically, rosemary is associated with the sun and the sign of Leo. Magically, rosemary is said to bring not only protection but also healing, purification, strength, clarity, and love.

Sage (*Salvia officinalis*) The sage I am talking about planting in your tarot space is garden sage. White sage is a protected plant and is used traditionally by Indigenous peoples. Garden sage, however, is a common kitchen herb, and using it as an incense or wash can be very beneficial to your magic. Even the name implies wisdom, and planting it in your tarot garden can help impart wisdom and success to your readings. Garden sage does best in full sun and can easily be grown from seed. Place it in well-draining soil and water the young plants frequently.

Tarot Garden for Love

If you end up becoming a professional tarot reader, or even just try your hand at reading for others, chances are you will get many people coming to you with questions about love. To help improve your insight and clarity surrounding these readings, you might decide to create a tarot garden for love. While there are hundreds of plants that are associated with love magic, the following is a short list to get you started.

Bergamot (*Citrus ×aurantium* ssp. *bergamia*) This herb grows easily in most spaces and conditions. Certain varieties are highly prized and used in expensive perfumes and cologne. Bergamot is known to grant happiness, joy, and love.

Carnation (*Dianthus caryophyllus*) The genus *Dianthus*, which comes from Greek, means "flower of Zeus." Carnations are easy to grow anywhere is USDA zones 5 to 9. They grow best from transplanted starts in full sun. In your magic, they will provide both love and healing.

Daisy (*Leucanthemum vulgare*) Daisy has long been used as a flower of love. Many a young lover has pulled the petals, saying, "They love me, they love me not" as a simple divination to see if their loving feelings are being returned. They are easily planted from seed and need a spot with partial sun. Magically, they are associated with truth and romance.

Dandelion (*Taraxacum* spp.) Most people think of dandelion as some kind of weed. The reality is that it is one of the most useful plants you can have in your garden. This helpful little herb goes by several different names: priest's crown, Irish daisy, piss-a-bed, and lion's tooth. Its resemblance to a lion's mane probably accounts for its association with the astrological sign of Leo. Dandelion is connected to the element of air. This makes it a great plant to use when performing divination or magic for clarity and insight. It is also known to grant wishes and joy.

Freesia (*Freesia alba*) This is an indoor plant except in zones 9 to 10. Place it in indirect light conditions and make sure it stays over 40 degrees Fahrenheit at night. It has an intoxicating scent and can be used in magic for both love and friendship.

Gardenia (*Gardenia* spp.) Gardenias can be trees, vines, or shrubs. They grow in full or partial sun in zones 7 to 11. They can be grown with some knowledgeable care. Be sure the soil has a pH of 5 or 6, and remember they don't take well to transplanting. They have a strong and sweet fragrance that can bring pleasure, joy, and romance to your magic.

German Chamomile (*Matricaria chamomilla*) Chamomile is another easily grown plant that should find its way into your garden if possible. The fad lately is even to use it as a ground cover for a bee-friendly alternative to the ubiquitous lawn. The tiny yellow flowers are known to help with sleep, dreamworking, and gentle love.

Heliotrope (*Heliotropium arborescens*) This delightful purple plant does best with morning sun and rich soil. It is hardy outdoors in zones 9 to 11. Its very name tells us it is associated with the sun and fire magic. Heliotrope can be used to help with love, dreamworkings, and peaceful thoughts.

Hibiscus (*Hibiscus* spp.) This plant comes in both tropical and hardy varieties. It is fairly easy to grow as long as it receives adequate sun and moisture. It is known to grant love, joy, and peaceful thoughts.

Honeysuckle (*Lonicera* spp.) There are many different types and colors of honeysuckle, and almost all of them can be grown easily in most gardens. They prefer full sun, and these vines will readily climb up almost anything nearby. Added to your altar or shrine, the flowers are said to foster kindness and affection.

Jasmine (*Jasminum officinale*) This sweet-smelling plant is said to give love and happiness to all who use it. There are summer- and winter-blooming varieties, and all are climbers that will need support. In cold climates, you may need to grow it in a pot and bring it indoors if there is a danger of frost. Magically, it is also known to attract beneficial spirits of all kinds.

Lavender (*Lavandula angustifolia*) Lavender is a delightful all-purpose plant that is suitable for many different environments. It is especially effective when placed with your tarot cards or burned as an incense before a reading. Plant it from starts in the spring after all danger of frost is over. Lavender needs plenty of sunlight and well-draining soil.

Peony (*Paeonia* spp.) This stunning wedding flower needs at least four to six hours of sun and well-draining neutral soil. It grows from bulbs and should be planted in its permanent location, as it dislikes being transplanted. In love spells, it is known to grant devoted love and dispel all negativity connected to your relationships.

Pot Marigold (*Calendula officinalis*) This particular type of marigold produces big and bold blooms. It is traditionally used in Hindu culture as a blessing for weddings and love. It can be grown from seed or starts and should be placed anywhere from full sun to partial shade.

Rose (*Rosa* spp.) Rose is the number one plant associated with love. It can be used in your magic to attract love, marriage, devotion, and more. There are many different types of roses, and some of the wild types are easier to grow than the hybrid cultivars. But never fear—there is a rose out there for everyone as they even come in miniature varieties that can be grown indoors.

Individual Tarot Card Garden

An individual tarot garden is a fantastic way to connect with your cards and understand them on a deeper level. You can choose to grow the plants associated with a particular card. You might also choose ones that remind you of the card based on the colors you see depicted, the scents that evoke the same feeling as the card, or whatever else you desire. You can also incorporate statuary or stones in your garden that represent your cards. Creating this type of space, even if it is only in a flowerpot or window box, allows for an intensive level of connection. You may choose to use herbs or flowers from this garden on your tarot altar. You may choose to gift them to people who are getting tarot readings from you. You may even choose to sit near or in the garden while you do your readings.

If you are wondering which card or cards to choose, consider using the one that most often represents you. Alternatively, you could pick the card that has been showing up repeatedly in your readings to better understand the wisdom it is trying to share with you. For example, say you are getting the Empress card frequently in your readings and you decide to make a flowerpot for her. In most decks, this particular card's imagery depicts a lush and verdant garden ripe with possibilities. Start with a pot that is round. This is a nod to Mother Earth and the fecund power of the Empress energy. One plant that is frequently connected to this card is rose. You may wish to start with a miniature rose to place in the center of the pot. Next, you can add other plants that are associated with her. One good suggestion is oats; they grow easily and form a grass that will fill up the pot and create some depth. Another possible choice is the herb mother-wort. It provides many benefits and also shows off lovely purple blooms. You could go on to include other related, plants such as morning glories for psychic connection or clover for luck. The possibilities are endless, and you are limited only by your imagination.

Chapter Thirty-Two
Tarot Questions and Spreads

Tarot questions and spreads are the building blocks of every reading. A tarot reading is only as good as the question. The clearer the reader is on these things, the easier it is to obtain answers and insight. Sometimes when you are reading for others, or even for yourself, the question can be unclear. My best advice is to do some thorough soul-searching to find out what it is you really want to know before you pick up the cards, and try to find solutions or information connected to the situation at hand. If you don't, things can get even more confusing.

I tend to think of it like a trip to the doctor's or other professional's office. If you don't define what the problem is, then you won't know where to look for a solution. Author and psychic Mat Auryn explains, "I firmly believe that asking the right questions is crucial when seeking guidance or insights. It is an art that requires practice, patience, and a willingness to look beyond the surface of things.… Asking the right questions can help us receive more specific answers or guidance when seeking insights or solutions. It allows us to focus our intentions and energies on what truly matters and opens up new possibilities for growth and transformation. As I have learned from my exploration of spiritual, metaphysical, and occult methods, the power of asking the right questions is essential for unlocking the wisdom and insights that are waiting to be revealed."[30]

---

30. Mat Auryn, interview conducted by Lilith Dorsey, April 25, 2023.

Many years ago, I took part in a few divination panels at an event that no longer exists in Virginia. The panel was full of highly knowledgeable authors and psychic readers, including Dorothy Morrison, Robin Wood, Awo Robert Ogbe Di, and others. Some great conversations were had, and one of the take-aways I have, even after all these years, is that a well-designed question is just as important, if not more important, than the reading. In theory, this may be hard to understand, but when you look at people's questions, in actuality you can see where you are looking is just as vital as how. When I first started as a professional reader, I had a client who would call very upset about her money problems. She was hyper-focused on winning the lottery. She had overdue util-ity bills and was afraid they were going to shut off her electricity and gas. The woman was convinced that the only way to pay them was to win the lottery. We did some readings and some spellwork, and she eventually won enough money to pay her bills. Unfortunately, during this time, her husband became very ill and died unexpectedly. Now, I don't think her spell workings caused his death, but her focus on money woes meant that she was allowing larger prob-lems to go unnoticed.

One thing a lot of people also hear as a professional reader is questions about love. Does my partner love me? Every reader has heard these words, but if we look at the larger picture, maybe that individual should be asking, is this relationship good for me? Is this person going to support me mentally and emotionally? Is this person healthy mentally and physically? One of my own spiritual teachers always recommended phrasing the question to include the seeker's most highest good. For example, is this partner, home, dog, job, etc. for my most highest good? Do your best to be mindful when composing your own questions and helping your tarot clients form theirs.

What happens if the seeker who sits down at your tarot table doesn't have a question at all? In this case, I usually recommend a few things. The first thing I suggest is doing a reading about a specific amount of time. For example, how are the next six months to a year going to unfold? I put this time limit on it, as the accuracy of most readings decreases once people start talking about more than a year in advance. Part of the reason for this is that there are many other variables that can unfold and change the situation. I also suggest the seeker ask if there is anything they need to know right now. Any of these questions will help to give an overview with what is occurring right now in the life of the seeker.

A Word about Querents

A querent is simply the person who consults the tarot. When doing a reading, Many people choose a querent card first to represent the person seeking the reading. This can be helpful when starting out and doing readings for others, as it allows the cards to understand that there is another person seeking answers and guidance. You can choose a querent a few different ways.

- Pick a card that represents the astrological sign and age of the seeker. If the person is a fire sign, choose a wands court card that reflects their age. Water signs can be represented by the court cards of the suit of cups. Air signs are represented by the swords court cards. Last, earth sun signs are represented by the coins court cards.
- You can ask the client to choose a card themselves from the deck. They can choose one that resonates with them personally or aesthetically. Alternatively, they can spread the cards out in front of them face down and just choose one that feels right. This is a good way to get both the seeker and the reader familiar with the situation at hand.
- You can choose a querent card for them that represents them or, alternatively, the situation they are asking about. For example, if someone was asking about a relationship, you could choose the Lovers or Two of Cups card.

However, not all readings call for the use of a querent card. I have known successful readers who use them all the time and readers who don't use them at all. Ultimately, it is always up to you.

Tarot Spreads

For me, tarot spreads are like a springboard toward insight and understanding. Every reader needs a fair number of spreads in their wheelhouse to begin to determine information and solutions. These can be found for themselves and others through the different tarot card spreads.

Yes/No Spread

Yes/No Spread

I believe that it is important for everyone to have a good yes/no method for asking questions with tarot cards. The most common method for doing a yes/no reading involves aces. First, gather your cards together and organize them so that they are in order and all upright. Next, shuffle the cards three times and cut the deck three times as well. Then take the cards in your left hand and speak your yes/no question out loud. Then, using your right hand, start turning over cards, counting as you go. Stop when you reach an ace or when you count out to the number thirteen. When you get to that point, start a new pile to the right of that, again stopping when you reach an ace or when you count out to the number thirteen. Finally, start a third pile, again to the right. The same rules apply: stop when you reach an ace, or when you count out to the number thirteen. Now look at the three piles in front of you. Do you have three aces showing? If so, you can interpret the answer to your question as follows.

> 3 aces upright = definite yes
>
> 2 aces upright/1 ace reversed = most likely yes
>
> 1 ace upright/2 aces reversed = most likely no

If there are no aces showing, that means there is not enough information to answer at this time. If you like, you can wait twenty-four hours and ask again. Most situations, however, are a bit more complex than just a yes or no. Mat Auryn offers some advice on this subject: "I also believe that it is more important to explore possible choices and outcomes by rephrasing questions rather than simply asking for a yes or no answer. By rephrasing the question, we can open up new possibilities and gain deeper insights into the situation at hand, empowering the client with more personal sovereignty in their decision-making."[31]

---

31   Mat Auryn, interview conducted by Lilith Dorsey, April 25, 2023.

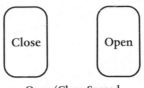

Open/Close Spread

Open/Close Spread

This is one of the easiest spreads that you can do, and it only involves two cards. Shuffle and cut the cards whichever way you prefer. Some readers like to shuffle three times and cut three times to the left. You may use that technique or another you feel more comfortable with. If you are right-handed, choose a card with your right hand from somewhere in the deck and place in front of you. Then take your left hand and choose a card from anywhere in the deck and place it to the left of the other card you have chosen. The card on the right that you chose with your right hand will be what will open the way for you in the situation. The card on the left will be what holds you back and prevents you from moving forward in the situation. If you are left-handed, reverse this process. Consequently, the card on the left will be what opens the door to the situation, and the card on the right will be what shuts it down.

Past/Present/Future Spread

Past/Present/Future Spread

The focus of this spread is three piles that represent the past, present, and future. It can also be adapted to any situation that has three parts, like me/you/us or mind/body/spirit, for example. Begin by shuffling and cutting the cards thoroughly in whichever way you prefer. Then cut the cards into the piles to the left using your left land. Flip the cards over. The pile on the left represents the past. The center pile represents the present. The pile on the right is for the future.

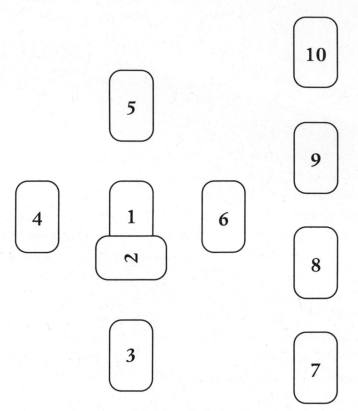

Celtic Cross Spread

Celtic Cross Spread

Chances are if you pick up almost any book about tarot written in the past fifty years, you will see this spread. It includes ten cards. Shuffle the cards well and cut them with your left hand. Then lay them out as shown above The first card represents the question or situation. The second card is what is going to hinder or help the situation (depending on what card is). The third card is representative of the foundation of the matter. The fourth card tells of the past influences on the matter. The fifth card is what your strength in the matter is. The sixth is the near future, in my experience the next two to three weeks. The seventh card represents the opinion of others involved in the matter. The eighth card is the environment surrounding the matter. The ninth card is your hopes and fears concerning the situation. The tenth is the final outcome of the situation.

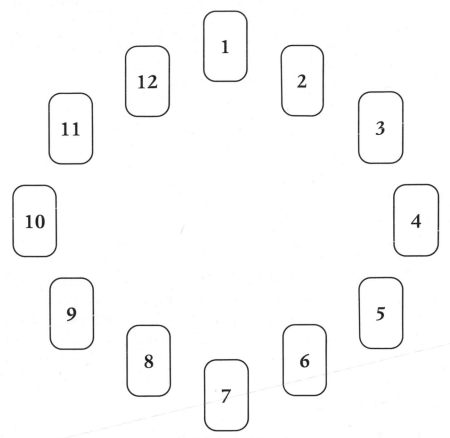

Wheel of the Year Spread

Wheel of the Year Spread

This reading is designed to show you how the next twelve months will unfold surrounding the issue you are asking about. Begin by shuffling the cards in the usual manner. Then, starting at the top of the table (or your tarot shrine, if you have one), lay the cards out clockwise from one to twelve. Turn them over. Card number one will represent the first month, number two will be the second month, and so on. This is a great reading to do on birthdays, holidays, or even New Year's Eve. As you are going through the months, you may need clarity about a particularly confusing card that comes up. In this case, feel free to pull an additional card from the deck and lay it on top of the puzzling one; this will help give more clarification.

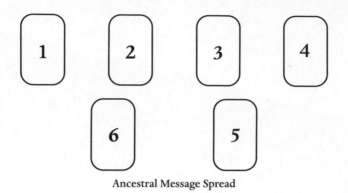

Ancestral Message Spread

Ancestral Message Spread

Here in my spiritual house, we always say, "Ancestors first, last, and always."
Ancestors are the reason you are here now, and they are the spirits who have
the most invested in your success in life. This simple reading uses six cards to
help clarify which ancestral energies are surrounding you right now and how
to best connect with them. Shuffle thoroughly and cut the deck. Lay four cards
out in the top row, and two beneath those in the bottom row. Turn them over.
The first card will represent how the ancestors are trying to contact and communicate with you. This will give you guidance about what signs to look for
as you go through your day. Many beginning Witches tend to try to find signs
everywhere, and that can become overwhelming very quickly. This card will
let you know exactly what you are looking for. The second card is all about the
lessons your ancestors are trying to teach you at this time. The third card represents what unnecessary obstacles may be in your path right now. The fourth
card represents the gifts your ancestors have given you or will be gifting you in
the near future. The fifth card represents how to access these gifts. The sixth
and final card represents the next steps the individual needs to take for success.
This is a great reading to do on Samhain or other ancestor-related holidays.
However, feel free to do this reading whenever you visit the cemetery or have
reason to seek clarity around messages from the dead.

Daily Tarot Spread

Daily Tarot Spread

Performing a daily tarot reading is good practice for both newbies and veteran readers alike. It will help you have the best possible day and avoid any unnecessary issues that may come up. Some people just choose a single card in the morning, but this reading gives you slightly more clarification. It involves just three cards. Shuffle and cut the deck in whatever way you choose. Place the first card in the center of the space before you. Then place the second card pulled to the left of that. The third card goes to the right of the first. The first card will represent the day to come. The card on the left will represent what you need to leave behind on this day. The third card will represent what help you will receive this day. It is as simple as that.

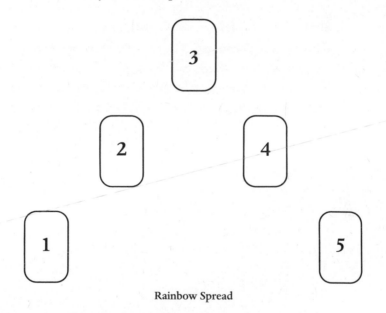

Rainbow Spread

Rainbow Spread

This spread lays out five cards in in upside-down U or rainbow shape. It can be done as a specific spread to help you figure out exactly what energies are surrounding a situation, or it can be used as just a general spread to discover what lies ahead. In either case, be careful with the phrasing of the question so you can receive the most clarity about the cards involved. This spread represents a journey. The first card will be the beginning. The last is the ultimate outcome that lies at the end of the rainbow. Begin by shuffling and cutting the deck thoroughly using your preferred method. Then lay out five cards face down in a rainbow shape. The first card will be at the bottom left, and the second will be placed slightly higher and to the right. The third card will be in the center at the top. The fourth will be below and to the right of this, and the last will be on the right opposite the first card you place. Turn them over one at a time. The first card represents the situation at present. This is different from a querent card, as it will show you exactly what is occurring right now. Very often, you will find this is unclear to the seeker, because otherwise they wouldn't be doing a reading to begin with. The second card is representative of the current expectations in the situation. The third card is for what isn't expected in the situation. This can be either helpful influences or hindrances depending on the card. Pay attention to the differences between the second and third card so you can have a better idea of how things will play out. The fourth card indicates what will happen next in the situation, while the last card will be your final outcome. All the cards in this spread are highly interrelated. See the story unfold through these five cards, and determine for the seeker exactly how best to proceed with this knowledge.

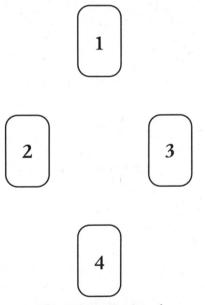

What Is Happening Spread

What Is Happening Spread

I almost titled this the WTF Spread, but I thought better of it. Sometimes situations arise that leave you confused and baffled about what is actually happening. This simple four-card spread will help you to gain clarity and insight into these situations. Shuffle and cut the deck whichever way you prefer. Draw out four cards face down on your tarot altar or shrine. Place the first card in front of you toward the center of the space. Place the second to the left and below that. Put the third across from the second. Put the fourth and final card directly below the first. The first card will represent what you really need to discover about the situation. The second will be what will help you in this situation. The third card is what you don't need in the situation. The final card will tell you where this matter is headed.

```
 ┌─────┐  ┌─────┐  ┌─────┐  ┌─────┐  ┌─────┐
 │     │  │     │  │     │  │     │  │     │
 │  1  │  │  2  │  │  3  │  │  4  │  │  5  │
 │     │  │     │  │     │  │     │  │     │
 └─────┘  └─────┘  └─────┘  └─────┘  └─────┘
```

Spiritual Path Spread

Spiritual Path Spread

When I first started reading professionally, I thought people were going to come get readings for all different reasons. The reality is most people have questions about either love or money. Maybe one out of a hundred asks about their spiritual path, when almost everyone should be asking these types of questions. This spread will help you discover and define that path for yourself. African traditional religions urge their devotees to ask this question often. However, I feel that people, no matter what tradition or type of spirituality they identify with, will ask themselves these types of questions periodically. The spread involves five cards. Shuffle and cut the deck however you choose. Then pick five cards and place them face down. Turn the first card up. This represents where you are on your spiritual journey right now. Next, move on to the second card. This second card is where to look for teachers and guides. The third card is what is blocking your spiritual path. The fourth card is where you need to look to find what it is you're seeking. The last card is the outlook for your spiritual journey in the future.

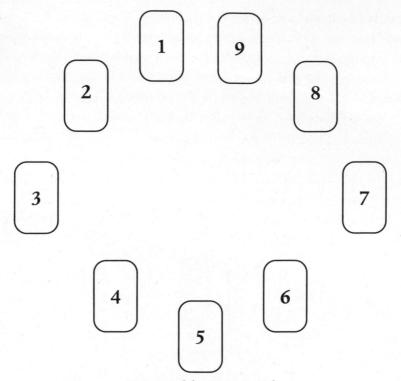

Ring around the Faeries Spread

Ring around the Faeries Spread

This particular spread may appeal to those who identify as Faery or Fae Witches. It gives insight on what the faeries may want to communicate with you at this time. To do this spread, you will lay out nine cards in the shape of a circle just like a faery ring. Begin by taking your cards to your tarot altar or shrine. Alternatively, if you like, you can go outside and do this reading in your faery garden. Shuffle and cut the deck however you like. Then take the cards with both hands and gently throw them into the air and catch them. This allows the deck to be in the hands of the invisible world with the faeries. It may help to put them back in your tarot bag for this particular blessing. Then, starting at the top of your space, lay out nine cards counterclockwise, forming a circle. The first card is what secrets are hidden from you at this time. The second card is what you are seeing clearly at this time. The third card is the best you can gain from the situation at this time. The fourth is what help you can get from the visible world. The fifth is what help you can expect from the faery world. The sixth card is what to give back to the faeries in return for their help. If you are unsure what this means, consider leaving an offering of one of the corresponding herbs or crystals that are listed for this card in this book. The seventh card is what you don't need to worry about at this time. The eighth card is how the situation will play out. The ninth card is seen as an extra message that the faeries wish to give you at this time.

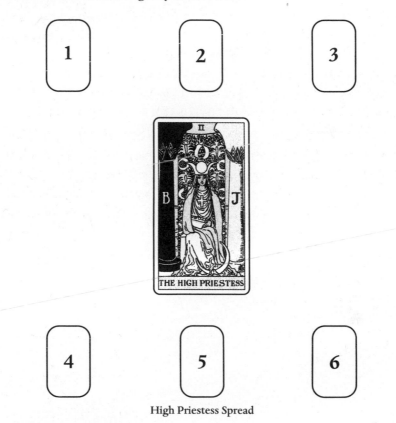

High Priestess Spread

High Priestess Spread

For many readers, the High Priestess card is their favorite. It speaks to intuition and the sacred feminine. Use this spread to access this power and learn to understand how it operates for you. Begin by removing the High Priestess card in the deck. Place it in the center of the tarot altar or shrine directly in front of you. Next, shuffle and cut the deck thoroughly with whatever method you choose. Choose six cards from the deck. Place the first three in a straight line on top of the High Priestess. Take the remaining three and form a straight line underneath the High Priestess card. The first card represents how you best can relate to the energy of the High Priestess. The second card is what will help you develop and trust your intuition. The third card is what is stopping you from developing your magic. The fourth card is how your own spiritual journey is progressing. The fifth card is who can help you with your goals. The sixth card is the special gifts the High Priestess holds for you.

Create Your Own Spread

Once you are comfortable with the basics of tarot and reading, consider creating your own spread. This can be as complicated or basic as you wish. Very often, I will create my own spreads based on the question. For example, if you are doing a love reading for a married couple, consider choosing one card to represent each partner. Then place one card above one partner's card in the spread and one card below. The above card will represent the best that partner can hope for in the situation, and the below card will represent what that partner has to let go of in the situation. Repeat this with the card used for the other partner. Each question is going to lead to more unique questions specific to the situation. Don't be afraid to alter the spread to get at the answers you need.

Conclusion
The End and the Beginning

Tarot Every Witch Way has come to its end. Each of the cards has been explored, and hopefully, everyone has a better idea how to strengthen their Witchcraft through the cards. No matter what kind of Witch you are, there is a way you can use tarot to help expand and improve your magical practice. In these pages, there is advice on every aspect of the sacred art and practice of tarot. Witchcraft is personal. It's about navigating the sacred world you find yourself in, capitalizing on the talents and strengths you inherently possess. Every single one of these strengths can be used with your tarot practice too.

Remember to use both your intuition and insight. Mat Auryn, author and psychic, reminds us, "It is also important to trust the process and trust whatever comes to you during a reading. While it can be tempting to second-guess yourself or doubt the information that is coming through, it is often the seemingly random insights that can be the most powerful and transformative for the client. I believe that it is important to approach each reading with an open mind and a willingness to learn and grow. By remaining curious and open to new perspectives, we can gain deeper insights into ourselves and the world around us. Ultimately, the goal of divination is to help individuals tap into their own inner wisdom and intuition, so they can make informed decisions and navigate life's challenges with greater clarity and confidence."[32]

Tarot can be used to predict, but it can do so much more. It can also help us learn, especially about ourselves and the situations we find ourselves in. Author and reader Courtney Alexander says, "I prefer to not use tarot to predict. If I read for anyone or myself, it is always with the premise of empowering the receiver. There is no system of divination that can overpower my ability to make decisions or manifest in my life. It cannot replace my free will. All it can do is give me a forecast. From there, I always have the power to make decisions that align with my soul growth. It is an informant of sorts. So with the philosophy in mind, it keeps me from falling into the trap of believing tarot has some special power to control my life. That's how many who read or go to readers are disappointed. However, when we see tarot as a teacher, we are in a much better place to receive the lessons we need to learn."[33]

Your interaction with the cards can be anything and everything you want it to be. The exercises, spells, recipes, and journeys within these pages are included to help you get in touch with your cards on a deep and abiding level. Readers may not choose to sleep with their cards, but hopefully they have internalized the messages presented here. They can use the spreads and meanings they find here to springboard their practice to a whole other level. They can use their readings to help themselves and others navigate difficult or challenging times.

I hope Love Witches have found love here. I hope Kitchen Witches found something tasty here. Cooking with the cards is something not only Kitchen Witches can do, and I hope everyone gets a chance to make some of the tasty recipes found here. Green Witches and Earth Witches may have found ways to go deep and get the real dirt on tarot magic. Cosmic Witches can now combine astrology and their knowledge of the planets with their practice of reading tarot. And I hope the rest of you fantastic Witches found something meaningful here too. With tarot, there are no limits to what you can learn about yourself and the situations you find yourself in. I hope you take the words found on these pages to tell your own magical tarot stories to the world.

---

32.   Mat Auryn, interview conducted by Lilith Dorsey, April 28, 2023.

33.   Courtney Alexander, interview conducted by Lilith Dorsey, October 16, 2016.

Recommended Reading

There are hundreds of tarot books that have been written. Some are better than others. The following is my curated list of books and websites cited and consulted and also extras that should be added to your tarot library. The study of tarot is a life-long pursuit. Each reading brings new challenges and insights, and hopefully, this book as well as the ones explored here will help you understand and uncover everything you need.

Holistic Tarot: An Integrative Approach to Using Tarot for Personal Growth by Benebell Wen. With over eight hundred pages, this is one of the most comprehensive tarot books on the market. Almost everything you want to know is shown here, along with delightful pictures and diagrams.

The Tarot Apothecary by Ailynn E. Halvorson. This book incorporates the magic of aromatherapy into the practice of tarot. A relatively new book, this work speaks to my soul. People tend to gravitate to their strengths, and this would most certainly appeal to anyone with an interest in aromatherapy and the sacred power of botanicals and their scent. Halvorson gives us energies that are present in each card as well as the essential oil that resonates with it. There is also an in-depth portion instructing how to create your own blends based on both elemental energies and tarot influences.

Tarot Dictionary and Compendium by Jana Riley. This book has been one of my most treasured texts about tarot since it was published. The beauty of this book is that it compares several different decks and their respective creators. The classics are all here: Rachel Pollack, Vicki Noble, Aleister Crowley, R. J. Stewart, and more all grace these pages. By comparing these different outlooks, a greater grasp on meaning and understanding can be had. A bonus in the book comes at the end, where a detailed examination of correspondences is given. Not only are similarities between cards found here, but Qabalah, chakras, runes, music, and more all find their way to these pages, providing a holistic understanding to the cards.

Tarot for Relationships by Jocelyn Almond and Keith Seddon. Although this was published in 1990 and is therefore a little dated compared to modern ways of thinking about relationships and gender binaries, it still contains a lot of helpful information. Many people turn to the tarot to find answers and solutions to questions about their romantic relationships, and this book provides insight like no other.

Ancestral Illumination: A Guided Journal for Black Tarot by Nyasha Williams. Many who choose to record their readings in a simple journal may not see the benefit of a book like this. That is, until they open it. In my opinion, this is one of the most fantastic tools on the market for readers of all skill levels. It allows the reader to record their readings in a single place and also allows space for monthly reflections as a whole. This book even comes with stickers.

Bibliography

Alexander, Courtney. *Dust II Onyx: A Melanated Tarot*. 2nd ed. Self-published, 2018.

Almond, Jocelyn, and Keith Seddon. *Tarot for Relationships*. London: Thorsons Publishers, 1990.

Artaud, Antonin. *Antonin Artaud: Selected Writings*. Berkeley: University of California Press, 1988.

Di Giammarino, Luigi. *Surrealist Tarot*. Torino, Italy: Lo Scarabeo, 2021.

Dillon, Julie, and Leeza Robertson. *Mermaid Tarot*. Woodbury, MN: Llewellyn Publications, 2019.

Doré, Gustave, and Charlie Westby. *Gustave Doré Tarot*. Torino, Italy: Lo Scarabeo, 2022.

Fiebig, Johannes. *Dalí Tarot*. 2nd ed. Los Angeles: Taschen America, 2019.

Ford, Henry J., and Jaymi Elford. *Tarot of Tales and Legends*. Torino, Italy: Lo Scarabeo, 2023.

Giglio, Gero. *TV Series Tarot*. Torino, Italy: Lo Scarabeo, 2018.

Giles, Cynthia. *The Tarot: History, Mystery and Lore*. New York: Fireside, 1994.

Glassman, Sallie Ann, and Louis Martinié. *New Orleans Voodoo Tarot*. Rochester, VT: Destiny Books, 1992.

Hall, Judy. *The Crystal Bible.* Iola, WI: Krause Publications, 2003.

Halvorson, Ailynn E. *The Tarot Apothecary.* Woodbury, MN: Llewellyn Publications, 2023.

Jodorowsky, Alejandro, and Kazan. *The Way Jodorowsky Explained Tarot to His Cat.* Torino, Italy: Lo Scarabeo, 2021.

Lechner, Renata, and Jaymi Elford. *Millennium Thoth Tarot.* Torino, Italy: Lo Scarabeo, 2020.

Listrani, Fabio. *Santa Muerte Tarot.* Torino, Italy: Lo Scarabeo, 2017.

McQuillar, Tayannah Lee. *The Hoodoo Tarot.* Rochester, VT: Destiny Books, 2020.

Miss Cleo. *Miss Cleo's Tarot Power Deck.* N.p.: Radar Communications, 2001.

Riley, Jana. *Tarot Dictionary and Compendium.* York, ME: Weiser Books, 1995.

True, Rachel. *True Heart Intuitive Tarot.* New York: Houghton Mifflin Harcourt, 2020.

Wen, Benebell. *Holistic Tarot.* Berkeley, CA: North Atlantic Books, 2015.

Williams, Nyasha. *Ancestral Illumination.* Philadelphia, PA: RP Studio, 2022.

Contributor Biographies

❧•❧

Over the years, I've conducted many interviews about divination and tarot for my blog, *Voodoo Universe*. This valuable information from some of the leading authors, deck creators, and readers can be found throughout this book. For more information about these fabulous people, I've included short biographies from them here.

Courtney Alexander,

Courtney Alexander, creator of Dust II Onyx Tarot, is a multi-media artist, writer, publisher, and public speaker. Her artistic practice is an ongoing ritual of expansion and emancipation. Through her self-portraiture, she challenges the politics and narratives of her identity as a fat Black queer femme, moving beyond just the exploration of her physical reality into expressions of herself as a timeless spirit. Less than a year after graduating with her BFA, she developed her series of paintings, Dust II Onyx, which she crowdfunded over $30,000 to self-produce and publish as a tarot deck (and later raised $50,000 for a second printing)—making history as the first Black person to create a widely distributed deck and selling three thousand copies to date. The series is made up of seventy-eight mixed-media paintings depicting the complexities of Blackness as humanity, as a race, and as a color story. It also includes a hardcover two-hundred-page monograph that serves as a catalog as well as guidebook.

Mat Auryn

Mat is the multiple-award-winning author of the internationally best-selling *Psychic Witch: A Metaphysical Guide to Meditation, Magick, and Manifestation*, translated in over ten languages. He is a Witch, an occult teacher, a highly sought-after speaker, and a retired professional psychic based in the Bay Area of California.

Bernadette Montana

Bernadette has over thirty years of experience teaching and practicing Wicca, the tarot, and Native American practices. She considers herself a progressive Witch under Janet Farrar and Gavin Bone. She is a third-degree high priestess in the Alexandrian tradition, an ordained interfaith minister, a tribal member and pipe carrier of the Sun Bear tribe (an all nations tribe), and a tribal member of the Baramaya tribe (Taino bloodline). Bernadette Montana is also the proprietor of Brid's Closet in Cornwall, NY.

Dorothy Morrison

Originally from Texas, Dorothy Morrison now lives the magical life in Louisiana with her family. Dorothy is a member of the Pagan Poet's Society and a charter member of MAGIC, a magical writer's and artist's organization. Dorothy is a Wiccan high priestess of the Georgian Tradition and has been an avid practitioner of the ancient arts for more than twenty years. She founded the Coven of the Crystal Garden in 1986 and spent many years teaching the Craft of Wicca to students both in the United States and in Australia. A former state championship archer and bow hunter, Dorothy's current interests include tarot work, magical herbalism, stonework, and computer networking. Dorothy's work has been published in many journals and magazines, including *Circle Network News*, *SageWoman*, and *Crone Chronicles*. She is the author of the acclaimed *Everyday Magic, Magical Needlework, In Praise of the Crone, Yule, Bud, Blossom & Leaf: The Magical Herb Gardener's Handbook, The Craft*, and *The Craft Companion*, among other works.

Deborah Lipp

Deborah is the author of *The Way of Four, Tarot Interactions, Bending the Binary, Magical Power for Beginners,* and several other titles. Deborah Lipp has been teaching Wicca, magic, and the occult for over thirty years. She became a Witch and high priestess in the 1980s as an initiate of the Gardnerian tradition of Wicca. She's been published in many Pagan publications, including *new-Witch*, *Llewellyn's Magical Almanac*, *PanGaia*, and *Green Egg*, and she has lectured on Pagan and Occult topics on three continents.

Andrieh Vitimus

Andrieh is the author of *Hands-On Chaos Magic*. Vitimus has been a practicing magician in multiple systems for over twelve years. He has taught metaphysical classes at Alchemy Arts in Chicago and at conventions including Aeon, Ancient Ways, Real Witches' Ball, ConVocation, and Sirius Rising.

To Write to the Author

If you wish to contact the author or would like more information about this book, please write to the author in care of Llewellyn Worldwide Ltd. and we will forward your request. Both the author and the publisher appreciate hearing from you and learning of your enjoyment of this book and how it has helped you. Llewellyn Worldwide Ltd. cannot guarantee that every letter written to the author can be answered, but all will be forwarded. Please write to:

Lilith Dorsey
℅ Llewellyn Worldwide
2143 Wooddale Drive
Woodbury, MN 55125-2989

Please enclose a self-addressed stamped envelope for reply,
or $1.00 to cover costs. If outside the U.S.A., enclose
an international postal reply coupon.

Many of Llewellyn's authors have websites with additional information and resources. For more information, please visit our website at http://www.llewellyn.com.